EVERYTHING IS BROKEN

The Coming Age of Abundance

Anthony Fieldman

For Mia Jordan Fieldman and her generation,
who will inherit what we leave behind.

I love you more than anything. —Dad

TABLE OF CONTENTS

"Broken But Together", by Michael Benisty © Anthony Fieldman 2019

PREFACE
Why Write This Book

At age fifty, in 2019, I was in a very dark place. By then, decades of unresolved traumas had calcified aspects of my character, and I was largely running on autopilot. From age three, I had experienced abuse so many times, at the hand of my family, trusted adults, and peers alike, that I had buried myself deep inside layers of armor to protect whatever was left inside of me.

It didn't work, of course. But doing so was wildly successful in preventing me from feeling profound joy, and from forming healthy bonds with nearly anyone.

Without community, whether we define it by a single life partner, a group bonded by purpose, or a posse of besties, we are lost. And I felt extremely lost.

By outward appearance, I seemed to be #winning. Income, job, family, friends, lifestyle... All boxes were ticked. But inside, I felt broken, mostly because—I now know—I had never resolved my traumas, and thus dragged them with me into every encounter, where they invariably corrupted relationships, and perversely *manifested* my deepest fears.

I had no one to blame but myself for ignoring the lessons each of these people and situations had come to teach me about my own triggers and wounds; about where, and how, I was broken.

But I didn't know it at the time.

In Spring of that year, I was designing a hotel-and-member-club concept for an unusual client named Tony who had aspirations for fostering community *and* personal transformation within the building. Early on, Tony hired a charismatic consultant to help us envision activities that could lead to transformational experiences for the guests. That consultant, Jamie Wheal, was a renowned expert on creating what he called *communitas*: "the creation of community through shared rite of passage." In our conversations, the form of human bonding he described was precisely the kind that escaped *me* in life, and I was rapt. At one meeting, he looked at us and said, "You know, if you really want to understand what we're talking about, what communitas looks like in action, you should consider going to Burning Man."

After months of planning, Tony and I headed into the desert.

What happened at Burning Man that August was nothing less than a forced reconsideration—an *invalidation*—of every negative story I had told myself about human beings over the preceding decades. Kindness was everywhere. Acceptance was without its usual caveats, or the need for shared traits or labels. Everything was given for free, joyfully, and without expectation of reciprocity. The level of creativity, from mutant vehicles, large-scale artworks, performances, fashions, and what-crazy-thing-can-we-do-in-the-desert-to-foster-delight-and-bond, was unlike any thing I'd ever seen, including years spent at a storied art school. Not even close. There on an ancient lake bed, an inclusive, participatory, optimism-fueled and fear-free attitude permeated *everything* everyone did, every moment of the day for a glorious week, in a makeshift city that had been whipped up in as much time, from nothing.

I was so unmoored by the whole thing, that back home, all I could think about was that I *had* to figure out what the hell had just happened out there, because for the first time in a half century, I felt deeply optimistic about the world and the people in it.

As I told my friends upon my return, Burning Man effectively *renewed my faith in people.*

Post-Burn, somehow, I felt brave enough to resolve to face myself in the mirror head-on, naked without armor, to meet my traumas and begin—I hoped—to finally make peace with them, so that I could feel as I had in the desert, but in everyday life.

It seemed, for reasons I couldn't understand, that Burning Man had landed on a formula for fostering human community between people with vastly different economic and cultural backgrounds that had improbably succeeded, where most others fail miserably.

Perhaps it was reaching middle age that finally awakened me. I certainly wouldn't be the first. It could also be the voracious reading I began to do upon my return, about the human condition; or, my decision to begin experimenting with psychedelics for the first time, as an instrument for self-healing; or, the special alchemy of Burning Man itself.

Of course, it was all of these things.

For no particular reason that Fall, I began writing every day on the subject of thriving. I wanted to explore the human propensity toward goodness I had just experienced "on Playa", as the large swath of desert where Burn happens is affectionately called, and I figured writing would force me to look at it more closely both inwardly and around me, to understand it and perhaps even apply those lessons to daily life.

A day turned to a week, then a month, and a year, and finally five. In all, well over one million words spanning hundreds of pieces on far-ranging subjects have materialized from that simple decision to write. This protracted exercise has resulted, over time, in something I can only call a form of *clarity*.

A big part of it came from books. Dozens of them. They included weighty tomes on thriving and the things that *prevent* it from materializing it, like **Man's Search for Meaning**, whose author, Victor Frankl, watched countless people die around him as members of his ethno-religion were being targeted for eradication during World War II, and whose insights about his own mind and perceptions helped him to survive, choose to devote his life to helping others, and ultimately develop the first major branch of psychotherapy since Freud. Frankl's logotherapy is based on the premise that the primary motivational force of an individual is to find a meaning in life. Then, there's **Meditations**, by Marcus Aurelius, who as a Roman Emperor was nonetheless dogged by the same questions as those with absolutely nothing: Who am I? Why am I here? What really matters, past amassing trinkets or power? One of the most powerful books I read was **Psycho-Cybernetics**, a titanic volume by Maxwell Maltz, who was the first, really, to articulate the power of positive thinking over 60 years ago, and how reality itself was no more than a manifestation of *stories we told ourselves about ourselves*, and which we could choose, at will. And finally, there's **Finite and Infinite Games**, by James Carse, who intuited that all of human interaction fell into one of two categories: **play to win**, which leads to all human struggle, or **play for enjoyment**, which leads to all human connection.

This quartet's—and countless other titans'—ideas lifted me out of a deep despair, and for the first time in my life, I began to understand what was broken in me, see a path to healing that brokenness, and understand that the root causes of our outward brokenness stems from the struggles within us. Through writing, I began to see patterns.

Five years on, I barely recognize myself. While I am still often haunted by old demons, I have met and healed so much trauma that I have regained a form of agency in my own life. Even when trauma does take over, its visit is shorter, and its power less crippling. The world looks very different, and infinitely more promising, than it used to. And not surprisingly, my relationships have also transformed as a result of the fact that I have *finally* learned many of the lessons that past abusers had been there to teach me, whether or not they knew it.

Not that the lessons are over. There is simply room for new ones now.

Marcel Proust comes to mind, from *Remembrance of Things Past*:

> *"The only true voyage of discovery, the only fountain of Eternal Youth, would be not to visit strange lands but to possess other eyes, to behold the universe through the eyes of another, of a hundred others, to behold the hundred universes that each of them beholds, that each of them is."*

Today, I possess other eyes.

In the process of trying to heal myself, a funny thing happened. I found beauty and creativity in places I didn't realize existed. Moreover, and the chief reason I am sharing this story, it is the *rediscovery of people's inherent goodness* that led me to the decision to write this book.

It seems to me that pain, unhealed, is what leads us to seek people and acts that *feed* that pain (thank you, Eckhart Tolle). There is a lot of pain amplifying itself out there right now, leading, I believe, to our most destructive behaviors—toward planet and one another. These are behaviors we cannot escape reading and despairing over, these days.

Chaos—the "meaning crisis", as John Vervaeke calls it—is everywhere, leading us to record levels of anxiety, depression and suicide[1], and a seeming inability to bridge over our differences to find enough common ground to thrive together on a planet where outcomes are increasingly global in reach.

At the same time, in spite of it all, there are people tapping into their inner reserves of creative capacity to put *good* into the world in both small and large ways, leading to *profoundly restorative alternatives* to the problems we have largely wrought, and which deserve a larger audience to bolster our collective optimism and **inspire us to participate in creating our own prosperity**.

This book is about those people and ideas, and just as critically, about meeting our demons head on so that we can begin to relegate them to the back seat, in order once again to flourish together as a human community.

The National Museum of American History, designed by the author while at SOM © Eduard Hueber 2009

INTRODUCTION
What This Book is About

If it feels as though everything is breaking at once—our climate, our economies, our institutions, our sense of meaning—you're not imagining it.

What's unusual about the present moment is not merely the number of crises we face, but their simultaneity. Housing, food, health, education, work, politics, and the environment are all failing in parallel, often in ways that appear unrelated on the surface yet feel oddly coordinated in their timing and impact. This book begins from a simple premise: that these failures are not independent, and that understanding their shared roots is the key to fixing them.

I didn't arrive at this conclusion as a theorist, economist, or activist. I arrived at it as a **systems designer**, and, later, as a human being forced to confront the limits of the stories I had been telling myself about how the world works.

For most of my life, I believed what many of us are taught to believe: that scarcity is natural, competition inevitable, and that survival requires constant extraction: of resources, of labor, of advantage. These assumptions are so deeply embedded in our institutions that they rarely feel like choices at all. They feel like physics.

Then, slowly and unintentionally, those assumptions began to crack.

Part of that reckoning came through multiple personal traumas, and their long shadows. Part came through my professional work as an architect who specializes in designing complex environments, in which small structural choices reliably produced large behavioral consequences for those who live, learn, work, and play in my buildings. And part came through exposure—sometimes accidental—to communities and systems that operated according to entirely different rules, and yet worked.

What emerged from that convergence was not a single answer, but a clearer question: what if the systems we live inside are no longer aligned with either human nature or technological reality?

This book argues three things.

First, that abundance, which I've defined as reliable access to the basic conditions for human flourishing, is no longer a speculative ideal, but a technical possibility. Advances in energy, automation, computation, logistics, and biology have dramatically reduced the marginal cost of providing food, shelter, knowledge, and even care.

Second, that this abundance is systematically suppressed by economic and institutional frameworks designed for a far more resource-constrained era, and those frameworks reward extraction over regeneration, competition over collaboration, and short-term gain over long-term viability.

Third, that beneath these systems lies a psychological layer we rarely examine: fear. Unhealed trauma, insecurity, and status anxiety scale upward into institutions that hoard, exclude, and defend long after such behaviors cease to serve us.

Throughout the chapters that follow, I return repeatedly to a set of lenses: scarcity versus abundance, finite versus infinite games, and systems designed around fear versus those designed around trust and collaboration. These ideas reappear not because they are rhetorical devices, but because they are structural patterns.

This is not a book about utopia. It is not anti-markets, anti-technology, or anti-work. It does not assume that politics will suddenly become benevolent or that power will voluntarily dissolve. It is, instead, an attempt to map the terrain of what is now possible, what is presently blocked, and what would have to change for a different future to emerge.

In Part I, we examine how the world we inherited came to be, and why systems that once made sense now reliably produce harm. In Part II, we explore how those same systems could be redesigned to reflect the reality of abundance rather than the myth of scarcity. And in the Epilogue, I offer a glimpse of what such a world might look like, not as fantasy, but as a plausible destination if we choose to change the rules we live by.

If everything feels broken, it is because the old operating system is failing. The question is not whether a new one is needed, but whether we will design it consciously, or allow it to emerge through collapse.

PART ONE

How It All Broke

"At The Beach", Lake Ontario's record-high water level © Anthony Fieldman 2017

1 Everything Is Broken: An Overview

The world appears broken in two distinct, but deeply connected, ways.

The first is how we interact with **the planet**. The natural ecosystems that gave rise to our existence and supported our explosive growth for millennia are being depleted at unsustainable rates, due primarily to the pursuit of competitive control and economic gain.

The second is how we interact with **one another**. Of late, the human systems we have invented to guide both individual and societal acts are increasingly hostile, turning individuals and nations against one another, fueled by toxic narratives and our resulting decrease in perceived kinship, understanding, and empathy.

Even though our planet will invariably find new equilibrium, having survived five mass extinctions, oxidation, and five ice ages, our actions are supremely problematic to *our own* survival in key ways.

Our Broken Planet

As the science overwhelmingly suggests, the planet on whose predictable and relatively benign systems we have relied for 300,000 years has been grossly disfigured by human activity and becomes less hospitable every day. The planet now regularly experiences "worst-ever" natural events such as wildfires, floods, earthquakes, hurricanes, droughts, mudslides, atmospheric rivers, and extreme heat events, to say nothing of the eviscerated glaciers, plastics-laden rivers, contaminated water supplies, destroyed habitats, acidified oceans, carbon dioxide-choked skies, and depleted aquifers for which we are at least partly responsible.

By and large, the climate no longer supports either the ways or the places we live today and as such, there will be a seismic upheaval among human societies in the decades to come. Gaia Vince's *Nomad Century* is an alarming treatise precisely because nearly all scientists now agree that our actions will precipitate the forced migration of between one and three *billion* people fleeing increasingly inhospitable climates for the shrinking Edens that will still support our thriving. By 2100, they posit, the *only* truly habitable landmasses will be those of Northern Canada, Russia and Scandinavia.

Nature always finds harmony among the elements, and it does so in the most efficient way possible, unburdened by human concepts such as ethics, morality, wealth accumulation, sovereignty, in- and out-groups, belief systems or hierarchical judgments related to survival itself (such as 'who deserves what'), all of which drive modern human behavior.

The planet we share has been endowed with the most remarkable ability to recover from relentless change, and has done so for billions of years, again and again, since its fiery birth. That's a period so long that it is without practical reference for human understanding.

In 2013 one of my heroes, the nature photographer Sebastião Salgado, addressed an audience I was in, during the vernissage of a show he named after the biblical Eden: GENESIS. Salgado had become famous after decades spent documenting war, famine, and genocide across the globe, and had finally had a nervous breakdown after witnessing that much inter-human savagery. For GENESIS, Salgado traveled the world for eight straight years, searching for places that hadn't yet succumbed to human desecration, in an attempt to regain faith in the future. The images he took were his love letter to the Earth.

After the talk, someone asked if he "felt better now," which elicited a big grin on Salgado's face. Addressing us, he said, "Absolutely. Because now I know: the Earth will be just fine. It is only ourselves we are killing."

This book is, first and foremost, about what we can do to improve the *human* systems that not only led to the disfiguration of the physical world, but also to the degradation of ways in which we interact with one another, because it is those broken systems that have driven us to the brink.

A statement made by E.O. Wilson nearly 100 years ago, in 1929, always comes to mind when I turn my thoughts to this subject:

> *"The real problem of humanity is the following: We have Paleolithic emotions, medieval institutions and godlike technology. And it is terrifically dangerous, and it is now approaching a point of crisis overall."*

The reason that the 20th century was more destructive than all those that preceded it, and that while the 21st is just getting started, it may yet be our end run, is the fact that the tools we now employ to fuel those "medieval institutions" are indeed approaching "god-like" and, realized in full, could destroy us.

As such, our top priority *must* be the replacement of our broken systems.

Our Broken Systems

The inescapable fact is that the systems we humans created to support our collective thriving as a species are all showing advanced signs of stress.

That's *good* news.

Why?

For context, humankind is given to great bouts of inertia, or "resistance to change", even if the benefits of new ideas are clear. Regardless, the timeline of change is *always* the same:

- Innovators dream up ideas, then attempt to find backers.
- Their early adopters share a unique capacity to see both significance and benefit quickly embrace and advance them.
- Once new ideas have been "de-risked", early and late majorities join in over time, according to means and readiness.
- Eventually, outmoded ways disappear, dragging holdouts, or laggards, into the fold
- Once an innovation works its way through the system, inertia sets in again. Invariably, however, *new* innovators challenge "the new normal", and the process repeats itself.

Everett Rogers termed this process **The Diffusion of Innovations**. A key reason that shifts to prevailing paradigms follow this pattern is that most of us don't like change, or at least what we consider *unnecessary* change.

Change is difficult because it requires a serious investment of thought, time and action. Change is also scary to those who don't understand it, or fixate on the short-term impacts on their lives today instead of the greater good it may bring tomorrow. For some, there's good reason. It's hard to be generous when you're starving. But for most, it's the lack of insight, understanding, resources, energy, will and/or trust that typically gets in the way of the new.

Until there's no choice.

Rogers' Diffusion of Innovations, illustrated below, is an elegant device that uses the brilliant bell curve to explain the long trajectory of change. While Rogers applied it to commercial markets, it frankly applies to every sphere of human activity.

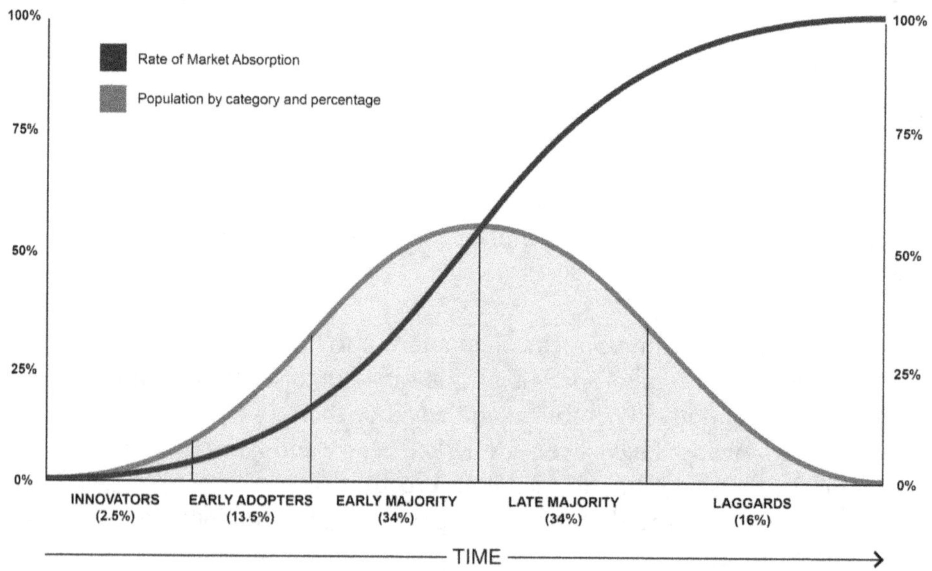

Based on Everett Rogers' Diffusion of innovations (1962). © Anthony Fieldman 2024

Changing major systems that impact most of us is hugely difficult because of its customary high cost to our short-term comfort and gain, and because it forces us back to the drawing board for things that took ages and countless resources to create in the first place. Most of us don't have the stomach for that kind of upheaval; and if we're honest, most of us don't know how to approach the ideation and implementation of something that might be better than what exists, even if we were to somehow agree that the current paradigm was worth replacing.

We rarely agree on much.

Fear has a central role in this, as well. As H.P. Lovecraft said, "The oldest and strongest emotion of mankind is fear, and the oldest and strongest kind of fear is fear of the unknown."

Or, as the ancient proverb goes, "Better the devil you know than the devil you don't."

And so, how is the fact that everything is broken *good* news?

It is good news precisely because when things are broken *enough* we are forced out of our passivity, and at that point there is a small window of opportunity for us to improve upon things before we settle back down again into business as usual.

The COVID-19 pandemic has therefore, in my view of it, created a once-in-our-lifetime opportunity. Not only did it force us up out of our chairs for fear of dying (see: Lovecraft), it also showed us what was broken, and even *how*.

Leonard Cohen put it magically in his song *Anthem*:

> *"Ring the bells that still can ring*
> *Forget your perfect offering*
> *There is a crack, a crack in everything*
> *That's how the light gets in"*

It is time to let the light in.

The structural issue here is that our rigid conceptual and institutional systems, and our inertia itself, stand at odds with the reality that natural systems continually change. And instead of embracing a "flux mindset" (to borrow April Rinne's term for "unsticking your mind from the constructs and assumptions that you hold unconsciously"), we use most of our faculties to prevent change from happening, at all costs. We do this not only with the physical world, but also with our own psychological inclinations.

To illustrate the idea, let's look at land ownership. Most individuals, institutions, and nations strive to source, purchase (or steal), hold, develop, and defend fixed land assets, then either exclude others' access to that land (as we do with real estate and borders) or charge people for the privilege (as is common with commercial and governmental assets).

The indigenous Lenape didn't understand our concept of land ownership[1] when the Dutch traded them wampum for New York City, in 1626. In its appraisal of a Smithsonian exhibit, *Native News Online* wrote:

> *"The Lenape believed they were receiving gifts to share their land with new neighbors. As stewards of the land, they didn't believe it was theirs to sell."*

The first thing we did, of course, was build a wall to keep them out, and called it Wall Street.

Our Finite Games

The problem with fixed land ownership is twofold. First, it prevents us from dynamically responding to climate events, as we used to. By 2100, nearly half a billion people are at risk of forced home abandonment, as sea levels rise[2] and coastal storms increase.

The so-called "share economy" shows the path toward two phenomena that could help alleviate these threats. First, dynamic housing systems like AirBnB, Nomad Stays, Outsite, Anyplace, Ukio, Selina, Boundless Life, Knowmad Tribe, Landing, and even conventional time shares and hotel operations are all mechanisms—albeit commercialized ones—for dealing with the dynamic ebb and flow of people in real time, globally. Second, pooling resources and sharing in the costs of property purchase, development, debt-servicing, use and/or operation are all potential pathways toward reducing the overall cost burden of being housed.

As we will see in Chapter 15, we have put access to shelter out of economic reach for too many. Causes include the artificial suppression of supply, the inflation of prices, punishing regulatory barriers, a lack of adequate focus on innovations in fabrication, prohibitive financing terms, and the lack of limits on the economic opportunism that is endemic to the real estate development market. We hoard not only land, but also objects, rights and labor for our exclusive control and use. We then leverage our power over others to maximize personal gain instead of sharing what we've created, or secured.

Ever since our societies expanded beyond relational clans, we have chosen to compete with one another for access and rights rather than collaborate in order to amplify them for everyone, in spite of the likeliness that we are hard-wired for empathy[3].

To borrow Carse's term for it, we have elected to play *finitely*—competitively—with one another for pieces of a *conceptually* limited pie.

'Resource limits' as commonly framed in economic discourse are an increasingly misleading concept. The outcome of this thinking, as most of us know and accept, is the creation of winners and losers. This construct is not only toxic, it is unnecessary. While competition may be benign enough in sports contests, it is decidedly less benign when what's on the line is our physical or mental health. When we compete for access to housing, food, medicine, education, and jobs, or struggle to find love, acceptance, friendship, support, community and connection, *everybody loses*.

The notion that there are inherent limits to supplying the basic conditions for human flourishing is, in light of current technology, increasingly false. In fact, everything listed above is abundant at the margin once foundational infrastructure exists, even if coordination and governance remain nontrivial. We simply *choose* not to share resources and ideas with one another freely, because as we'll see in Chapters 10, 11, and 12, the economic paradigm we've designed discourages it.

The chief exception to our interpersonal game-playing is how those with a healthy family life treat their children, or parents. Simply put, we invest countless hours and resources in our progeny for decades, expecting nothing in return but the satisfaction of having nurtured and loved another human and empowered them to live fully. For parents, the investment *is* the reward. For the children, it's another matter entirely. When it comes to end-of-life inheritances, more than 70% of families fight over estates[4].

In an economically incentivized society, the temptation for gain is simply too great to ignore.

Unsurprisingly, what drive nearly all finite games we play are two things. First is the economic model we've invented, which is traditionally supercharged by something I call "**the myth of scarcity**" because scarcity, as we apply the term to basic human needs in advanced technological societies, is largely manufactured because our willingness to provide for everyone is limited by competing economic and political forces. Most of us accept these as facts instead of seeing these geopolitical and regulatory bottlenecks as *design failures*. Second is the notion—false, in my view—that *all* humans are better than *non*-human creatures, and that *some* humans are better than *other* humans.

Finite games have led to a world divided by competition between factions rather than united by the fact that there is only one world, and everything on it shares a single fate.

The economic model that prevails globally today has pitched humans against one another in a bid to maximize extraction as cheaply as possible, rather than invest in resource amplification and sharing. To say it again, there is enough productive capacity to meet everyone's needs. We only *elect* to artificially compete for pieces of it then extract it unsustainably, rather than take the natural steps necessary to pool our resources to create and share in true abundance, managed sustainably.

The result of our systemic game-playing is a human population whose daily lives are a struggle against the natural world *and other humans* for survival, rather than an eight billion-strong army of collaborators, managing the endless bounty of planet Earth.

So What's Broken, Exactly?

A central driver of our current crisis is our unexamined fealty to money and the economic abstractions built around it.

This manifests in myriad ways.

Housing is broken because we've made the fundamental need for shelter the single most unattainable (i.e.: expensive) asset[5] in human societies. **Food** is broken because in search of hegemony we have turned food into the biggest killer on Earth[6], while simultaneously disfiguring 51% of global habitable land[7] to achieve it. The **environment** is broken insofar as how hospitable it is for *us*, because we have relentlessly focused on short-term gains via resource extraction and use, rather than long-term sustainability. **Education** is broken because we've honed people into specialized instruments for profit generation, robbing us of our inherent capacity for creative polymathy, and even made *that* a privilege for those who can afford it. **Work**, too, is broken for much the same reason: by and large, graduates become cogs in a globally splintered workforce of specialists without a unifying framework for human thriving, or true consideration for individual needs and passions.

Chapters 14 thru 25 are devoted to dissecting the underlying causes of systemic stress, and an appraisal of healthy alternatives within each category that exist and point the way to possible solutions.

It's important to keep two things in mind as we chart our path toward improving what's broken.

First, as I mentioned earlier, the natural world remains *unbroken*. It's simply different from the one we inherited. We will adapt as we always do to its increasingly inhospitable climate. If our forebears could do it during the stone age on a frozen planet with nothing but spears and animal skins, we can, too.

Second, given that human systems are nothing more than fictions, most of which are *mere decades or centuries old*, we can and should replace outdated competition-based systems with collaborative ones that take advantage of the physical and conceptual resources at our current disposal. And our technological resources are *god-like*.

This is where our collective energies need to go. If we are to adapt to a planet we disfigured we must advance the failed systems that brought us here, focusing on an approach that maximizes our collective, long-term thriving. The world has become too small not to, and our tools have become too effective to ignore the fallout of their potential misuse.

A New World

In the Epilogue, I share the world I dream of when I'm feeling confident enough to let my mind go there. I call it **The (Potential) Path to Abundance**.

The solutions presented in the rest of this book are technically achievable with existing tools, though politically and psychologically resisted.

All Before One

The cost to produce energy and goods could be borne by a planetary array of humans, machines and A.I. working together to optimize the generation, distribution and repair or resources, which would allow us to then share it all, *freely*.

It wouldn't take us more than a few years of working together to devise a plan for truly free energy generation and distribution, in perpetuity. Tesla invented such a system 100 years ago, before J.P. Morgan stopped financing it, and to pay off Tesla's debts, demolished it for scraps.[8]

Tesla was eventually undone by what he called "ignorant, unimaginative people, consumed by self-interest": powerful men who sought to protect the immensely profitable low-tech industries they had spent a lifetime building.

Tesla succeeded elsewhere. While little known, he actually invented over a dozen patented technologies that Guglielmo Marconi borrowed[9] (and took credit for), which led him to manifest Tesla's dream of *free* global transfer of communications and ideas. We still enjoy it, today.

It's called radio.

Money—"the root of all evil"—doesn't actually need to be replaced. It simply needs to evolve. The fact that the world's richest billionaires could end extreme poverty several times over[10] is just one advanced symptom. The combined productive output of powerful machines, a planetary digital network, artificial intelligence, and human ingenuity (for invention and optimization) can not only provide for the needs of all humans today, but the cost for doing so is quickly approaching zero. That is, it is all inherently **deflationary**, as eloquently presented in Jeff Booth's book, *The Price of Tomorrow.*

In it, Booth lays out that the concepts of inflation and growth—two metrics that galvanize nation-scaled activity, globally—are not only ill-conceived, they are *unnatural* insofar as they contravene the fact that everything is becoming inherently less expensive with time. Thus we are now in an entrenched paradigm of creating artificial growth through the creation of very real and crippling debt. As we discuss in Chapter 12, it now costs us $3 of debt to create $1 of GDP growth, globally.

We may have to reconcile these things soon, regardless of how we feel about money, given that the natural outcome of these systems is an increasingly unemployed and unemployable human species.

The Rise of the Useless Class

In Chapter 25, we'll see that we are quite likely on the doorstep of hosting a global population of unemployable people.

With the right leadership, this could trigger widespread prosperity.

Pew Research summarized a gathering of 979 technology pioneers, innovators, developers, business and policy leaders, researchers and activists[11] thus:

> *"The experts predicted networked artificial intelligence will amplify human effectiveness but also threaten human autonomy, agency and capabilities. They spoke of the wide-ranging possibilities; that computers might match or even exceed human intelligence and capabilities on tasks such as complex decision-making, reasoning and learning, sophisticated analytics and pattern recognition, visual acuity, speech recognition and*

language translation. They said "smart" systems in communities, in vehicles, in buildings and utilities, on farms and in business processes will save time, money and lives and offer opportunities for individuals to enjoy a more-customized future."

An unemployed population supported by a non-human workforce that needn't eat, sleep, take time off, be trained, receive payment or be emotionally mollycoddled, is the *exact* mechanism that could finally render the conversation about "working to live" moot.

The marginal cost of life is reducing dramatically. It is economic systems that are preventing the savings from reaching *all of us*. The release from artificial growth mechanisms will unlock untold potential for humans, who will finally have the time to do what they *love* instead of what they think is *marketable*. In his book, Booth writes:

> *"We are trapped in a system where we don't know what we would do with ourselves if we didn't have jobs… allowing abundance without the jobs might actually open an entirely new enlightenment era where we have time to enjoy the benefits that technology brings."*

Forbes, a bastion of finance, industry, investing, and marketing ideas, wrote the following, about the topic of Booth's book[12]:

> *"Humans will probably always work, in the sense that we will always have projects and goals. But what a sad species we would be if we always needed that work to be in the form of jobs, directed by other people, with a need to generate revenue. There are three types of people who prove that you don't need a job to have meaning: aristocrats, comfortably-off retired people, and children."*

Think about it. What wouldn't we all give to live like an aristocrat, to retire from the grind, or to play like children do?

It's not only possible, it's the answer.

If we were to finally stop fighting one another for scraps, to live in the abundance created by deflationary technologies and a planet-wide system of distribution shared freely, the finite games of war, competition, greed, social climbing, extraction, and patriotism would be largely defanged. As a result, poverty, sickness, deprivation, homelessness, hunger, and many forms of human stress would crater automatically, because unlimited access to human, capital, technological, and physical resources would become marginally free.

As would we.

Final Thoughts

Economics is not only broken, it is an underlying cause and key accelerant of other problems. The good news is that robust alternatives exist, and point the way to fixing *other* broken things.

Housing is broken but can be fixed once we simply create enough homes for everyone and simplify the currently prohibitive means of attaining one: affordably in the short term, and free thereafter.

Food is broken but can be fixed once we stop subsidizing the production of unhealthy food products and give up resource-depleting practices; and once our efforts focus on maximizing health and access once again, as they did when we lived in clans.

Climate is broken but can be fixed once we embrace the sustainable infrastructure investments required to do so, for which robust solutions exist today, in every ecosystem.

Education is broken but can be fixed once we fully leverage existing digital networks, remove the impediments to their access, and focus efforts on students' *passions* rather than their potential earning power.

Work, too, is broken but can be fixed once we embrace technology-enabled abundance and no longer "work to live", at which point transactional relationships will be robbed of their primary fuel.

Each one of the foregoing broken systems is the subject of multiple chapters in this book. And while the following aren't covered in depth, they're worth a mention, because they, too are very broken.

Healthcare is broken but can be fixed once impediments to access are removed and we retool our institutions to focus on *prevention*, rather than treatment.

Public safety is broken but can be fixed once money no longer drives desperate acts, once we give up on toxic fictions, and once we understand that the fate of our wellbeing is co-dependent.

Politics is broken because it is powerfully exploitative. Once leaders truly understand how inextricably linked our collective fates are, they can leverage their platforms to retool institutions and global relationships to pool the human, capital, natural, and technological resources that will be required to fix everything else, and share it freely.

At that point, things will no longer be broken. Once we've fixed them all—and we can with the tools at our disposal *today*—we can finally turn our free attention to the very thing people excel in, beyond anything we've ever achieved: **creating meaning**, and sharing it with others in the name of collective thriving.

To repeat: it's time to let the light in.

But first, we need to understand what's getting in the way.

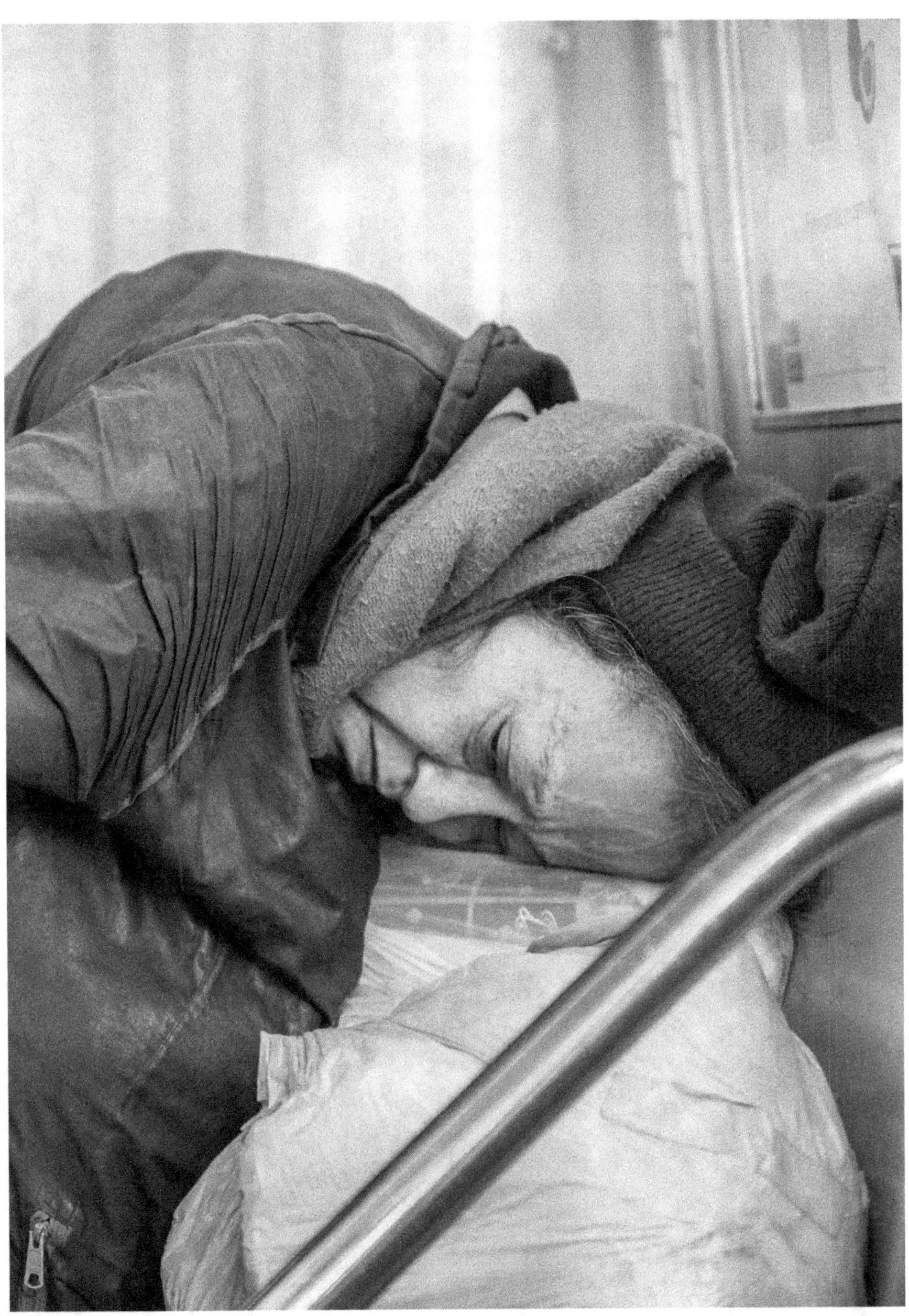

Homeless on the subway © Anthony Fieldman 2016

2   An Audit for Project Human

Everywhere I look these days, the sky is falling. Oceans are dying. The planet is warming. Weather is extreme. Forests are burning. Freshwater is disappearing. Wild animals are going extinct. Physical and mental health are cratering. And in spite of this—in the context of an avalanche of data telling of our impending demise from every corner of the Earth—we continue to make choices that are self-centered, small-minded, greedy, xenophobic, murderous, and *easy*.

How the heck did we get here, and how do we move beyond it?

Water Water Everywhere

Landmark research by an Edinburgh-based research team[13] has found phytoplankton and zooplankton concentrations to be down by more than 90% from expected values, which, as the foundational food chain nutrient, could lead to the loss of food supply for three billion people. The researchers, funded by the Global Oceanic Environmental Survey Foundation (GOES), concluded:

> *"An environmental catastrophe is unfolding. We believe humanity could adapt to global warming and extreme weather changes. [But] It is our view that humanity will not survive the extinction of most marine plants and animals."*[14]

These researchers had trolled the oceans in 13 boats over a two-year period and found that everywhere they looked, plankton and phytoplankton were critically endangered and on the brink of collapse. They concluded that nearly all of it will be gone by 2045, little over 20 years from now.

Why do phytoplankton matter? Read what the researchers had to say:

> *"Plankton are fundamental to life on Earth as they form the bottom rung of the food chain. It is consumed by the krill which are fed on by the fish that, in turn, provide nutrition for terrestrial animals including billions*

of humans.

"They also perform a vital role in regulating climate change by helping oceans absorb carbon dioxide and giving off the chemical dimethyl sulphide, which assists in creating clouds.

"If we destroy plankton, the planet will become more humid, accelerate climate change, and with no clouds it will also become arid, and wind velocities will be extreme."

Remember: these are scientists' words:

"We have two choices. We can choose to wake up, understand and address the real issue or choose the game-over button for humanity come 2050."

I never realized that plankton created clouds (they do; some 60% of them), and that without these micro-organisms, there would be no solar heat gain reflection (via clouds), ergo no rain, plants, trees, or animals, including the humans who depend on all of it.

Like many others, my attention had hitherto been focused on trees' role in environmental health. Most of us already know that trees are vital to our survival as a species.

In spite of this knowledge, as I share in Chapter 16:

"We have cut down half of the world's trees—three trillion of them—since we began practicing agriculture 12,000 years ago. Half of that loss, or 1.5 trillion trees, has occurred in just 125 years. The biggest culprit? Deforestation for grazing livestock."

An article in *Nature* put it dryly: "No Trees… No Humans."

Trees absorb human CO_2, while we breathe in their oxygen. They also stabilize the soil so that we can grow things in it; keep temperatures cool by preventing the ground from drying out; create habitat for the world's terrestrial creatures; scrub the air of toxins like carbon monoxide, sulfur dioxide, and nitrogen dioxide as part of the carbon cycle; and provide the raw materials for our homes, our heat, our packaging, and a thousand other things.

Well, the impacts from the looming collapse of plankton could apparently *dwarf* those of the destruction of our forests.

You see, in addition to producing clouds and thus food, potable water and life, the oceans, it turns out, produce 50% of the world's oxygen supply, nearly half of which comes from microscopic phytoplankton[15]. So, even if you think scientists can come up with aluminum suits to protect us from atmosphere-free solar radiation and food-like capsules to tend to our biological processes on an animal-free rock, a significant proportion of the animal kingdom wouldn't be able to breathe on it.

So, I ask again: How the heck did we get here, and how do we move beyond it?

The Root Cause of Our Destruction

Have you ever stopped to ask yourself why it is that we seem to consistently choose exploitation over conservation, which is another way of saying "now" over the "future"?

Because to me, it's been clear for a while now.

The prevailing global economic paradigm leads to market mechanisms optimized for extraction rather than provisioning, which mechanisms have largely failed to deliver equitable outcomes.

2,000 years ago, St. Paul supposedly said:

> *"For the love of money is the root of all kinds of evil."*
> —Timothy 6:10

He was right.

Why else would we fish the oceans until they're empty, trolling its floors until everything we scrape against dies, and toss the things we catch but can't sell?

Why else would we pump oil from the ground and release 18 million tons of it into the seas every year, which breaks up into tiny particles that are toxic to plankton, and all other ocean life?

Why else would we clear-cut most of the Earth's forests to grow cows everywhere in spite of the fact that they have the largest environmental footprint on the planet[4], and have a debatable impact on human health?

Why else would we produce things as cheaply and toxically as possible, design them to break so we can force people to replace them, and center an economy around the idea of tossing out what we have, to replace it with something we don't?

Why else would we treat the Earth like a bottomless dump, tossing out bagfuls of trash daily full of plastics—PE, PP, PET, PS, and PVC—that could take centuries to fully biodegrade,[16] often only *after* it has killed off the remaining fish in our oceans?

And why else would we make human-to-human interaction as extractive, transactional and predatory as it is, the overarching result of which is an increasingly expensive and decreasingly accessible life?

The global growth narrative and profit motive that have driven late-stage capitalism are subjects we'll cover in Chapter 9 through 12. The erstwhile belief that resources are unlimited is a subject we'll visit in the next chapter. These frameworks have supercharged our destruction of the world. If they didn't, I am convinced that many, if not most, of our choices would look very, very different.

So what to do?

Fix Project Human

The good news is: solutions exist for all of it. We not only know how to fix things, *we have many means for doing so*, extremely cost-effectively. And with the right socio-political will to overcome entrenched patterns, we can realistically implement most, if not all of them.

We simply need the courage to do it.

Step 1: Change Our Relationship to Money

Fantasy? Impossible?

Jeff Booth, whose book, *The Price of Tomorrow,* I introduced in Chapter 1, warns us that we are dangerously wedded to an outmoded economic system that made sense in a pre-technological era "that counted on growth and inflation, where we made money from inefficiency;" and that while these forces are no longer the primary drivers of cost, we have yet to recognize the profoundly deflationary bounty that today's technology-fueled world has created.

What Booth is telling us, and what the evidence suggests, is that in reality, most things have become *less* expensive over time to produce and distribute, as operations, labor, and supply chains have all become more efficient, and as technology has become increasingly powerful. That includes "needs" like food, energy, shelter, education and health, and even frivolities like entertainment.

As a result, Booth points out, the cost of life *should* be approaching zero. But it's doing the opposite.

We will revisit Booth's ideas in Chapter 12, in detail.

The amount of disposable income we spend on food has plummeted[17] from 24% in 1930 to approximately 10% today, with the rise of scale, food science, technology and distribution networks. Yield/acre has increased threefold since 1948[18] while new farming technologies are emerging that can deliver a *hundreds-fold* increase in return/acre[19] over conventional farming, as we'll see in Chapters 18 and 19.

So why is food getting more expensive?

The cost to educate, too, is nearly zero, in reality. We produce content that can reach everyone on the planet instantly, any time, and have mechanisms to allow for discourse around the lessons, for the price of Internet access (which could also be free). The world's greatest academic institutions have created MOOCs—massive open online courses—that distribute some content freely, as we'll see in Chapter 21, while subscription-based courses like MasterClass and others abound. And YouTube, anyone? The latter is a veritable how-to for nearly everything we can conceive. So why is a formal education becoming less and less affordable for the masses, with 13% of global respondents citing the ability to pay school fees as their single greatest worry, according to the World Bank's 2021 Global Findex Database?[20]

We can build homes for next to nothing as New Story does; 3D-print them for a few thousand dollars as ICONBuild does; or construct them 'conventionally' while employing renewables and industry-optimized resources to reduce costs, as we'll see in Chapter 15. So why are home costs skyrocketing?

We can produce and distribute energy *nearly* for free from sun or wind or tides or ground heat. This was even true in Nikola Tesla's time, 100 years ago, as I referenced in Chapter 1. So, why don't we?

Health, too, is cheap. Adopting prevention protocols could make the overwhelming majority of maladies and their associated costs evaporate overnight even *without* subsidies from our governments (or maybe faster, because doing so would level the playing field). The wholesale cost of medicine too is, as evidence suggests, a tiny fraction of what we charge for access to it. Remember "Pharma Bros" like Martin Shkreli, who jacked up the price of AIDS medicine by 5,000%, just because he could[10]? They were only the public face of the industry's pervasive markup.

Just as bad, the culture of "more" that we live in mandates continual upscaling and upgrading, when in fact the majority of the things we own are perfectly fine for our needs. It is only market-driven narratives that spur us to consume and toss goods we used to pass down, to chase dreams of "arriving", or "keeping up with the Joneses", as we'll see in Chapter 8. Why on Earth would we choose *more* over *enough*, when biologically we are hardwired for the latter?

And with respect to entertainment, there is little true cost to playing games or performing. We *could* play for fun and let people watch us for free, because if we're honest we *like* performing, and all the attention it brings to us.

Taken together, these trends indicate that most if not all of life could be far less costly, if not marginally free, while the evidence suggests its *true cost* is plummeting with every step of technological and scientific advancement. This applies to sustaining, housing, healing, educating, and providing goods and services to a planetary array of human beings, without ever-decreasing numbers of dollars or yuan changing hands. So why don't we embrace that fate?

We tend to resist natural deflation under conditions where economic gains is incentivized. As long as survival is contingent on monetary extraction at scale, destructive incentives reliably emerge.

But we *could* embrace deflation, by changing the game we play from a finite one to an infinite one, which would necessitate a system redesign. We'll visit one such system in Chapter 10.

Step 2: Change Everything Else

We've seen that everything we need in life is within grasp for everyone, if only it were made widely available according to its *true costs*. Qualitatively, every person on Earth could enjoy food, shelter, education, health, and fun; and quantitatively, we could pay for it with the fruits of whatever labor, creativity and output it is that we *chose* to make with our time and energies, once we no longer had to labor to pay the bills. We will dive into that topic in the book's final chapter.

If we accepted the evidence that the true *cost* of living (as distinct from its price tag) is profoundly deflationary, then we could invert the age-old narrative of "I work to live" into "I live to work." Only here, "work" would be borne out of our passions for contributing to the wellbeing of our communities in ways we *chose* to participate, on our terms. This is called purpose, a subject we'll revisit in the Epilogue.

An ideological shift from "working because I *have to*", to "working because I *love to*" would be profound. Choosing how to contribute one's time and efforts according to one's skills and passions rather than chasing promotions and raises "so that I can really enjoy my life on weekends and after retirement", is a plausible and next step in human evolution.

The best decision I can see us taking to survive the cannibalizing paradigm of 'competitive transactionalism' is to *replace it*. If not, we risk continuing to extract everything on Earth that someone is willing to pay for and competing against one another for scraps of it until it is gone, in lieu of partnering in the creation of things to grow, maintain, and share freely.

One name for this idea is the 'gift economy'" A primitive if imperfect version exists at Burning Man, which continues to be studied by a variety of urban planners and economists. An article in the *Brown Daily Herald* explained it thus:

> *"Compared to the market economy in which people build a relationship based on the items traded, the gift economy focuses on building a relationship between the people trading... Rather than accumulating material wealth, participants in a gift economy grow richer through obtaining social capital."*

Another name for this concept is 'relationship economy'. One of the world's most successful companies has operated in this manner for generations. We'll discuss them in detail in Chapter 10.

Charity, generosity, philanthropy, and hospitality are cousins of the gift economy. Parenting is perhaps the most pervasive expression of a relationship economy. In healthy families, what is given freely returns in some form, as needs arise. This is the true nature of human community.

In business, purpose-driven enterprises like non-profits, ESG frameworks, impact investments, B-Corps, and co-operatives are all structures that not only exist today, they are growing. In fact, according to a white paper by Jump Associates, "purpose-driven companies [have] provided shareholders with a 13.6% CAGR [compound annual growth rate] return on average over a twenty-year period. That's three times their closest industry competitors and five times the S&P 500."

Slowly, we are getting there.

Final Thoughts

In our audit of Project Human, an important choice lies before us: evolve and retool our economy to embrace the plausible creation of abundance, or remain at war with one another over scraps to fuel *the myth of scarcity*, and accept that if we do, it may well lead to our end game.

Before the last tree falls, or the last phytoplankton dies—both of which systems have been critically degraded by humans—we need to develop the courage to make the right choices, or embrace those with the ideas and means of incubating them.

As we'll see in the next chapter, the greatest impediment to achieving these things may not be money, per se, but the lack of adequate investment in mitigating what *drives* us to act in the first place.

3 This is What the Inflection Point Looks Like

If it feels as though every man-made and natural system on the planet is at an inflection point, and that the decisions we make next could deliver us to long-term, sustainable prosperity or result in the collapse of our species, it's because the evidence suggests that this is exactly what is going on.

The good news is that we are not *solely* to blame for the state of the world. Believing so is a conceit borne of the concept of human exceptionalism. Rather, from the 50,000-foot view, we are little different from fruit flies, trees, or yeast. That's because all living systems follow the same general path as we have: one that starts flat while incubating kinetic potential; then uses that energy to fuel explosive growth and prosperity; and finally, slows at some point due to either external limits (in fuel) or internal ones (our own choices). Once this happens, we invariably employ one of two forces to determine what comes next: resistance to changing paths, which is followed by collapse; or re-invention, which ushers in a new period of equilibrium.

If "what comes next" is a question we are likely all pondering right now, we're not alone. An unrelated trio of philosophical luminaries whose work I came across has advanced our collective thinking on the matter. Theirs are ideas worth sharing.

Just 40 years ago, Jonas Salk (of polio vaccine fame) and his son Jonathan employed the use of the sigmoid curve in a neat little book called *A New Reality*, to demystify the complex trajectory of our species.

The Salks' principal goal was to help us understand how the choices we make today will either result in our collective long-term prosperity tomorrow, or in collective catastrophe.

We'll come back to the Salks shortly.

Just a few years ago, shortly before he died, Swedish physician, academic and Gapminder founder Hans Rosling published the optimism-filled book

Factfulness. It made such an impression on Bill Gates that in 2018, Gates offered a free copy to every graduating American—all four *million* of them. In the book, Rosling uses the sigmoid curve and decades' worth of data to prove that the inflection point of the human species is not only upon us *right this minute*, it is both normal and good news, insofar as we are collectively transitioning from a point of explosive growth (the bottom half of the 'S') to one of global stability (the upper half).

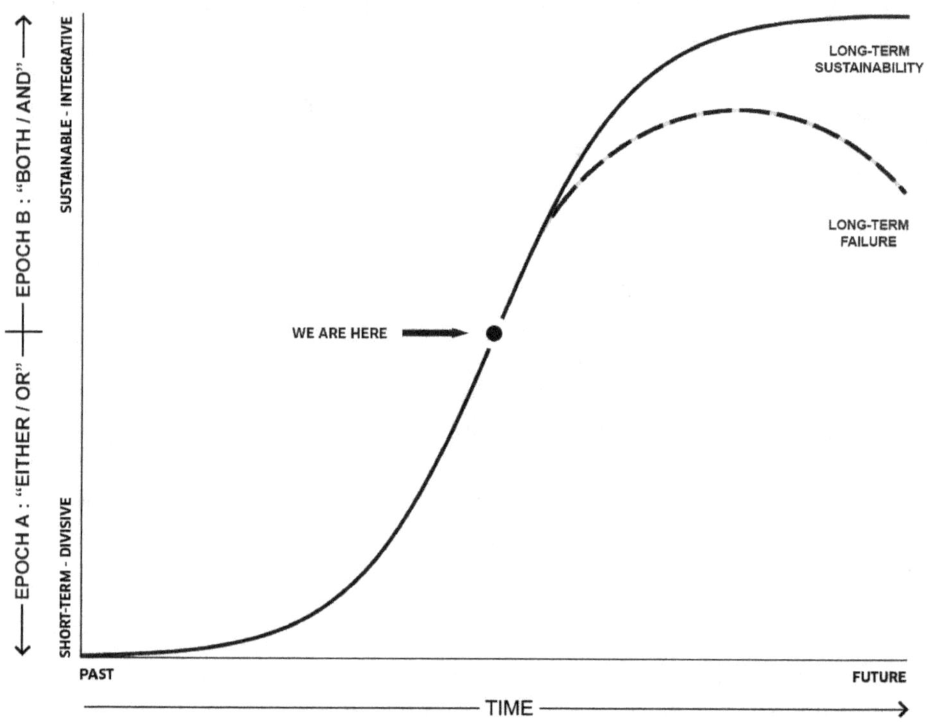

Based on Jonas and Jonathan Salk's work © Anthony Fieldman 2022

But it was the Salks that got me thinking, as I finished their book, and unsurprisingly, their work aligns well with Rosling's.

What the father-and-son team illuminated, for me, is that right now, we are living through the *very center* of the inflection point that every species experiences. That fact makes this either the most exciting period in history, or its most terrifying.

Or both.

I have felt for some time that we are drinking from the fire hose of karma, by which I mean the compounding consequences of delayed feedback across ecological and economic systems. The planet we have depleted of resources (soil, water, trees, ice, fauna) and filled with waste (the detritus of a throw-away culture) on the mistaken assumption that resources are infinite and the planet is too big for us to destabilize, is showing us with biblically proportioned insistence that we are dead wrong.

Epoch A and its Finite Games

The Salks referred to the phase of explosive growth that ended just a few decades ago as "Epoch A", which runs under the assumption that we can take whatever we want without repercussion, to serve "us and ours". They explain that Epoch A is characterized by persistent expansion, short-range planning (for maximum short-term gain), competition, sub-division (or narrowed focus), independence and power, transactional relationships, and an "either-or", "win-lose" mindset.

You know: basically, the past 150 years.

The Earth is showing us the error of that thinking.

But rather than use their insight to indict us, the Salks show us that Epoch A is *designed* to deplete resources. Or, at least, in that sense, we're no different from fruit flies or yeast, all of which keep gobbling up resources until there are none left.

The good news is that unlike fruit flies, we don't *need* to have a mass die-off. We have agency in our lives, and can make choices.

And the specific choices we make, in their words, could yield vastly different results.

The Salks and Hans Rosling have one major thing in common, apart from the use of the sigmoid curve. All of them are unabashedly optimistic about what comes next.

As an antidote to the Epoch A mindset, they point toward what they believe to be an inevitable future of socio-cultural human evolution. Pragmatically self-preservative, they believe that Epoch B will be characterized by dynamic equilibrium, long-range inter-generational planning (for maximum sustainability), collaboration, integration (or polymathic thinking), interdependence and consensus, deep connections, and a "both-and", "win-win" mindset.

The Salks say we are already there, and that what we are feeling is growing pains associated with this shift.

They illustrate this shift with the use of resources:

"[Through] *industrialization in both Europe and the United States, resources seemed limitless. They could be exploited without regard for the effects either of consumption or of the disposal of waste. This would correspond with Epoch A, in which positive value was placed on growth, consumption, and unlimited use of resources.*

"*In the last 50 to 70 years, however, there has been increasing awareness that resources are limited and that unfettered consumption, along with disregard for the effects of waste products, endangers our survival. Our adaptive response has been to place increasing value on awareness of limits, conservation, and on sustainability.*

"*Thus, the conditions of Epoch A support and are consistent with the values of unlimited growth and consumption, while the different conditions of Epoch B lead to the different values of sustainability and conservation.*"

In other words, the Salks don't believe our values will change due to goodwill. Rather, they will out of simple self-preservation. That is, they foresee more and more humans playing infinite games henceforth because we will *have* to, if we want to survive.

Thus, we will refocus human ingenuity with a new set of drivers that invests for long-term viability in a resource-finite world.

No Pain No Gain

The second critical point that the Salks make in their book is that there is no gain without pain. One cannot expect eight billion human beings to simply jettison their existing systems and lifestyles and start again without difficulty, resistance, and/or mutiny.

But.

The change is generationally inevitable. Millennials, the largest generation in human history, were the first to be *born* into Epoch B, with the tacit understanding that resources are in fact finite, and that our actions do in fact bear consequences.

To them, it's not abstract or faraway. It's record-breaking environmental calamities saturating their media feeds daily; and nation-sized plastic gyres, mass extinctions, chart-topping man-made mortality rates, and a yawning abyss between the haves and the have nots.

With this change "from accelerating growth to decelerating growth, a major shift must occur in human values, attitudes, behaviors, and relationships."

And so, the Salks illustrate that:

"...the tension we feel at this time [is] *an inherent part of this developmental and evolutionary process.* [It is] *not necessarily a sign of the impending end of the human species but instead reflects **the process of inversion in values**."*

Epoch B and its Infinite Games

Here, what the Salks describe is a future that tracks closely with a perspective that's emerged during my five years of research-fueled writing. Sociologically, they posit, our future will come to resemble those of pre-modern societies that were based on 'traditional' ways of "child-rearing, care of the elderly, conflict resolution, family relationships, and sustainable adaptation to the ecosystem—fit conditions of relative equilibrium."

Once these Epoch B value sets are applied to the complex, industry- and technology-powered institutions we've built in Epoch A, "the creation of altogether new societies for the future" will emerge, because they will need to.

Epoch B is characterized by infinite games, which some also refer to as "Game B". Jim Rutt, entrepreneur and the former Chairman of the Santa Fe Institute—one of the world's top science and technology think tanks—gives a great primer on Game B.

> *"To give a brief description of Game B: if Game A is the current Western civilization status quo, then Game B is a new civilization-level social operating system that at least hundreds of millions of people can live in. It's not something for just elites or outliers.*

> *"Game B is something that doesn't yet exist; it's what comes next. Some of the principles of Game B are that it is self-organizational (not top-down), network-oriented (not individualist), decentralized (not centralized), meta-stable (evolving but not volatile), oriented towards human flourishing, and towards the flourishing of non-human life as well."*

Well, Game B is being incubated everywhere:

- Online, with decentralized resources like all "Wiki" sites and the Internet itself;
- In business, among non-hierarchical companies such as Automattic, Valve, Cloudfare, and MorningStar;
- In corners of the physical world, where non-hierarchical social structures like kibbutzim and the Navy Seals have thrived for decades; and
- In new corporate governance models such as B-corps, cooperatives, and collectives, in which people beta-test communal structures that prioritize the collective good and common access

Thus, the 'brave new world' of Epoch B is not a repudiation of the existing order; it's a reappraisal of the things that must drive those gains if they are to be sustainable.

It will take the best of both worlds, and remake it.

Final Thoughts

All of the following human systems are broken, or breaking: economics and the transactional nature of human relationships; housing and its affordability; dietary and environmental health; how and why we educate; and the means and even reasons we work. And all are symptoms of the end run of Epoch A.

Therein lies the opportunity, and our transformation.

So, while nearly no one likes change, it is already upon us. We have passed the inflection point of our own evolution; and with the right choices, it's only going to get easier from now on.

Seen optimistically, as the Salks and Rosling did, we are living *not* through the most terrifying time in history, but rather at its inevitable inflection point, for which we have not only front row seats, but *steering wheels*.

Let's go for a tour of the trigger event.

Then-Brooklyn Borough President Eric Adams, at a Black Lives Matter protest © Anthony Fieldman 2020

4   2020: The Great Reset

Our current dystopia was *bound* to arise, for a number of reasons. First, modern life just keeps getting more complex, thus largely 'unknowable'. Second, this leads to an intensification of *fear*. Third, media has hijacked our amygdalae to cash in on the "attention economy". Fourth, our respective life experiences run the gamut, fueling mistrust and discontent. Fifth, the majority of things we "know" are in fact acquired secondhand from friends, family, teachers, books, blogs, and media, increasing our risk of manipulation. And sixth, the source material for all of these things has gone into hyperdrive since the advent of portable communications devices.

The Power of Ideas

Let's put the transmission of knowledge in perspective, for a minute. Humans have existed for just 300,000 years. The very first piece of 'writing' was created in Mesopotamia around 3,400 BCE. It was a piece of cuneiform carved into stone in pre-modern Iraq, which the Egyptians picked up two hundred years later and developed into the hieroglyphs we all studied in school. On the human timeline, this occurred during the last 1% of history. Much later, in 1440 CE—just 586 years ago—a German goldsmith named Johannes Gutenberg created the printing press. It is widely considered the greatest invention in history by scores of scientists, historians, engineers and entrepreneurs.

In an article named "Which is the Greatest Invention of All Time", *Destination Innovation* writes this appraisal:

> "[Gutenberg's] *invention of mechanical movable type printing started a revolution in communication throughout Europe. It facilitated the spread of knowledge in the form of printed books and pamphlets. This fueled the Renaissance and the Reformation. There followed the Age of Enlightenment and the sharing of Scientific Knowledge.*"

Gutenberg did no less than **democratize information** for the first time in the history of civilization. The printing press put more power into the hands of 'everyman' than anything before it. That's because access to sources of knowledge fuels human power, and reach.

There are two more statistics worth sharing, on the topic of dispersion of ideas. *Forbes* writes[1]:

> *"There are 2.5 quintillion bytes of data created each day at our current pace."*

and,

> *"Over the last two years alone 90 percent of the data in the world was generated."*

That's two years out of 300,000 of them that we've been "us".

This means that 90% of the world's data has been produced in one *one-hundred-and-fifty-thousandth* of human history.

So, the definitive reason that it feels as though we are living in a topsy-turvy dystopia right now, unfolding in real time, has mostly to do with both the speed with which our complex minds and our personal contexts are being spoon-fed information, as well as the overwhelming quantity of time we spend absorbing it. On average, according to Nielsen, adults now spend eleven hours—nearly half of our days— staring at a screen[2].

If we assume that people sleep on average 8 hours a day, then we are spending fully two thirds of our waking lives engaged with some form of media.

You don't need to be a scientist to intuit this. You need only look around you: on the street, in elevators, at dinner, at work, driving a car, out with your kids, or even in bed with your spouse.

What does all of this have to do with the idea of a "Great Reset?"

Well, *because* 90% of the world's data has been produced in just two years;

because we now spend far more time absorbing whatever our screens are feeding us than we spend ruminating, discussing, or researching; and *because* the sources of our information are severely dramatizing all of it in a blatant effort to profit from it, primarily by how much time we spend on any given site or channel; then to say that *people now inhabit distinct realities* is less hyperbole than *effectual truth.*

Given that the human brain's predisposition for fear is falling prey to the unyielding daily onslaught of highly selective data contained in the distinct worlds, or multiverses, of the Internet, our realities have suddenly become, in the blink of an eye, nearly irreconcilable.

The Worst Year Ever

It would be impossible to unpack just how distinct our worlds have become. So, let's look at just one world view. It was a conclusion that shaped countless realities in 2020 and everything that arose from it, and was neatly captured on the cover of the December 14, 2020 issue of *Time Magazine.* On that cover, a giant red crayon "X" symbolized the editors' attempt to negate the existence of the year itself, abetted by the issue's feature article, declaring 2020 to be "The Worst Year Ever".

Really?

For as long as COVID-19's acute phase menaced the world, I told anyone who would listen to me that for those whose lives *weren't* lost to the virus, or whose livelihoods *weren't* severely impacted or decimated by it, and who have recovered and remain alive and well today, 2020 will most likely be remembered, over the long term, as **the best year in modern history**.

How?

Well, a funny thing happens when we spend eleven daily hours absorbing what factions of humans are yelling at us while a virus courses its way through every nation on Earth, rattling the foundational structures of the civilizations in which we live: this egregious "stress test" begins to reveal the fault lines in what we've wrought, and those are seismic differences in our beliefs, trust, access, capacity, competitive edge, resolve, values, and priorities.

2020, I'd posit, will likely be remembered as the year that a large number of us finally woke up to discover that our lives were running on autopilot. While the dust has partly resettled by now, it was nonetheless a year in which *enough people* glimpsed the cracks in many of our systems and the behaviors that they sponsor. That includes, critically, the fact that the business world didn't crater when more than half of the workforce was forced to stay home... and *liked* it.

On this last point, an increasing number of us now realize that after 150 years of assembly-line thinking reinforced by reductive labels like "consumer," "user," or "tech head," to borrow my own profession's label of choice, we may have gone just a wee bit too far. And now that our mobile lives allow many of us to live from anywhere and *still* participate in economic life, many people are doing just that: reconsidering foundational decisions: where to live, how to live, how to collaborate, what matters to us as individuals and as a species, and *how to get there.*

And the very thing that has conspired to cleave reality into countless fragments and splinter our worlds has, much as Gutenberg's printing press did before it, *also* democratized power, once more.

That "thing"—the Internet—is connecting every human being on Earth to one another through an unbreakable and *non-hierarchical* web of emerging relations no one yet controls, or possibly even *can*. The emergence of the Internet puts systems and the know-how for creating them under the sphere of our own increasing influence, and is already greater than at any other time in history. I am referring to systems for living, protecting, educating, powering, healing, recycling, up-cycling and producing food: all of them enablers of human thriving.

Which Side of the Divide Are You On?

This will conspire to place human beings on one of two sides: the side of the living future—Epoch B— or the side of the dying past—Epoch A. Moreover, this period, which began in 2020, is now unfolding so rapidly that it is unlike anything we have ever seen. And enough people are now adequately unnerved to take notice of it.

This is a *great* thing for humankind. We are experts at inertia: the disinclination to change. Because of this, we historically deepen existing tracks until we are stuck in ruts we can no longer escape. Today's extractive systems comprise our deepest rut yet.

But the scale of environmental destruction, the COVID-19 virus, and some pathologically committed global political and business leaders have collectively led us to the Inflection Point. Ironically, given the latter's bid to control our future, they have handed us the reins of universal empowerment by creating catastrophes so dire that it will force the changes we need to survive, let alone thrive.

What we do with this opportunity is another thing altogether, and here's where we meet the mindset divide.

One side has largely given in to fear and mistrust. Some insist that the virus was a hoax or man-made, and that life-saving vaccines are in fact a deep state elite-fueled plot to control and even rewrite our DNA. Others determined that the penultimate U.S. election was totally stolen by a cabal of left-wing extremists. Many have doubled down on fossil fuels and 64-oz. sodas, and will ride these things to six feet under, if given the chance. They have taken advantage of digital soapboxes to rattle nerves and force black-and-white interpretations that make enemies and allies out of *everything*. And yet another group tossed up their hands in the hopes that their gods would sort it all out for them, or decided that this may be the Great Cleansing, Rapture, or some other form of End Times that will finally deliver their hard-won rewards.

But they are not the *only* groups.

The other side has chosen courage and optimism. They spend at least a few of their eleven daily onscreen hours harnessing that global human intelligence called The Internet to rethink norms, starting with their own life choices. They have rolled up their leisurewear sleeves and begun the hard work of incubating new models of human activity to replace the fractured old ones. In lieu of subdividing and conquering in pursuit of power, status, wealth, possessions and competition—all "finite values" that conspire to subdivide human beings and turn them adversarial—many are basing their new systems on "infinite values" like collaboration, community, empathy, trust, inclusivity, connection, health, vitality, hope, trust and compassion, from which words one cannot contrive a loser because they lift all boats. These are the people at "the head of the curve" that we examined in Chapter 1.

And others are following them, the way Rogers explained it.

Final Thoughts

If you choose the status quo, you are dooming yourself to suffer needlessly. The "old world" will remain for a while longer, well past the seismic reboot of 2020. But the world of economics-fueled competition and extraction is making its end run. 2020 has shown it to lead to woeful unpreparedness and to fuel more death than has been necessary. The global network we now plug into has allowed us to meet this challenge better than at any time in human history. And still: more people died than needed to because some of us sowed chaos in order to conquer, in lieu of shoring one another up to survive together.

Alternatively, you can choose the path to the future. It's already here. Entire sections of the Internet, fueled by those who have created—and still largely create—the structures through which we collaborate, consume, or conspire, are already moving on. So-called "Game B" communities based on infinite values are incubating and thriving online, and looking to recraft analog living offline, in Dunbar-sized groups of 150 people[23]. Proponents are testing new models of post-industrial education in line with such values, with post-extractive value creation. We'll discuss a few of these in Chapter 13. Others are rewriting how we diagnose and even administer health[24]. Yet others are incubating new business paradigms, complete with digitally powered manufacture and supply chains[25]. Many are learning to grow food in small scale, in our living rooms or on our roofs, through interdependent systems of animal and plant food production and waste. We'll see large-scale initiatives in Chapters 18 and 19. Innovators are cleaning up the planet with new systems of energy and waste management/reversal[26]. And countless protesters are sidestepping traditional forms of governmental control and/or influence by connecting directly with collaborators to chat the path to greater freedoms, in spite of government censorship and often, disinformation.

The Arab Spring was the most conspicuous version of this last point. "Nearly 9 in 10 Egyptians and Tunisians surveyed... said they were using Facebook to organise [sic] protests or spread awareness about them," according to UAE's *The National*.

The power is increasingly with people who are fed up of being used as pawns and are now in possession of every tool needed to rapidly create new modalities of living and thriving in a digitally connected age, to make sure that the next time we are ravaged by a natural virus—one in which, it must be said, we had a hand in creating, at least as a *byproduct* of our existing systems—we have the ability to handle multiple fallout across the sphere of human activities better, wherever we are, in our Brave New [Connected] World.

Every small act has an impact we can scarcely measure, as we'll see in the following chapter. Therein lies our power.

No Kings Day protest, New York City © Anthony Fieldman 2025

5   The (Real) Butterfly Effect

To say "we are all connected" is more than metaphysical kumbaya. It is a factual comment about cause and effect over time that applies not only to the natural world's ecosystems, but to human history, as well. To say it is to understand that every single act by *every single person* who ever lived helped to create the world in which we live today, no matter how seemingly trivial.

And the permutations are near-infinite.

Edward Lorenz, MIT math professor and meteorologist, and the man we can blame for how we predict the weather, proposed a concept in 1972 that has to be among the most heretical concepts since Copernicus proposed his heliocentric model of the universe, relegating humans to the back seat of the cosmos.

Lorenz introduced the concept of the Butterfly Effect, essentially suggesting that some systems, like weather, were inherently *unpredictable*, and therefore "small variances in the initial conditions could have profound and widely divergent effects on the system's outcomes." In the process of combining math and meteorology into the theory of the Butterfly Effect, Lorenz was repudiating the world that the Father of Science himself, Isaac Newton, had set in place nearly three hundred years earlier: that nature is *deterministic*, and runs like a clock, predictably.

Lorenz's ideas founded a new branch of mathematics called Chaos Theory. Equally unorthodox, Lorenz suggested that if he were wrong, and the rest of the world were right about nature's predictability, then "Nothing would be uncertain and the future, as the past, would be present to our eyes." He observed "that nature's interdependent cause-and-effect relationships are too complex to resolve." He used this theory to conduct "parallel simulations" for things like the weather. We're all familiar with his work when we see scientists attempting to predict a range of outcomes for hurricane landfall, strength and damage.

Lorenz's theories have application far beyond meteorology. They apply to humans and human behavior, equally. As I prepared to write this section of the book, I shared a thought with a friend to illustrate the idea: "You know, for every famous person, there are millions of others whose acts, however modest, *needed* to occur in order for that person to do what they did." Then I added, "I'm convinced that every single act by every single person on Earth matters, because we can't appreciate the complexity of relationships between what the world looks like today and the things it took to make it that way."

To make my point in a decidedly un-rigorous way, I cited everyone's favorite genius, Steve Jobs. I said that every part of Syria's history had to play out exactly as it did, or we never would've had iPhones. (Jobs' father was Syrian.) If we scratch even the surface of this man, we see cause and effect everywhere, even by looking at just a few permutations of his history. What inputs did it take to make Jobs' biological father Syrian rather than something else, which exerted a fundamental cultural influence over the man he became? What did it take for the same man to decide to become an activist? Or to leave Syria to pursue a PhD in the U.S.? Or for him to meet and fall for a Swiss-German woman there, whose ancestors' own origins and choices are equally complex? Or for *her* father to become anti-Muslim, pressuring her to leave her then-boyfriend? Or, as a result, for her to decide to decamp to San Francisco without telling anyone, when she became pregnant with the future Steve Jobs? Or for her to decide to give Steve up for adoption, once she realized she couldn't "go it alone"? Or for the first couple to whom she offered him to change their minds and decline? Or for the second couple to choose the adoption agency where they met Joanne—Jobs' biological mother—after Clara Jobs had suffered from an ectopic pregnancy, leading them to pursue adoption? Or for Joanne to rescind her offer, only to have the eager Jobses file suit, and win custody of the future, as-yet unborn inventor?

Ignore for a moment what happened in Jobs' own life: the millions (billions?) of choices *he made*, and which had to be exactly as they were, influenced by a lifetime of personal experience in reaction to other human beings who abetted, challenged or otherwise influenced his own choices. The same applies to his biological and adoptive parents, and everyone down their own ancestral *and* socio-communal lines. All of these choices has to occur in order for Jobs to exist, let alone influence the choices he made. And assessing it all is mathematically and deterministically impossible. Regardless, the fact remains that if every Syrian didn't do exactly what they did, or every Swiss-German, or every American, and likely every other person who influenced those people and histories, then there'd be no iPhone, which I use as a proxy for walking around *with the world in our pockets.*

Simply put, we are the product of everyone and everything that ever existed, down to the most modest act.

Lorenz called it Chaos Theory. We could just as easily call it humanity. Chaos theory stipulates that "within the apparent randomness of chaotic complex systems, there are underlying patterns, interconnectedness, constant feedback loops, repetition, self-similarity, fractals and self-organization." To me, that sounds a lot like life. In fact, *Wikipedia* cites Chaos Theory's current *centrality* to the stock market, road traffic, computer science, anthropology, sociology, meteorology, physics, environmental science, engineering, economics, biology, ecology, philosophy, and even pandemic crisis management. Right now, scientists and researchers are applying it to cryptography, robotics, celestial mechanics, quantum physics, team-building and group development.

I am not a mathematician, but it sounds as though it applies to pretty much *everything* humans do.

In 1994, a work colleague named Neil introduced me to Stephen Wolfram's book *Cellular Automata and Complexity.* Neil was a computer scientist. He showed me that on an empty grid with just one black-filled cell, *the rules that one chose to create* to determine whether the adjacent cell would fill or remain empty resulted, once an algorithm had been written to auto-populate the grid according to your rules, in complexity that quickly and furiously morphed into ever-changing patterns, with no single pattern *ever* being replicated. This richness resulted from a *single decision.* Wolfram, Neil told me, was able to run simulations from this seemingly simple cell logic to recreate—randomly, not with intent—every single pattern found in nature, from the structure of leaves to that of snowflakes.

Neil and I used it to compose building façades. That was our modest aim. But Wolfram's studies stuck, because they helped me to understand the seeming randomness of cause and effect, even if that randomness were based on a set of deterministic rules. The *Wikipedia* page on Chaos Theory, at the time of this writing, includes a mesmerizing graphic on the right-hand side, with a hinged pair of red lines acting as a pendulum, tracing random and non-repeating patterns.

It's beautiful.

Lorenz's theory was mischaracterized in Hollywood by people who insisted "the flap of a butterfly's wings in Brazil could set off a tornado in Texas," citing Lorenz's own words. But that was never his point. He was saying only that one could not predict what would happen, but rather that every act mattered in determining the outcome. Even the flap of a butterfly's wings.

So why the science, math and geometry lesson? It seems obvious to me. We are all connected, more deeply and more fully than we can ever understand.

I'll share one more example. A psychologically deranged man in Pakistan put a bullet through the skull of the headstrong daughter of an educator, who then went on not just to survive, but to tirelessly champion women's rights everywhere, inspiring tens of thousands of other girls *worldwide* to self-advocate in every corner of the Earth. We cannot undervalue what made this girl who she is without first understanding how everyone who came before her in her own lineage fits into the picture. The fact is that she exists, she inspires, and countless girls will do things they may not have dreamed of if they hadn't read Malala's book. Her own influences certainly include modest people about whom we will never learn but who Malala assuredly remembers and values for the part they played in shaping *her* life, as well as the gunman himself, for playing the part of a catalyst.

Again, this is just a tiny example.

Every single moment of every day we are met with choice. In a book called *Bad Moves*, authors Sahakian and LaBuzetta posit that the average adult makes about 35,000 choices a day. Separately, Cornell researchers Wansink and Sobal say we make 227 of them about food alone. Let's give them all the benefit of our doubt. That's 273 trillion individual decisions collectively made, every day, by people on Earth. Do my decisions affect those of anybody around me? Of course they do. There are no markets without customers, no domination without submission, and no destruction without an army and all the people in it. Our choices exert a counterinfluence over others' choices. In a very real way, human beings can be seen as a single organism whose choices are near-infinite, and all-powerful.

Even the tiny ones.

It was a momentary slip-up in miscommunication, after all, that led an unprepared East Berlin Politburo member named Günter Schabowski to *mistakenly* declare at a 1989 press conference, "As far as I know, the border is open immediately," a few hours after which Checkpoint Charlie was flooded by thousands of East Germans, as border guards staring in awe and confusion opened the gates, let the hordes through, and East and West Germans brought down the hated Berlin Wall, presaging Germany's reunification, and the fall of the Iron Curtain.

Butterfly flap, indeed.

I was there the next day.

Final Thoughts

So, what can we take away from all this, apart from a headache? We can be more humble than we are. We can realize that everyone we come across is a person with needs, wishes and a personality, just like us. Personally, I still have much to learn in this regard; but I'm trying. We can realize that no matter what we do, the way in which we act toward any one of them will impact them, as well as decisions that *they* will make afterwards. In its destructive form, we call that game "Kick the Cat".

We can realize that if we put good in the world, the world will become better. We can realize that the most modest act can have a major impact on all of humanity. So while a butterfly could ultimately, mathematically, precipitate a tornado in Texas, a human smile, a donation, words of support, or any act of kindness that comes from a place of caring, humility, shared humanity, empathy, understanding, acceptance, or love can move mountains.

It not only *can* change the world, it *does*.

And conversely, every act that serves to weaken human beings cheats us of our potential to move mountains together. So, the next time you look at someone famous or rich, or who seems to be #winning in one way or another, and the next time you look at someone homeless or ill who seems to bear the weight of the world on their shoulders, just know that you had something to do with their successes or failures, and that your very next act can equally have an impact on them, both directly and indirectly.

With every one of our 35,000 daily choices, we are omnipotent.

Generosity begets generosity. Kindness begets kindness. When good things happen to us, we feel invincible. And when bad things happen, we are more inclined to act in kind.

On page 350, in the epilogue of his simultaneously heartbreaking and optimism-fueled book, *The Body Keeps the Score*, author, psychiatrist and trauma expert Bessel van der Kolk finally says it:

"Trauma breeds further trauma; hurt people hurt other people."

To understand this is to understand the root of our broken systems. Internalize it, and take responsibility for your power. Understand that for all the inequality in the world, others' power is no more than the result of past acts we all brought into being; and that acts in the present and the future can change things drastically, in ways we cannot imagine.

We have the agency to choose our futures.

The rest of this book is a deep dive into each "broken thing", with a focus on "unbroken" initiatives being developed meaningfully and at scale, that operate from just such a place.

The author hammering away at the Berlin Wall on November 10, 1989 © Timm Oberwelland

PART TWO

How To Fix It All

"Black Lives Matter" Protest, NYC © Anthony Fieldman 2021

6 How Everything Broken Could Be Fixed: An Overview

If you've paid close attention, you'll have noticed that since COVID-19 first arrived almost six years ago, everything has changed. Or, more accurately, everything has *begun* to change. I'm referring to where and how we work, live, learn, and socialize; what we value and thus invest in and prioritize; how we view ourselves, our communities, and the planet at large; and how these perceptions are shifting the ground underfoot across the spectrum of human activity, and will likely result in an effective rewrite of a century (if not twenty) of behaviors.

In Chapter 4, I referred to the pandemic as The Great Reset because human behavior is remarkably consistent and because the path to any "new normal" starts, progresses and ends the same way, every time.

And as we saw in Chapter 1, Everett Rogers brilliantly codified this phenomenon as The Diffusion of Innovations to explain how everything humans create transforms from an idea to a new and entrenched reality.

The pattern of change has been remarkably consistent, over time.

COVID-Fueled Innovation

The pandemic can be seen as the de facto catalyst for a multi-system rewrite. It was that rare event that was big enough to shake things up globally: *enough* for the cracks to appear to *enough* people, then disrupt the status quo just *enough* for us to begin doing something about it. The reason it took such a seismic upheaval is because the overwhelming majority of us favor what we know over what we don't know, and are hard-wired to fear.

To repeat a quote I shared in Chapter 1, "The oldest and strongest emotion of mankind is fear, and the oldest and strongest kind of fear is fear of the unknown."

Our biological underpinnings predispose us as individuals and groups to favor inertia. We often protect business as usual while fighting change and challengers, mostly out of fear that we'll be left behind or that we'll lose control over resources we've amassed in order to protect the things that benefit us. And because our amygdalae fire any time we feel threatened, too few of us stop fighting change long enough to ask ourselves whether the way things *are* is the way they *should be.*

Often, they aren't.

COVID-19's impact on the status quo was seismic. Well beyond those whose lives were tragically lost or ravaged as a direct result of the pathogen, nearly everyone on the planet was affected in significant ways. Overnight, work, health, play, and education were all crippled. For some, the impacts were catastrophic, while others escaped the worst or have recovered, in whole or in part. For a small subset of people, life actually improved. Regardless, no one was spared change because the pandemic unmoored us all from our usual patterns, if only because "usual" was no longer an option.

This is where opportunity exists for those given to meeting the future head on, to participate in the creation of "a better tomorrow".

Not everyone will.

When it comes to groups of any kind, there are nearly always more people near the center than at the extremes. In fact, the very words "normal" and "extreme" make that logic pretty clear.

The bell curve upon which Rogers' ideas are based is a great tool for charting the adoption of anything new. That's because no idea will ever make intuitive sense to everyone, and even if it were to, not everyone would readily toss something familiar for something whose safety and benefits haven't been proven, let alone widely adopted.

Our appetite for risk varies greatly, but biologically favors self-protection.

Within the paradigm of innovation, there are really three human populations: those who **lead** (whom Rogers calls innovators and early adopters), those who need to **be led** (the early and late majorities), and those who **refuse to play ball**, no matter what others do (the laggards).

Wherever we sit on the curve, every human system we consider normal today began as a disruption, and they all followed the same pattern of absorption until they eventually replaced the status quo.

As I wrote in Chapter 1, I believe we are now faced with a once-in-a-century opportunity to fix systems whose failure to meet enough people's core needs were revealed by the pandemic, whether those systems are simply ripe for an upgrade, are obsolete leftovers from another era, or never worked for a broad cross-section of human beings in the first place.

Improving or replacing these systems is important because they touch or govern most areas of our lives, including **housing, nutritional and environmental health, education,** and **work**, as well as the **economic system** that drives them all.

In spite of our considerable ingenuity, most pervasive paradigms have failed to produce outcomes that prioritize access, equity, and quality over personal gains and hegemony, largely due to the actions of powerful individuals, companies, and political bodies who wage legal and economic wars to prevent new ideas (and competitors) from undermining that which is in their self-interest.

But in spite of our best efforts to thwart change, every human system we now take for granted began, grew, and ultimately flourished the same way: in accordance with the bell curve.

As the adage goes, "Time and tide wait for no man".

Eventually, innovation usually wins.

What remains to be seen, and could decisively alter the arc of coming innovations, is the **moral framework** we will adopt to guide them. This is where the planet's dominant economic system comes into play. For example, will we pit resources against one another in competitive acts of subterfuge, the way we have for ages? Or will we finally synchronize the collective capacity of eight billion humans in a bid to bring as many contributors into the mix as possible? Said another way, will we continue to play zero-sum "finite games" in which losses equal gains, with those gains becoming increasingly concentrated in fewer hands? Or will we use our outsized brains to create such positive-sum "infinite game" structural systems as brilliantly conceived by innovative thinkers like James Carse, and championed by acolytes like Prof. Nikki Harré and Simon Sinek?

In a 2018 report on the state of global capitalism, *The Economist* observed the following:

> *"High profits across a whole economy can be a sign of sickness. They can signal the existence of firms more adept at siphoning wealth off than creating it, such as those that exploit monopolies."*

This dominant economic paradigm presents a moral dilemma. In appraising A.I. for *Buzzfeed*, futurist Ted Chiang wrote:

> *"There's a saying, popularized by Fredric Jameson, that it's easier to imagine the end of the world than to imagine the end of capitalism."*

He goes on:

> *"Who pursues their goals with monomaniacal focus, oblivious to the possibility of negative consequences? Who adopts a scorched-earth approach to increasing market share? A hypothetical strawberry-picking A.I. does what every tech startup wishes it could do—grows at an exponential rate and destroys its competitors until it's achieved an absolute monopoly."*

The challenge, then, isn't so much whether a new innovation will disrupt existing systems. Few would argue the perception that Silicon Valley is the poster child for innovation. It's whether or not, as our tools and reach both expand exponentially with the "god-like technologies" E.O. Wilson observed we increasingly possess, we will endow our systemic creations with a moral backbone that favors maximizing public good (infinite play) over scorched-earth capitalism (finite play).

Our (Possible) Future

Each broken system deserves to be dissected and appraised in detail, and the rest of this book is devoted to that task. To introduce them, I'll summarize select key drivers and innovations being developed today which could, if informed by the right moral framework, lead us to a proverbial Eden.

So, what would that look like, exactly?

Housing

Shelter is truly one of our most basic needs. Without a home, we cannot function. Without a *safe* one that supports us within the context of our cultural community, whether it's a Mongolian ger, a Korowai treehouse or a unit in New York City's public housing, we are robbed of the means to participate in daily life from a place of stability.

And yet: across much of the world, we've made home ownership one of the least affordable basic needs, impacting 1.6 billion people, and making 90% of cities "unaffordable"[27]; moreover, it has been found to be *the* leading driver of homelessness[28].

The solution to housing everyone is threefold, and rests on supply, mindset, and policy.

Supply is simple to fix, if the priority is to house everyone: build enough homes for the population. And yet, this basic, self-evident metric languishes in most countries, due to governmental and economic constraints.

There are two notable exceptions: Germany and Japan. The real cost of housing in both countries—nearly flat over decades, unlike other G7 nations[29]—is primarily the result of having built enough of it for prices not to spike. In Germany, 97 construction permits are issued for every 100 people it adds to the population, balancing demand with adequate supply. If this seems like an obvious solution, it's *not* common practice, elsewhere.

In Japan, "…centralized national control over housing and zoning has yielded cities with so many modest homes in transit-centered, low-carbon neighborhoods that rent has been flat for decades."[30]

Self-preservation is another barrier to broad home ownership in many places, counter-intuitively. In the U.S. and Canada, for example, we want property values to *increase* because decades back, society began to conflate "home" with "investment". Why? Our definition in those countries shifted when governments deregulated housing and privatized retirement benefits. Soon after, people were scrambling to drive up prices so they could secure their own financial futures for when they no longer could (or wanted to) work, since the then-dominant "social contracts" no longer existed.

We will revisit this idea in depth, in Chapter 15.

In fact, equity in one's home is the greatest source of wealth generation in the United States for those lucky enough to own one, comprising 50-70% of total wealth for the three middle-income quintiles.[31]. While in absolute dollars, retirement accounts hold more value than real estate does[32], this is only due to the fact that one third fewer people own a home, primarily due to lack of affordability.

If The "Economics of Enough" took hold—a concept I'll cover in Chapter 8—we could find ourselves in a situation more like Germany's or Japan's.

Lastly, there is the problem of direct subsidies. In referencing Pulitzer Prize-winning author Matthew Desmond's book, *Evicted*, Maggie Talbot shared the following take in *The New Yorker*:

> *"The payout to homeowners* [via mortgage interest deductions] *in 2020—a hundred and ninety-three billions dollars—far exceeded the fifty-three billion dollars in direct housing assistance that the government gave to low-income families."*

As framed in the book and article, this means that *most* aid goes to those who need it *least.* Nearly four times as much, to be exact. What if those resources were redirected toward holding land costs down, or for funding innovations in next-gen, affordable housing?

The good news is that private industry is now doing exactly that, in spite of government policy. A large contingent of architects, engineering, technology and construction companies are dreaming up solutions to this problem by modernizing the act of constructing a home, whether its for a single family or a multi-unit building. Finally, the momentum is building for a century-old idea: that homes should be like cars: fabricated (and largely assembled) in a factory, where incremental improvements in quality and efficiency can be leveraged, and the associated reductions in price passed onto customers. In another novel approach, some companies are moving the factory to the job site, with devices like massive 3D printers and robots.

I've been telling my architectural partners for a few years now that there's no defensible reason a home should cost more than a car. In the United States, a *five-year*, $45,000 mortgage on a $50,000 home, even at a 7% interest rate, would cost an owner roughly $890/month. That's significantly less than half the average rent across the U.S.,[33] and after just five years, they would own it outright. If that financial burden was still too great, then for a mere $300/month, it would be theirs at the end of a common 30-year term.

Today, $100,000 homes—twice my dream price, yet less than one quarter of the median home price in the U.S[34]—are popping up everywhere. A $100,000 home would cost the unsheltered no more than the average rent in the United States does today.

At the time of this writing, MiniMod, Avrame, FabCab, Modscape, KitHAUS, Koto, ICONBuild, IdeaBox, BuildCover, PlusPuu Houses, and Boxabl all have high-design, ready-made homes on the market today, for a fraction of the cost of a stick-built one. These may not be luxe, but they are quality-built answers to homelessness and *unsafe* housing. The latter point is important because 5% of U.S. homes are classified as inadequate[35], while as many as 40 to 45 percent of U.S. homes in metropolitan areas have at least one health or safety hazard, such as mold, pests, or lead paint.[36]

As companies continue to innovate, barriers to home ownership should continue to lower, even while quality continues to improve, as long as individual and corporate greed are not allowed to drive the price.

Enter the moral imperative.

A $50,000 home is conceivable in the near future, as the movement gains steam. In fact, ICONBuild's Vulcan robotic printing system recently built a community of 65 homes in Nacajuca, Mexico with real estate partner New Story at a cost of just *$5,000 USD apiece* for a group of ultra-poor, homeless families who had been living huddled under open-air tarps with dirt floors and without running water.

While it hasn't published the costs, ICON later used the same technology to 3D-print a well-publicized project called "House Zero" with architects Lake|Flato. It was a gorgeous 2,000 sq. ft. 3BR/2.5BA net-zero house in Texas that should make *anybody* happy.

Of course, government will have to play a role because no matter how a home is built it needs land on which to sit, and for the moment, a free market propped up by profit-driven developers and government subsidies still largely establishes the value of that land in the sale of places to live. Too often, it puts home ownership out of reach. Policies like Japan's point the way toward flattening prices, over the long term.

The United States has stepped in before. The Homestead Act of 1862 offered *160 acres of free land* to anyone intrepid enough to claim it, then build and live on it for five years[37]. It's a policy that ran for more than a century, broadly ending in 1976, and in 1986 in Alaska.

Land aside, more home innovators like ICON are coming and attracting early adopters like Lake|Flato and the individuals who purchase what they create, thus de-risking and normalizing the idea for the early and late majorities that will eventually bring the laggards kicking and screaming into their affordable future.

We will do a deep dive into both homelessness and housing in Chapters 14 and 15.

Health

I've written about food for nearly eight years now. To repeat key statistics I shared in Chapter 1, two of the most important ways in which food is broken are that (i) it eats up more land resources (51%) than anything else on the planet, with tropical deforestation alone producing 20% of all greenhouse gases[38]; and (ii) industrialized, profit-driven food products are literally killing more of us (one of out five global deaths, or 11 million humans per year) than anything else.

Fun fact: according to the Global Burden of Disease, which is the most comprehensive worldwide observational epidemiological study, three times as many people die each year from *overeating* than from malnourishment[39].

Chew on that for a minute.

Food, along with housing, is foundational to our wellbeing. Yet here, too, we have gamified nutrition in the name of economic profit. Putting orange juice in our gas tanks would destroy our car engines, so none of us do that. Why, then, do we readily pay to pour the equivalent of gasoline in our own bodies and destroy the planet on which we depend in the process?

We can do much, much better.

The solution to a broken food system necessitates growing real foods responsibly and efficiently, getting them to people affordably, and educating and incentivizing the public to avail themselves of the bounty.

Like housing, food production is undergoing a renaissance. So-called vertical farming companies are coming online, seemingly monthly.

At the time of this writing, Plenty, Aero Farms, Altius Farms, Bowery, HydroGreen, Dream Harvest, Farm.One, GrowPod, Square Roots, Vertical Harvest, and Vertical Roots are operational and comprise just a handful of established innovators.

There are tons more.

Some are innovating at the scale of a consumer appliance we can purchase and install in our homes, like Canada's Nutritower. Others, like France's Agricool—the world's largest, at the time of this writing—are working at an industrial scale as an alternative to inefficient, land-depleting open-field agriculture.

We are firmly at the leading edge of the bell curve. Even at this early stage, however, the vertical farming market could well quadruple or quintuple in market value in the next five years, as it tiptoes toward normalizing[40].

The longer-term upside is massive.

Beyond how we grow foods, the decentralization of our food system from the ten mega-companies (the "Big Ten") who currently control nearly everything we eat[41] into a pervasive constellation of smaller operators is one strategy to return food to its roots. It wasn't that long ago that *nearly all* of us—90%, that is—were farmers[42].

Instead of backbreaking work, however, growing food could well be as easy as activating an A.I.-fueled farming system with our phones.

Food's decentralization will also help mitigate the risk of cyberterrorism. Called "one of the most glaring cracks in Canada's national defence [sic]" in an article[43] a friend sent to me a while back, the food sector represents a new geopolitical weapon, with evidence of state-sponsored attacks from Russia, China, North Korea and Iran having gained control over farms' computer systems in Canada alone, since it expressed its support for Ukraine.

Those systems increasingly control temperature, soil moisture, animal nutrient and antibiotics delivery, air flow, etc., even in *conventional* farming. And so, innovation in the food sector, plant and animal, alike [air protein, anyone?[44]], will require us to invest the same amount on cybersecurity and human resources that we lavish on our phones and laptops today.

We will examine food innovations in depth, in Chapters 18 and 19.

Any appraisal of physiological health must include an assessment of the healthcare system that underpins it.

Sickness is big business. The constellation of co-conspirators is vast and includes farmers, food scientists, food and beverage companies, restaurants (fast and slow), marketers, agricultural businesses, chemical companies, investors, retailers, transportation businesses, advertisers, regulators, media, clothing companies, insurance companies, drug companies, doctors, authors, lifestyle and fitness companies, and the government itself, who makes the most money of all through taxation and kickbacks.

This, in itself, may be the biggest impediment to improving health outcomes across the board because until economic gains no longer drive us to profit from others' sickness, too many of us will be disincentivized from sharing our inventions freely.

Leading the world, Americans spend $4.9 trillion each year on direct healthcare costs alone. That's $14,570 per person[45]. Most wealthy countries spend half of that, which is still too much, in my view. We also spend $264 billion on physical fitness[46], in spite of the fact that for this world-leading investment, Americans rank 20th in physical activity[47]. Agrochemicals for conventional produce add another $235 billion to the national economy[48]. And Big Pharma spends $30 billion just on marketing their products to Americans alone[49].

The list goes on.

And yet: largely because of technology, we are on the precipice of innovative systems that could upend sickness and return us to health. The costs we will charge would-be patients for the privilege of access, however, remain to be seen.

mRNA vaccines have prevented millions of hospitalizations and millions more deaths in the US alone since the pandemic started[50]. The speed of sequencing genomes is now one of our greatest weapons, and the only one we've devised that moves as quickly as mutating bacteria. For now, people have benefited from <u>free access</u> to these life-saving medicines because governments have so-far determined that it is in their best interest to do so, as they've done with the flu shot for decades.

There is no reason that the trend cannot expand and for governments to prioritize investing in their citizens' health *beyond* fighting a pandemic, beginning with *prevention.*

Stranger things have happened.

Artificial Intelligence is one of the most interesting frontiers in medical science. In breast cancer care alone, the use of A.I. for imaging analysis is reviewing mammograms 30 times faster than conventional doctors and diagnosis historically have, and with 99% accuracy[51].

The A.I. market in particular could plausibly transform healthcare. At the time of this writing, there are many such indicators. In Mexico, my good friends Alan and Josh recently pioneered A.I.-powered, 100% automated IVF technologies and processes that is already outperforming manual analogues. Their company, Conceivable Life Sciences, aims to drastically reduce cost barriers to pregnancy while simultaneously improving outcomes.

In the U.K., eMed aims to "put an accessible and affordable health service in the hands of every person on Earth". U.S. Freenome aims to use A.I. to test blood for early cancer detection. Singapore-based Bifourmis employs predictive patient monitoring to detect personalized patterns of health deterioration. U.S. Zymergen, recently acquired by Ginkgo, uses A.I. to engineer microbes to make useful molecules. Insistro and Exscientia both focus on machine-learning driven drug discovery and development. And many companies and universities are pioneering nanobots, nanofibers, and nanotech wearables to bring the future *inside of our bodies* to do the work we cannot.

That list, too, goes on.

Biomedical investment illustrates Rogers' Diffusion of Innovations theory perfectly, with U.S. Healthcare Generative A.I. Market returning a projected 37.6% CAGR, according to Grandview Research[52].

Education

A healthy, well-fed and housed population is nothing without being armed... with mental resources. Like housing in the United States, the cost of an education has increased precipitously over time, outpacing wage growth there eightfold since the 1980's, according to *Forbes.*[53] Accordingly, American student loans are now second only to the country's housing debts, and on par with auto loans[54].

Per that same *Forbes* article:

> *"Many young professionals are having to choose between saving for retirement or repaying their loans. Add in the pressure to buy a house, and it's easy to see why savings rates are nearing all time lows."*

This, in the world's richest country.

According to NPR, the prime drivers of cost increases are colleges' investment in teachers, facilities, and programs that allow them to complete favorably against one another for prestige and human capital. It's the ultimate finite game. And the cost of play is passed on to students who are immersed in debt as a result, or cannot afford to join the game.

Here, too, however, innovations are abounding, thanks to the Internet.

Globally, according to *Forbes*, more than 6.04 billion humans, or 73% of us, now have Internet access.[55] That number is expected to reach 7.9 billion by 2029[56].

The reason this matters, as we'll explore in depth in Chapter 21, is that education has begun, and will likely continue, to move increasingly online.

The phenomenon even has a name: edX.

I've been using a hypothetical example for a while now to illustrate an idea. It came to me when, during the pandemic, storied institutions like Harvard, Yale, Oxford, Stanford, and MIT all offered free MOOCs to anyone with a web browser.

Let's say college costs $60,000/year. Sadly, this is a common ticket price for out-of-state tuition [I have a daughter in college, so this is a "fresh wound"]. An institution with an annual class size of 1,000 would thus gross them $60M in tuition fees. On top of this, they have to pay teachers, property taxes, mortgages or other real estate investments, utility costs, suppliers, and an army of asset-related non-teaching employees to manage facilities, security, etc.

Let's now say that instead of admitting 1,000 students at $60,000 apiece, the cost of college was just $1,000, and 60,000 students were admitted from across the globe. How? By putting college entirely online. A college's earnings from tuition would remain unchanged. Moreover, instead of paying for physical facilities, colleges could put a large chunk of that obsolete investment into advanced teleconferencing to connect students and teachers dynamically, leveraging AR and VR. As it is, more and more college resources are moving online. Why not learning itself?

The entire world was forced to do this during the pandemic. And even with v1.0's *significant* downsides in terms of retention and efficacy, students still mostly learned, and they graduated.

Well, the Metaversity is coming. Per *The Conversation*:

> *"In one of the largest efforts thus far, 10 U.S. colleges and universities have teamed up with U.S. technology company Meta and Irish virtual reality platform Engage to create 3D digital versions of their campuses, known as a metaversity."*

In the Metaversity paradigm I described, colleges could opt to spend a portion of their massive real estate and operational savings on lavish, monthly or quarterly in-person educational retreats, domestic and abroad, for students to bond, grow perspective, and gain mind-expanding experiences. [Gap year, anyone? It was awesome.] In these "intensives", students could gain valuable one-on-one time outside of the Metaverse with professors, while building social connections with fellow students that historically carry over into adulthood.

One could argue that learning occurs *at least* as much outside of a classroom as inside of one. That's been my conclusion after decades of designing institutions of higher learning. In this vein, month-long, service-focused international travel programs such as those offered by Putney Student Tours, which has been operating since 1951, often produce seminal educational *and social* experiences. In Putney's own words:

> *"Our programs take students around the world to immerse themselves in local cultures, communities, and landscapes, instilling a passion for learning and discovery that are new to them. This spark often ignites*

lifelong interests, serving as a springboard for students to chart their future course."

My daughter twice attended Putney's programs during high school, in both Costa Rica and Thailand, as her mother did before her. In my view, both gained a significant practical education in areas of skills-building, entrepreneurship, geography, economics, language, international relations, and self-awareness.

When college goes online, students will be able to access the material any time of day across time zones. Teachers will potentially *earn the same for less work*, creating digital content once and then focusing on mentorship, as we do at work regularly. If we did this, overall institutional costs would decrease dramatically, while *allowing sixty times the number of people to be educated for one sixtieth of the price*, in my hypothetical example.

In truth, the multiples could be far higher.

What impact would a sixtyfold increase in educated humans have on global prosperity?

The mind reels.

"But an in-person education is far better than an online one," I can hear you say. To this, I have two things to say. First, I am describing a rethink of college, not primary or secondary education. For those, in-person education is critical, though here, too, we could innovate significantly. We'll discuss that at length in Chapters 21 and 22. Second, most of what we now learn is *already* online, whether we like it or not. And the primary source of our youth's sense-making is no longer the college classroom (if it ever was), but the Internet. And the Internet is brimming with powerful knowledge, dynamically and interactively presented. *Parsing* the content is what now matters most.

Beyond institutional innovations, even the *necessity* for a general education, delivered conventionally, is not beyond scrutiny. Consider that some of our own era's greatest innovators didn't even have one. Thomas Edison. The Wright Brothers. Steve Jobs. Paul Allen. Bill Hewlett.

None graduated college. Some skipped it altogether.

Many non-tech superstars skipped college, too. Kobe Bryant. Madonna. Oprah Winfrey. Tina Brown. Maya Angelou. Tom Cruise. Jay-Z.

"Poor them...?"

How about titans of social impact? Abraham Lincoln, Benjamin Franklin, Michael Bloomberg, Andrew Carnegie, and Harry Truman *also* skipped college.

Whether we skip or reinvent it, educational innovation is here, on the Internet, and it's a matter of time before it upends what it means to learn. When that happens, education may finally be democratized, and in the hands of a globally empowered, well-fed, housed, and healthy population of human creators, for pittance.

Work

The last broken system I'll cover here, and in Chapters 23 thru 25, is work.

As a partner in a large company whose 600-ish employees hold wildly competing views about in-person vs. digital employment, and who design workspaces for a living, I am convinced that the future will not be one size fits all. Increasingly, people will vote with their feet (or fingertips) to prioritize *fit*, because they no longer *have* to submit to environments they don't like.

This growing phenomenon has been called "The Great Resignation". Countless others who haven't quite summoned the courage to leave yet are engaged in a related phenomenon: "quiet quitting".

We'll dive into specifics of work in later chapters. For now, what's worth noting are bell curve-leading innovations that point toward the future of work for all of us, wherever that is. As with the new classroom, the new workplace will be largely digital. While Zoom, Microsoft Teams, GoToMeeting, Google Meet, and WebEx all leave most of us personally wanting, they are no more than a way stop to the new. In the Metaverse, things will change, dramatically.

No longer just for sci-fi pieces like *Ready Player One*, the Metaverse will be where we increasingly gather to transact and play. The barrier to entry here won't be willing participants on any part of the bell curve, but rather the extent to which technology will allow us to give up our analog worlds.

Most of us are ready to.

Somehow, every time I leave home, I am still gobsmacked by our "new normal". Elevators, streets, restaurants, subways, and even parties all now center around our phones. No one is immune, from the three year old being "babysat" by videos to the fifty-somethings that comprise my demographic, few of whom can tell stories anymore without showing one another something on our screens, myself as much as anyone.

I've been known to put friends' phones in boxes when they visit.

The avatars are part of it. Snapchat makes them fun, and obvious. Lensa, Face Tune, and others are churning out falsified and idealized images of ourselves. At the time of this writing, the three top apps sold in the U.S. were all A.I. photo editors[57]. Think about that! Many of us now spend large swaths of time composing and digitally enhancing photographs of ourselves, then posting them on social media in order to project to the world the self we *wish* we really were. In fact, an increasing number of people are asking plastic surgeons to *make them look like their A.I. avatars*[58].

You can't make this stuff up.

What does this have to do with work? Well, apparently, a majority of us are ready to give up large chunks of corporeal life for a digital existence, at play and at work, because we like our idealized worlds (and selves) *better*.

Back in April of 2022, 64% of respondents said they'd consider quitting if asked to return to office (RTO) full time[59], while fully 8 in 10 companies surveyed admitted to losing employees over their RTO policies[60].

Why? The office always sucked.

The answer, it seems, is to innovate where people want to be: online, most of the time, with work hours reflective of our customized needs and desires.

Then, there's the Metaverse. A majority of knowledge workers worked remotely for much of the pandemic. And as more traditional in-person services move online (remote diagnostics, anyone?), it will plausibly expand the trend from knowledge workers to *most* workers. Which is where the Metaverse comes in.

Today, telephony is mostly 2D, with video of talking heads on teleconferencing platforms comprising the dominant exception. As the Metaverse gets built, however, we will not only be able to "optimize" ourselves via the avatars we love so much ("beauty" filter, anyone?), but the digital world will look and sound increasingly like our analog one—only one that is unfettered by forces like gravity, material costs, and even time. We may change our environment as easily as flicking a screen. Said another way, the "office" will finally become awesome.

Even without an established Metaverse, the writing is on the wall. Per one *Forbes* article[61]:

> *"The results of a recent McKinsey survey, for example, show that when offered the opportunity to work flexibly, 87% of workers would take advantage of this opportunity. Randstad's 2022 Workmonitor report also found it to be a top consideration for American workers, with 83% of respondents reporting flexibility in terms of working hours as important, and almost three-quarters (71%) see flexibility in terms of location as important to them."*

I don't know about you, but when nearly *all* workers want to opt out of the office life—permanently or part time, in decreasing order—it's time for a reboot.

Final Thoughts

The bell curve is one of the most ingenious inventions of all time, because it beautifully illustrates the trajectory of change. The reason I focus on it frequently is that awareness of it may help encourage us to stick our necks out, where obstacles may otherwise seem insurmountable. The bell curve tells us so.

Change is here and more is coming, where it's most needed: in **housing**, in **food** and **environmental health**, in **education**, and at **work**. These are the chief subjects of this book.

Bit by bit, human systems will shift as they always do, led by innovators who dream up ideas or invent technologies; embraced by early adopters who back, beta-test and/or refine them; and stabilized by an early majority given to jumping on the band wagon of tested, de-risked advancements. Once half of a the population is on board, it's simply a matter of time before a risk-intolerant, stuck-in-the-mud late majority led by fear shifts from protecting what it knows and has to adopting the new, if only out of fear of being left behind. And the laggards? Well, the innovators are already beta-testing the next generation of advancements before the laggards can get their pants on.

The ride is going to be epic. And with the right systemic support, which includes, ideally, a re-appraisal of predatory economic behaviors inflicted by individuals, companies, and nation-states, the world will continue to flatten, and as more core needs are met well, untold human creative potential will be unlocked. *This* is the moral imperative.

But before we dive deep, let's look at one more idea: an organizing principle to guide our behaviors: a "rallying cry" for the new era.

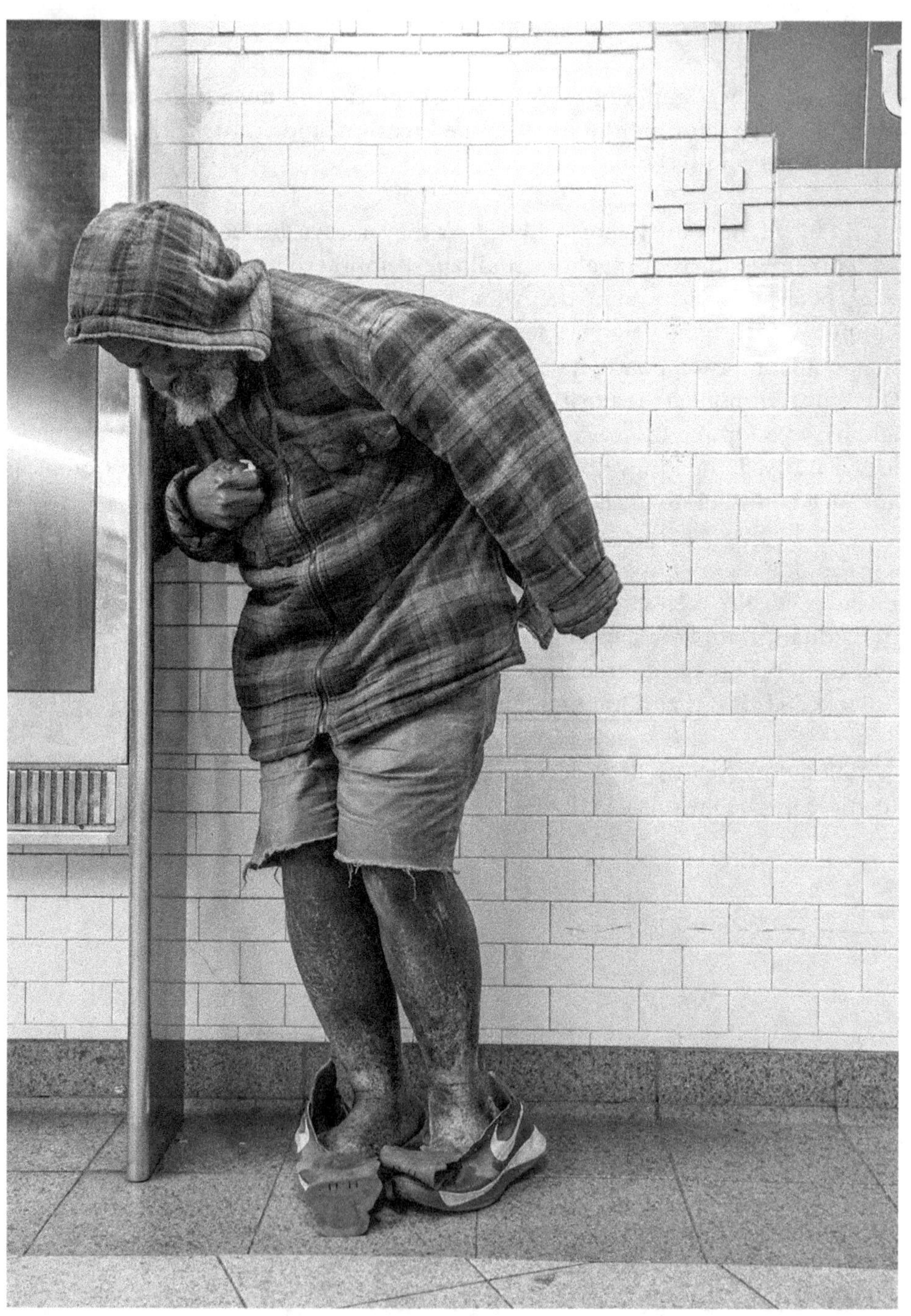

"Homeless on Halloween", NYC © Anthony Fieldman 2015

7   Do No Harm

We have been lured into destructive behaviors by a misguided notion I introduced in Chapter 1 as "the myth of scarcity". Critically, that myth significantly curtails our willingness to act in accordance with a "do no harm" principle. It is time for a new rallying cry.

Sometimes, I dream of a world in which the worst of human behaviors don't exist. In those moments, I envision crisp air, cacophonous forests; crystal-clear waterways, teeming oceans and snow-capped mountains, all gloriously free of industrial machinery. I dream of a world in which the machines that do exist emit nothing but light, air, or vapor—the very same things that power them; where strangers smile at one another, as if greeting an old friend; where curiosity, empathy, optimism, and ethics are the cardinal points of our behavior; where lawyers and their enforcers, politicians and their militaries don't exist only because there is *no need* for such things; and where everyone speaks to truth, acting in accordance with a singular, foundational tenet governing human conduct:

"Do no harm."

What a world that would be. If we measured everything we do by this metric, the world that we know would scarcely exist. Energy would become infinite, and freely available to all. Food would fill everyone's bellies and be nutritious once again the way nature designed it to be, not toxically debilitating, and unrecognizable. Poverty would disappear, as would crime, most diseases, inequality, broken promises, competition and zero-sum games, because these things are all *very harmful*, and our new rallying cry wouldn't allow them.

Greta Thunberg wouldn't have to lecture the world's leaders, pointing out their duplicity for applauding her publicly then doing nothing to fix the diseased planet they created, and which she is inheriting. With her powerful admonishment, "How DARE you," she showed us that she is more of an adult than we are; and that adulthood itself is now something she is right to mistrust, because, well, just look at us! Look at what nearly all humans do with our actions. We destroy the planet and one another in the name of profit and #winning, because **we have given in to the myth of scarcity: that to win, someone else must lose**. And so, we wreak havoc on everything and everyone in a bid to come out on top.

This myth is simply misleading. There is no limit to the sun, wind, ground heat, or waves. There is no limit to kindness or generosity, to our ability to create shelter and safety, feed and clothe everyone sustainably, or educate and heal every human. The only thing there is a limit to is our willingness to act with empathy rather than indifference or worse, toward one another; and to invest adequately in the governance and cooperative coordination that could lead to equal, universal access to limitless resources. In the absence of these choices, the prevailing narrative urges despoiling because it's cheaper, more profitable, more expedient, and/or more controllable. It leads us to compete for the natural and human resources we choose to mine and sell to one another, often killing one another in the fight for dominance, and control, rather than opting to **harness and cultivate infinite resources, then share them to seed global prosperity and true upward mobility**. The myth's "hook", of course, is money; more specifically, late-stage capitalism.

What creatures we are. No wonder Greta is angry.

To paraphrase Robert Oppenheimer, now *we* are Death, destroyer of worlds.

The Guardian columnist George Monbiot wrote a recent piece titled "Trashing the planet and hiding the money isn't a perversion of capitalism. It IS capitalism." He's not wrong. To underscore this point, he writes,

"Politicians condemn it as 'the unacceptable face of capitalism.' But it's not. It is the face of capitalism."

"Do no harm."

It's a simple sentence—one that demands we act on the better angels of our nature, rather than be driven by our demons. "Do no harm" commands us to make benign choices at worst, and net-positive changes at best. "Do no harm" compels us not to fell forests; poison waterways; hollow out the Earth; empty it of fish and other wild things; kill one another in the name of resource access, ownership, profit, market share, or shareholder return; and compete for jobs, food, housing, education, medicine, status objects, accolades, privilege, and adulation. "Do no harm" encourages us to harness and share the infinite because *not* doing so, when it's so readily available to us, would in fact cause egregious harm. To withhold is to harm, in many cases. To deny or usurp, hinder or impede, exact a price for the privilege of what could be freely shared is no different from "doing harm" to those who would otherwise benefit from something.

Call it whatever "ism" you wish. Words are dirty because we pervert them to suit our vested interests, and engage in acts of coercion or duplicity accordingly. "Do no harm" is much simpler because it precludes our need to supplicate to a self-proclaimed authority, commander, or deity.

But whatever you call it, as long as you live by its quiet appeal, "Do no harm" will result in the world of my dreams, and Greta will no longer need to be angry and point out obvious things to the adults in the room who have spent far too long causing irreparable harm.

All it requires is for us to make different choices.

Political scientists Chong, Citrin, and Levy wrote a paper in 2021, presented that September at the annual meeting of the American Political Science Association, that "focuses on the concept of harm in shaping public policy and in the growing determination that a paramount goal of public discourse is to avoid inflicting injury." While theirs is still no more than an emergent concept that has yet to have a material impact on how we interact with one another and the planet, the fact that *some* are seeing through the myth of scarcity and all the amoral and destructive behaviors that it elicits is good news, indeed.

Echoing their findings, a *New York Times* Op-Ed by Thomas Edsall[62] references "moral foundations theory", which argues:

"...that across cultures, several innate and universally available psychological systems are the foundations of 'intuitive ethics'. The five

foundations are care/harm, fairness/cheating, loyalty/betrayal, authority/ subversion, and sanctity/degradation."

If it isn't obvious, the first word in each pair is largely ethical, while the second is decidedly *unethical,* and, as Monbiot and others have pointed out, the traditional outcome of a scarcity mindset.

One final point. It was author April Rinne who really provoked my thinking on the subject of our behaviors with her wonderfully rich and optimistic book, *Flux,* which expands on Carol Dweck's seminal work on "fixed" vs. "growth" mindsets and applies it to a world in constant flux (i.e.: what we are experiencing today). In it, she argues:

> *"Contemporary mass-market consumerism and free-market capitalism fuel notions of never having enough, being enough and—by extension— working hard enough. That's how consumerism thrives, by making sure we never see ourselves as enough. Whether you accept this messaging, indeed if you even see it, is a function of your mindset. Are you questioning this system, or are you too busy hustling on its hamster wheel to notice that you may be running right past life?"*

Rinne is suggesting that we may not just be playing by the wrong rules, we may well be playing the *wrong game entirely*—one based on a false narrative of insufficiency. The behaviors that the myth of scarcity elicits lead to the outcomes Rinne has set out to help us recalibrate.

She goes on:

> *"The faster we produce and consume goods, the more we damage the environment. The more we look for happiness and satisfaction outside ourselves—a new car, a new dress, almost anything that allows us to "buy and display our way out of sadness," as psychology professor Tim Kasser says—the more likely we are to be depressed. We're taught to consume, consume, consume—and please don't think about the side effects, thank you very much.*

> *"Did you know that before marketing ate the word, to consume meant to destroy, as in "consumed by fire," and to squander, as in "to spend*

wastefully?"

Rinne, Chong, Citrin and Levy, Monbiot, Kasser, and our teenage Swedish dynamo have all converged around the dangers endemic to world-eating practices within capitalism. They are all, in their own manner, sounding the alarm. While capitalism has inarguably done much good in the world, that good has come at great cost; and like all systems we've invented, it's reasonable to suggest that it may be ripe for an upgrade.

It may be time to toss the gamebook and change the game we all play: from one that peddles false notions of scarcity and reinforce a consumerist mindset, to one that embraces the empirical plenty that surrounds us, guided by the tenet "Do no harm."

Final Thoughts

Rinne sums it up.

"For today's leaders, the stakes of running fast [her chosen metaphor for playing the consumption game without pausing to ask if it's the one we *should* be playing] *are high. At risk is not only one's well-being, business success, and health of the economy. The survival of Earth's life-support systems and the welfare of future generations are up for grabs as well. Against this backdrop, learning to run slower* [changing the game] *could solve a lot of other problems too. It's almost completely at odds with the old script, yet it's our best shot at staving off collapse."*

Three short words sum up the solution.

Do. No. Harm.

In the next chapter, we will revisit a prevailing and ultimately destructive mindset whose redefinition is, in a sense, a prerequisite to repairing most of what's broken.

8   The Economics of "Enough" — A Provocation

"Enough" is anti-consumerist. For one, it espouses limits. For another, it looks at needs, not wants. And above all, it values long-term societal health over short-term personal gain.

It just might save us.

Enough isn't a sexy doctrine. Far from the life of the party, it's the rational voice that tells you skip the nightcap and get a good night's sleep. While everybody knows it's right to think these things, nobody enjoys the reminder.

We'd rather party, and pay the price tomorrow.

Enough looks inward at need, rather than outward at want like consumerism does. *Enough* pumps the brakes when we are no longer hungry, cold, or alone. By contrast, consumerism floors the accelerator because there is always someone, somewhere to chase, fueled by consumerist envy.

My father, a top-tier über-consumer, used to read stories about billionaires and critique out loud what he called "abstract levels of wealth". "How many pairs of pants can they wear at once?! How many cars can they drive?!" In the next breath, he would chuckle about the six bagfuls of suits he just gave away because his enormous closets were overstuffed and, "it got a bit crazy".

My father is neither inherently selfish, nor insatiable. In fact, he is more often than not extremely generous. Rather, he is a victim of the "more doctrine" that demands upward mobility, economic growth and trophies.

The interesting part is, I wouldn't consider my father particularly fulfilled, in spite of his longstanding membership in the rarefied 1% Club. He is often *happy*, but I wouldn't call him *content*. More on this distinction later.

Enough is the fastest route to contentment.

Contrary to what many of us have learned, excess is bad for everyone. It's bad for our bodies, which buckle under the weight of gluttony while counterintuitively, they thrive in a climate of famine[63]. It's bad for the planet, which we destroy to feed our insatiability. It's bad for our feelings of safety and adequacy, which attempt to convince us not only do we never *have* enough, we never *are* enough, as Rinne pointed out in *Flux*. A society that advocates excess risks making us impotent in our own lives.

So why do most of us chase it?

Choose Your Path

We are not inherently consumerist as a species, in the sense that we aren't wired to poison our bodies, ravage the planet, or corrupt our minds without considering the downstream effects of unchecked consumption. The opposite is true. Biologically, our bodies are incredibly efficient, using nearly everything that enters them to cultivate a healthy equilibrium, while returning what is spent to fuel other things. The planet itself is a closed-loop, zero-waste ecosystem that uses no more than is necessary to power each piece of it, and redistributes all of it, at one point or another. Similarly, our minds are engaged in the nonstop act of economizing energy and effort, to maximize the efficacy and efficiency of processes and outcomes[64].

With that said, we are also storytellers. Our fictions are how we derive inspiration, dream, and aim ourselves. The world as we know it is the product of these stories. We have conjured gods, empires, ROI and other extravagances. And we too-often lie prostrate at their feet, frequently killing people and biomes in their name.

We are so good at this that we often confuse our stories for truths, and like the extra nightcap we began this story with, we find reckless story-chasing far more exciting than prudent needs-meeting.

Enough, and its cousins modesty, simplicity and restraint, are party poopers. We like that they exist, but secretly find them boring.

Consumerism is the life of the party. It rewards us with dopamine, which we mainline in its presence: "Just one more." But, like any other drug, dopamine is short-lived, and we always wake up at least a little bit regretful.

Consumerism, like other drugs, can lead to addiction and overdose, and on more than occasion, death.

Like temperance vs. bingeing, or contribution vs. extraction, there are choices to be made in the bid to find our *enough*.

The Doctrine of Enough

Like consumerism, *enough* measures the self in the context of others. *Unlike* consumerism, *enough* seeks to bring others to the party, rather than find a bigger or more exclusive one. In that sense, *enough* is tied to the ethics of generosity, empathy, inclusion, and fairness. *Enough* understands that others have needs, too, and sees excess as a bounty to share. When we feel we have enough—enough love, enough food, enough friends, enough "stuff"— those who subscribe to the "Doctrine of Enough" look for places to share their bounty with *others.*

Enoughers volunteer their time. They donate materials and things. They share their insights, ears, and shoulders in equal doses. They look for day jobs that allow them to practice their *enough* beliefs. *Enoughers* are committed to a lifetime of plenty, shared. Well, guess what? These things *also* release dopamine into our bodies, providing an alternate and powerful high.

Except that instead of suffering from hangovers the next day, *enoughers* wake up feeling love, connection, and purpose fulfilled. These are perhaps the only three forces stronger than our chemical temptresses.

Enough taps into our inherent evolutionary efficiency and interdependence. It accepts we are part of a larger ecosystem, and that together, we are stronger.

Consumers see only a world full of foes: pitted against one another, and against the planet, in a war for #winning. In it, everything is there to be conquered, so that we can stand apart, victorious, in spite of the fact that these ideas are frankly toxic.

Internal Needs vs. External Wants

There's another key difference between *Enoughers* and *consumers*. *Enoughers* turn inward to fulfill **needs**, while *consumers* gaze outward to seed **wants**. The only way to measure *enough* is against an *internal* barometer: to eat or drink one's fill; to feel warm or cool *enough*; to be protected *enough* from the weather; to feel *enough* love, purpose, or connection. Those things are non-transferable, solo assessments. No one can eat for us, or live our purpose. By contrast, wants fuel *more-seekers*, who only exist in the context of *others* because the word "more" itself is a *relative* concept. As in, more (or less)... successful/ rich/ beautiful/ powerful/ elite/ popular/ etc... *than* someone *else*. *More* is insatiable, because it ignores *enough*, and there are so many others who have more of something than we do!

It's an old problem. 2,300 years ago, ancient Greek philosopher Epicurus said:

> *"Nothing is enough for the man for whom enough is too little."*

In *Flux*, April Rinne applies a modern lens to Epicurus' sentiments:

> *"The truth is: no amount of physical stuff can ever replace your inner sense of worth, but it can easily bankrupt you. Yet the old script persuades you of the exact opposite. This is how today's consumerism is designed: the goal of "more" can never be fully satisfied, which keeps you tethered to the hamster wheel, clicking on ads and buying things that never fully satisfy.*

> *"But hold on. This is a script. And it's not a script that many people would opt into, if they actually paused and thought about it. Who wants to live for an unattainable goal set by others, that's exhausting and expensive, and often brings more jealousy than joy?*

> *"The new script sees through the mirage of more and says, enough is enough, once our basic needs have been met."*

Enough is Enough

The ancient Greek root for enough is enenkeîn, which means "to carry".

This made sense, given that for the longest time we were semi-nomadic, and having more than we needed was detrimental. It slowed us down; it limited our spontaneity; it made us a target for others' greed or exploitation; it was expensive; it gave us reasons to fear loss, damage, or devaluation; and it made us appreciate our belongings less, because with multiples of anything, each version of it is decidedly less special.

It still does.

An acquaintance of mine named David is a longtime restauranteur and entrepreneur in NYC. He told me a story some years ago as we stood in a new building he had recently bought in the Rockaways, in Queens. Nearby, he had just acquired a number of concessions on the beach and planned to turn them into food halls reflecting the diversity of the city. Soon after he closed on the agreement, he moved decades' worth of "stuff" he'd collected into enormous basements under the beachfront pavilions. Within weeks, Superstorm Sandy hit. In an instant, everything David ever owned was destroyed.

Within a day, he managed to internalize what had just happened. He told me:

"I never felt freer."

David, like all of us, had become prisoner to his *more*. No matter how cool or expensive his particular *more* was, it was a prison nonetheless. And now that it was gone, he was freed from the culture of consumption, and thankful.

It needs to be said that David never replaced his stuff. The last time I saw him, he was in the same outfit—coveralls—that he wore daily, and driving a rusted-up old pick-up that he had found abandoned after Sandy subsided. It didn't matter to David whether he was spending the day on the one-acre urban farm he ran, or in meetings with city officials, as when he consulted with me on a large-scale waterfront development I was creating at the time for Brooklyn's Red Hook.

David had found his own *enough* and had become, by my external measure, a very free man.

So, how can we, too, simplify our lives the way David was forced to? How can we disburden ourselves from our *moreness* and scratch our inner *enoughness*?

Be Content, Not Happy

Happiness is a widely understood as a temporary state of pleasure, while contentment is a long-term state of satisfaction, i.e.: *enough*. Similarly to our wants, happiness is induced by external experiences, whereas contentment emanates from within, like our *needs*. Contentment derives from contentus, or "to contain". Contentment is therefore within us, and is expressed as an "unconditional wholeness", according to Rinne, in *Flux*.

The path to contentment is the removal of obstacles that detract from our internal *enough*. The Buddhists have canonized this. Monk novices own nothing and live by the generosity of others, while ordained monks spend a life overcoming desire (or *more*) on their way to Nirvana.

They're onto something. While monasticism isn't for everyone and I'm not proposing a global population of novices and sadhus, there's a lesson to be learned between the extremes of "nothing" and "never enough", regardless.

Final Thoughts

Enough is radical. It's radical because consumerism reigns supreme right now, and the idea that *more* may not be better undermines no less than the global economy, as it's been designed. However, embracing a mindset of *enough* can lead to long-term prosperity and contentment, improve our outlook, and help our fellow humans have enough, too. The myth of scarcity, on the other hand, as applied to basic human needs in technologically advanced societies, is largely manufactured. We do, in fact, have the knowledge and tools to build and/or provide enough for everyone on Earth. We just choose not to invest in that outcome adequately, at scale, because we have given into the myths that supplies are inherently limited, that more is better, and that the things we covet, and by extension, *we*, are never *enough* as we are.

More demands to be fed until there is nothing left to consume.

The people who profit from this toxic narrative are the über-consumers, among them captains of industry, political leaders, and the financiers who back them. But in reality, everyone loses in this paradigm, including the #winners.

The price #losers pay should be obvious: their core needs go unmet in a climate that pits us against one another for control over excess. They lose out on *participation*, which is the basis for thriving.

But the #winners lose three times. First, contentment belongs to those for whom *enough* is enough, not to those who rely on excessive consumption to fill an insatiable emptiness. Second, connectedness and belonging come from sharing and contribution, while hoarding and extraction divide us. And third, we each have but one body and mind, and one planet to share. To desecrate any of these is to upset the balance of our inherent equilibrium. The Hopi have a word for this: "koyaanisqatsi": life out of balance. Its opposite is "suyanisqatsi": life of harmony and balance. Other traditions have similar words to describe an "optimal life." They all have just one thing in common.

That thing is *enough*.

ECONOMICS:

Exchange and the Finite Game

"Classmates", Jodhpur, India © Anthony Fieldman 2013

9   IROI

Most of us are familiar with the term ROI. That's because "Return on Investment", or net profit over cost, is widely understood as a key metric that drives much of the economic world. In fledgling ventures, half-baked ideas and "what if" pivots, future ROI is projected, and along with proof of past successes, generally informs whether offers to invest are either accepted or declined. Within existing businesses, ROI greatly influences whether ideas or projects get green-lighted or nixed. Among nations, ROI influences how leaders weigh potential regulations and subsidies, among other measures. And everywhere, ROI is why regular humans and mega-corporations alike rally resources and people around something from which we all hope to profit, most commonly in the near—or very near—term.

ROI relies on tangible metrics: costs incurred, units sold, and profit made, which in turn influence dividends and share price adjustments. These are all measures of efficiency. At the same time, they are outcomes that cannot be measured until they exist. "Upstream", ROI also often looks at fuzzier lenses through which to assess *potential* returns. These include trends; risk; scalability; competition; barriers; the team itself; the market; strategy; adoption and absorption rates; etc.

We are very good at measuring tangibles, as a means of evaluating risk and reward intelligently.

What we are markedly less good at is assessing—and thus, given our risk-aversion and penchant for numbers, less likely to invest as readily in—things that don't *directly* yield dividends but *could* do so "sometime down the road". That's because doing so would necessitate shifting our focus from the highly delineated near term toward a more distant and murkier horizon. We would also need to invest not only over a longer period of time, but also, potentially heretically, in a *person* rather than an idea, product, or company with an expected, weighable ROI.

The latter approach is how we invest in thoroughbred horses. We pay for pedigree and potential, but we are clueless as to whether or not a particular colt will mature into the powerful and profitable contender we hope it will. So we invest heavily in its development potential in a bid to actively maximize our investment. We do not simply pay a breeder, sit back and wait for revenues to pour in.

They'd never materialize if we did.

A second, if obvious, example of this latter approach is how we raise children. We don't invest time, energy and money in them because we look for fiscal returns, per se, though many of us hope *their* future successes will keep us comfortable, if and when we need help. Rather, most of us invest in our children because our pride in having contributed to their nurture is its own reward. Children are the longest, most open-ended, most effort-intensive and most gratifying investment most of us will *ever* make.

By marked contrast, in professional day-to-day life, when evaluating new ideas and investment opportunities, many of us will give prime focus to the numerical details that point *mathematically* to an "informed" decision.

Fewer of us, in these instances, consider the person or people peddling an idea *as much as* the quantifiable pitch, beyond track records and bonafides. That is, it's less common to focus primarily on a person's intangibles: their energy and thoughtfulness, how well their undeveloped ideas resonate with us, or even their human development potential, as people, and then, as a direct result of any of these things, open up our wallets and say, "I'm in," without first weighing the details of a business plan and/or a financial model.

Wouldn't that be nice.

By the same token, too few of us support or "green light" an idea and then *actively participate in its incubation* and future success with "sweat equity" in the form of direct work: contributions that could round out missing skills, enlist new collaborators, or provide critical strategic leadership. Doing this would require us to invest not just our dollars but our efforts toward *creating* the success we wish to see.

Conventional lending institutions don't do this, generally.

Not long ago, I had dinner with my friend Erin. She's a travel writer with a truly global set of relationships, nearly always engaging with interesting people and mind-opening activities. Somewhat out of the blue, while sitting at a sidewalk bar in the West Village talking about economics, she mused aloud:

> *"How much of what you put into life results in the kind of insights that allow you to move forward as a human being?"*

IROI

It was that sentence that got me thinking about an "IROI" concept, or **"Insight Return on Investment"**.

She wasn't speaking about investments in the narrow, financial sense, but in something much larger. She was referring to the idea that all the investments we make in *ourselves* build personal capacity toward things that are impossible to even imagine, let alone measure downstream. But we do it anyhow because with enough time and enough experiences, internalized, our ability to act and succeed strengthens.

What a beautiful thought.

An investment framework named StartLab attempted just that. Created by Itay Adam, who in 2014 became famous for closing $2M in funding from an international VC fund with just five slides and no idea (he even quipped about it in the interview, citing Seinfeld and saying his was a deck about nothing), StartLab focused on the quality of individuals and teams, rather than products. Of his approach, Adam provided a corollary:

> *"Take a child to the fair. Hand him an air gun and tell him he only has one chance to win the huge brown teddy bear. He will surely miss. Now, you'll start with the accusations and cripple his soul turning him to the sort of kid who will never try this again. Both of you lose.*

> *"Take another kid, hand him the gun and tell him he has 50 attempts. He will probably nail something on the fourth attempt. But, on the twelfth attempt he will start aiming for the very center of the target, and by 40 he will get bored and create a new gun. That's life. Create an empowering*

surrounding and you, too, will get empowered."

We forget that a large share of success isn't only the research we do, the work plan we chart, and the lessons we gleaned from our past experiences. It also comes from the open-ended investment we make in our own *undirected* development as people, because this feeds our contextual understanding of the world, inspires us, and primes our minds for *whatever* may emerge from these things.

Not everything has to be predetermined or directed toward a specific end. In fact, insights often, if not usually, emerge from seemingly unrelated places, within minds primed to think broadly about how we approach what we do.

I've long felt that someone who chooses their own path will invariably do a better job at it than by following one chosen for them. This applies to things as small as the methodology of any single task, or as weighty as one's career choice.

However we choose to funnel our energies into our work, and whatever our appetite for risk, there is no replacement for insights gleaned from things that have our full attention and passionate energies.

To refer back to what Adam highlighted, why do we typically tell children *what to do* and *what to think*, at home and in school, and teach them rote skills while censuring "wrong answers", instead of inspiring them to engage in open exploration and discovery? Aren't these the lifeblood of invention and creative acts? And aren't creative acts the *only* path to innovation?

Why do we do the same thing with adults, at work? We not only reprimand them for falling short of adequately servicing our priorities, we often fail to give them the chance to show us that they can add value and contribute in ways we didn't request of them, or even foresee. In other words, why don't we create space for people to "create new guns", to borrow Adam's metaphor, if the context is right?

When we invest, why don't we all do what he promoted with StartLab, which isn't all that different from how entrepreneurs within the Mondragón collaborative in Spain are evaluated, and funded? In Mondragón, investors admittedly focus more on traditional pitches than people potential, but at the same time, they invest decidedly for the long haul. Not only do they *not* scrutinize short-term gains, but they contribute expertise, via human capital, to funded ventures. They do so primarily to invest in ventures' success in the same way that we invest ourselves in our children and friends. In fact, the governing principle in Mondragón is that until the venture succeeds, they will continue to contribute *whatever is necessary* to ensure that it does.

The success rate of incubator projects there is nearly 100%.

We'll do a deep dive into Mondragón in the next chapter.

If our belief in a person is predicated on the ROI we receive on our investment, and further limited to the convenience and/or success of a business transaction, then we are making a clear statement about our belief in an individual: *we have none!* Rather, we are *transacting* with them, and our relationship is nothing more than a legal structure and a financial model. In that regard, these relationships are mathematical; they are not "human". Humans aren't spreadsheets. We are social. We are emotional. We are works in progress. We need encouragement. We more than occasionally need help. We blossom in collaboration. We seek *purpose.*

When we have these things, we thrive. When we have these things, we are far more likely to succeed than if we feel a target on our backs or a magnifying glass over our heads, or we are told that a predetermined outcome—a certain quantum within a fixed deadline—is expected, without which there will be dire consequences.

And yet, the lion's share of our business interactions follow that very formula: show me the idea; detail how much I'll get for my efforts, in how long; make me feel comfortable with the risk attendant to lending you money, or time, or agency; and then send the check here, and otherwise don't bother me. I'll be back for my money; and if you fail, you'll hear from my lawyers.

If we did that to our children, we'd seed a generation of failures.

In the case of our children, our success is a direct measure of the investment we make in them. We may try to do that by forging them into weapons, as so-called "tiger parents" do; but all of the "tiger children" I know, personally, suffer from the same tragic thing: they're broken inside. Their nervous systems are wrecks, and while they'll likely tell you they're #killingit, and by external measure, likely are, inside they suffer from deep levels of self-hate, usually without knowing it. Dr. Theodore Rubin, M.D., the former president of the American Institute of Psychoanalysis, makes a compelling case for this in his seminal book, *Compassion and Self-Hate*.

By contrast, when we allow children to explore their worlds without expectation, listening carefully to the internal cues they provide, helping when asked and sharing insights without expectation of reaction or outcome, then we seed the potential of unlocking parts of *their own internal engines*, and long-term flourishing. They may not know what they have in them. Most don't! It may take ages for their experiences to gel, to connect and lead to something exciting or valuable… or even game-changing. Everyone's path is different. Paths don't run on fixed timelines. They don't follow mathematical formulas, no matter how much we wish they did. They aren't prescriptive, because humans are unpredictable, and react as much from our hearts as we do from our wallets.

So the real question is: **why don't we treat others, personally and professionally, the way we wish we were treated ourselves?** I know I'm certainly very guilty of a double standard in this regard. More accurately, I often treat *myself* as badly as I treat *others*. I don't offer it as an excuse. It's a self-observation—one I actively work on overcoming. Some days, I succeed. But, however short we fall of the ideal for interacting, most of us do so to some degree, in professional life.

Why do we treat others by a yardstick we ourselves don't like, whether or not this is "how business gets done", as usual?

Why don't we redefine the default?

Said simply, why don't we invest in *one another* rather than specific ideas, and do so over the long term, rather than being led by ROI?

Why don't we invest in an *IROI*, acknowledging that insight is quantifiably *unpredictable* and stands a far greater chance of occurring in the right context:

not with someone breathing down our necks or measuring outcomes in the short term, but by rolling up their sleeves and *pitching in* with the investment of time, ideas, patience, and resources *personally*, without prejudice as to the short-term outcome?

Do we not all wish someone did that for us? Isn't there more to professional life than ROI?

I believe there is.

Ever the clear-eyed synthesizer, Simon Sinek said:

> *"We should invest in people, not ideas. A good idea is often destroyed by bad people, and good people can always make a bad idea better."*

If "good people can make a bad idea better," then you might ask, why invest at all in it? Who invests in a "bad idea"? The answer, I think, is in the first part of Sinek's provocation. We should invest in people, whether or not they have landed on an idea we can plumb for return… yet.

Insight is admittedly not the only measure of future success. **Sweat equity** counts equally. Ideas are a dime a dozen. Without adequate effort, they remain nothing more. **The right partners** are critical. "It takes a village," unless we're talking about a singular creative act. And **timing** can't be underestimated. Great ideas have failed because people's hearts and minds weren't ready. Apple's Newton, one of the world's first "personal digital assistants" that featured a touch screen, proprietary and third-party apps, and handwriting recognition, comes to mind. Apple started incubating it in 1987, and they hit the market in 1993, fifteen years ahead of the 2008 iPhone that one could say largely constituted a second stab at the same thing, and which has utterly transformed how we work and play.

The Newton *bombed*. What had changed in the interim leading up to the iPhone was *the public*. What underpinned *both* efforts was the investment Jobs' parents and mentors made in his development, which nurture famously helped shape the man Jobs became: someone who kept trying, until he changed our world.

The underlying engine for all of human endeavor is purpose. It must often be uncovered, coaxed, cultivated, reinforced and aimed. Sometimes, our efforts lead to dead ends, and sometimes we make the wrong decisions. When we do, we have a choice to make: punish errors and those who create them, or understand that mistakes are not only common, they are a chief means by which we learn, and improve.

Thomas Edison said of his eventual electric light, "I have not failed 10,000 times. I've successfully found 10,000 ways that will not work."

Final Thoughts

When these forces coalesce in a single person or group, and are supported by the community around them, then that person (or group) can maximally contribute to our collective wellbeing. It could be a small contribution, or a transformational one. There could be one of them, or a hundred.

We never know. There's no guarantee.

But I want to live in a world of people who invest in one another: not just financially but interpersonally and emotionally, over the long term. To do otherwise is anti-societal. To confuse people for transactions is inexcusable. It ignores half, if not more, of what generates success, both in the narrow financial sense, and in the broader sense of interpersonal enrichment, societal wellbeing, and long-term, collective reach.

The way we typically measure success, by and large, is not only misdirected, but toxic. We have lost the forest for the trees by treating people as currency. We need new, more empowering and more mutually beneficial humanistic measures of returns on our investments. It may be that "insight" isn't the only one, or even the best. But insight is the wellspring of ideas, direction, and purpose. Ergo, IROI. So, in my mind, it's as good a place as any to start.

Much as Bhutan developed GNH—Gross National Happiness—as a measure to broaden our definition of societal wellbeing, an IROI—or **Insight Return on Investment**—may lead to a greater measure of how well our investment in one another leads to the greatest currency of all: that which clarifies ourselves *to* ourselves, including that which can, with the right partners, and in the right context, fill us with purpose and transform the world.

Purpose, aimed, is a solid investment. This is precisely what one of the world's most successful conglomerates does so brilliantly, as we cover in the next chapter.

10 The Relationship Economy

Terry Mollner is one of the global pioneers of environmental, social, and governance (ESG) investing. For decades, now, his Calvert Impact has been among the world's largest impact funds with $37 billion under management. At the time of this writing, the fund supports 150 million people, 66% of whom are women. Mollner is a trailblazer in a new economy based on individual *and community* thriving—an infinite game and real-world alternative to the prevailing global model of finite, zero-sum, win-lose capitalism.

Mollner's two guiding lights are decidedly at odds with dominant business drivers across the commercial landscape. To Game A players, "wellbeing" and "the common good" may receive lip service, but frankly distract from companies' core focus. We know this because what businesses *actively measure* tells us where priorities truly lie, and those things are primarily market share, backlog, growth, productivity, efficiency, competitive victories (hit and capture rates), and of course, profits.

In corporations, wellness initiatives are often marketed to potential employees. But when you consider that large U.S. employers spend less than $716 per employee[65] on wellness incentives and programs, employee wellbeing is still scarcely more than a salve to keep workers *healthy enough* to continue generating profits. Less well known, employers also *gain a financial return* on their wellness investment. In fact, in the two categories employers measure, companies see a $0.50 ROI on every dollar spent on "lifestyle management", and a $3.80 ROI, or *fourfold return,* on "disease management"[66], according to a 2014 study by RAND Corporation on the subject. Wellness spending, it would appear, is both *minimal* and *good for the bottom line.*

With regard to the common good, there is significant room to grow. Fortune 500 companies, which collectively generate 2/3 of the U.S. GDP, spend a total of $20 billion on corporate social responsibility (CSR) initiatives, of their *$13.7 trillion* in combined revenues[67], according to a study by *Harvard Business Review.* Expressed as a percentage, their investment is just one-and-a-half *hundredths* of one percent.

I'm not clapping.

So back in 1973, Mollner set out to create an alternative—an antidote, really—to a business model he was convinced would eventually drive the planet and its people to ruin, if left unchecked. His goal was to prove that such a thing could exist and be "fully integrated into the modern world," as it is, today. As he writes in the astounding article, *Mondragón: The Loving Society That is Our Inevitable Future*, "I had been searching the globe for years for a Relationship Age society," and adds, "I had never expected to find such a mature and comprehensive example," hiding in plain sight.

Mondragón

He did. And what he found has been operating that way since its post-war inception in 1956, in war-devastated Western Europe, under the nose of Spain's great dictator, Francisco Franco. That was long before it became *the* dominant association of cooperative businesses in Spain. Today, Mondragón, named after the town in which it was founded, and centered, is comprised of more than 84,000 members. Collectively, Mondragón is Spain's top producer of industrial machinery and major home appliances, leads the way in heavy construction, furniture production, farming and high technology, and created Spain's computer chip industry. Their profitability is *twice* that of the average Spanish corporation, and worker productivity is higher than anywhere else in the country. Even more amazingly, it operates its own banks, schools, health insurance companies and food stores, in an ecosystem of community services and relationships. And as I hinted at earlier, their Entrepreneurial Division, which provides venture capital to new "relationship cooperatives", boasts close to a 100% success rate. When we set that against a global startup failure rate of 75% (or higher)[68], it's nothing less than astounding.

Put in a single phrase, their mantra is: **relationships for life**. They approach all business activities through this lens, not just because the owner-members are tied to their investments—people and capital—for life, but because of their inherently tribal feeling that they are *family*. They feel that way because they are *treated* as such, including their education, nurture, health, training, and work-life balance, as well as their *ownership stake* in commercial business life.

Consistent with the title of Mollner's article, *love drives business* in Mondragón.

What a strange concept: a business built on love. But that's exactly what it is. Mondragón, the business enterprise, is a modern community that was founded on infinite values like love, family, connection, honesty, relationships, trust, respect, safety, communication, and tolerance, by a young priest named Don Jose Maria Arizmendiarrietta, whose mantra was, "**people before things**."

When it came to making decisions, he was known mostly for the following question, "How can we do this in a way which works fully for those in the enterprise and those in the community rather than for one more than the other?" To him, the notion that there needed to be a loser in any transaction was a shortcoming of imagination.

Just a few concrete examples of how it works. At the time of this writing:

- Every member of the cooperative is also an owner. If they don't have enough capital for their initial investment (equivalent to $15,000 USD), it's loaned to them, and they pay it down with their work contributions.
- The salary differential between the lowest paid and highest paid manager in a Mondragón cooperative (there are many) can be no higher than 1:6
- Loans to finance new ventures that members incubate are made by the conglomerate's own financing arm *until the investment succeeds*. With every challenge faced and not met, the interest rates lower, not raise. If the fledgling business is in deep enough trouble, the bank will donate capital to the business. Eventually, most businesses succeed because they have been supported deeply until they do. Put metaphorically, a parent doesn't abandon its child until it can stand on its own two feet. At Mondragón, it's no different.
- Half of all profits made within the cooperatives go directly to the owner-member-employees. However, beyond a guaranteed 6% interest dividend, the remaining profits are reinvested in their individual "internal capital accounts", there to grow with the continued success of

the companies.
- Beyond this, 10% of all cooperative profits are earmarked for charity (against a 60-year average of 2% in the United States[69]).
- Unemployment insurance pays 80% of take-home pay in the case of a layoff, and a pension plan pays 60% of the same, until death—on top of their cooperative profits.
- The Board of Trustees is fully comprised of cooperative members.

The larger arc of this story is that a new model of business is emerging. It is one that stands at odds with what Mollner refers to as the Material Age structural priority order of "capital, then product, then managers, then workers". In a Relationship Age company, it's the opposite: workers, then managers, then product, then capital. Which is another way of saying:

"People before things."

The Finite Game (Game A)

Nearly every exchange mechanism we have created to manage XXL groups of people—nations and corporations—has followed a finite game model of win-lose relationships and activities that place profit before physiological and emotional wellbeing, in which people's productive lives are primarily aimed for achieving economic (or military, or political) success.

We see this fixation on money in every broken system today. Politics is largely run by lobbyists and is rife with corporate kickbacks, perhaps no place more than in the United States. Agriculture worldwide commonly pollutes and destroys limited land assets for short-term gains. Access to healthcare services and drugs is too-often predicated on one's financial means. In conventional media, content is largely selected on one criterion above all others and tailored to specific audiences we hope to lure with it: viewership, or "eyeballs" [online, it's views, reads, likes, shares, or comments], which of course drive revenues. Even social interaction is increasingly *transactional*; everyone's a brand or a network connection. And lastly, education's growing unaffordability means that it is increasingly the already-privileged who can access the tools that empower their futures, leaving too many others out in the cold, or with crippling debt.

The United States' response to the COVID-19 pandemic offers an excellent case study in overlapping crises borne of greed and profit motive. These were daylighted brilliantly by Ed Yong in his searing article, *How the Pandemic Defeated America*. The U.S.'s world-leading death toll, he wrote, was due to the "chronic underfunding of public health"; the "decades-long process of shredding the nation's social safety net"; the "millions of essential workers in low-paying jobs" who "risk their life for their livelihood"; the "fealty to a dangerous strain of individualism"; the uprooting of "the planet's animals, forcing them into new and narrower ranges that are on our own doorsteps," due to which "viruses have come bursting out"; the defunding of China-based US Centers for Disease Control and Prevention specialists, and the American epidemiologist embedded within China's own CDC; the profit-led "era of sick buildings" in which "pollutants and pathogens built up indoors", leading to the sacrifice of "designing buildings for people"; the chronic understaffing in 75% of all nursing homes; the "economic protectionist" policy of "reducing the influx of immigrants who make up a quarter of long-term caregivers"; the "national temperament that views health as a matter of personal responsibility rather than a collective good"; and the "chronically strapped local health departments" who "lost 55,000 jobs—a quarter of their workforce" that resulted from "budget cuts", which itself resulted from the fact that "the US spends just 2.5 percent of its gigantic health-care budget on public health".

In reality, *every critique* Yong levied resulted from a financial decision that cheated long-term health in favor of short-term gain, or the gain of the few over the gain of the many.

Yong wrote, "This profit-driven system has scant incentive to invest in spare beds, stockpiled supplies, peacetime drills, and layered contingency plans." He adds, "America's hospitals have been pruned and stretched by market forces to run close to full capacity, with little ability to adapt in a crisis."

Those problems go well beyond healthcare.

The Infinite Game (Game B)

The principle driving infinite games is simple. If you took any existing institution and convened a panel of extremely bright and diverse thinkers and experts, asked them to re-imagine it and instead of giving them *carte blanche* you established two unyielding "rules"—that every decision had to advance so-called "infinite values" from which one cannot construe a loser, and that business relationships were thought of as lifelong—then what emerged would likely look very different from what exists today.

It wouldn't take more than a single sentence, articulated with these principles, to see how each institution could be of more value to the *collective*. Let's try it.

- The better **capitalized** and supported an inspired idea is, the greater the likelier it will succeed;
- The more **ownership** people feel, the greater their commitment and contributions will be to its success;
- The more **settled** individuals are, the more robustly they can contribute to their communities;
- The **healthier** people are, the more productive they can be;
- The safer our **land assets** are, the fewer resources need to be diverted to mitigate the fallout caused by catastrophe;
- The more **educated** a population is, the more valuable its ideas become;
- The more **integrated** efforts are across the ecosystem of institutions that comprise a community, the better informed each will be, and the better decisions each will therefore be able to make;
- The more tailored the flow of **information** is toward collective benefit, the more targeted our energies can be toward what will make the biggest difference; and
- The **closer we feel** to one another over the long term, the more we will work toward mutual understanding, mutual benefit and shared goals.

In different language, I just described **entrepreneurship, economic participation, housing, human health, environmental health, education, collaboration, communications** and **social exchange**, in that order.

In Calvert Impact-funded businesses, the common good always trumps individual considerations, to the point where it insists upon "reasonable" profit caps, above which all excess profits are set aside and permanently managed for the common good.

In a 2014 article titled *The Differences Among Socially Responsible, Impact and Common Good Investing*, Mollner wrote about three existing models corporation harness to do something more than just generate profit:

1. In third place, **socially responsible** (SR) companies maintain financial return as the driving priority, while establishing a tolerance for investing in a form of "minimum socially responsible standards of behavior".

2. More meaningfully, **impact investing** (II) companies go a step further, focusing on "one or more good things that [the investing company] wants to perpetuate in society".

3. Mollner distinguishes both of these from **common good investing** (CGI) companies, which he believes to be "the inevitable future of all investing", because while SR is "less bad" than conventional solely profit-driven companies, and while II is focused on some "external good", only CGI begins with the foundational premise that the people doing the work are the primary value-creators, and thus should be the *primary beneficiaries* of the fruits of their labor.

What a novel idea. He explains it as follows: "If two people come together, they have two choices: they can compete or they can cooperate." He cites lions, tigers, and bears as apex competitors; while cooperation, he says, is "when all the parts give priority to the whole," forming a "human society".

Mondragón is just such a society, in which the greatest good is that which supports the community. As to the "full integration within the modern world" that he sought at the outset, the 84,000-plus people within Mondragón's cooperatives are well-paid, all have equity ownership in their workplaces, enjoy a solid educational and healthcare support network, have greater job satisfaction and less turnover and failure, are supported in their business ideas as budding entrepreneurs, are set up for life with a safety net that they contributed to, and outperform the rest of their own nation while doing it. Moreover, they've been doing this for three quarters of a century.

This isn't the stuff of fairy tales.

Players of Infinite Games do so because any game that is truly enjoyable is one that its players generally wish to keep playing, rather than concluding. When we are focused on concluding a game, it is because it's either boring, or we wish to win it. Not so for an endless / infinite game. Not to keep hammering it home, but our children are the obvious example of an endless game. We don't invest time and effort in them and bid them adieu, never to be seen again. Rather, we invest in them because the relationship is its own reward—one that continues to pay dividends in the satisfaction that we have contributed to someone's success, and for the joy of continued interaction and deepening ties.

We could say the same of our closest friends, as well as of that co-worker or teacher or nurse who with empathy, humility, and selfless service, transformed our lives and in the process became a trusted advisor, best friend, or even spouse.

We are social creatures to our cores, and when we service our relationships, we enrich our lives. It is only when we corrupt this joy with power plays, lack of respect or kindness, and conflicts over priorities or interests, then fail to invest the time required to resolve and align these things, that we devolve into animal behaviors, like the lions.

When people are so focused on their own interests that they will manipulate, deceive, and exploit others to achieve their goals, it easily leads to the breakdown in foundational human relationships. This pathology goes by the name Machiavellianism, and with its cousins narcissism and psychopathy, comprise what is known as The Dark Triad. While competition isn't part of the triad, per se, its cultivation nonetheless sponsors and reinforces the development of these dark traits.

In 1989, the Basque National Congress—the pre-eminent body of the autonomous Basque Country, technically still part of Spain, but largely self-governing—decided to officially adopt Mondragón's "third way" as the method by which economic policy would be developed and administered[70]. According to Mollner, "This may be the first nation in modern times to commit itself to the development of relationship economics."

A century-plus earlier, in 1833, the widely circulated and as widely criticized *Tragedy of the Commons* was the brainchild of British writer

William Forster Lloyd. In the Middle Ages, Britain was just one of many nations that held land and grazing rights "in commons"—that is, freely available to, and often managed by, the communities that benefited from and contributed to their upkeep. In his treatise, Lloyd *speculated* that this model led to the degradation of the land's value and bounty. He called this **the tragedy of the commons**. His musings stuck, however baseless they were, and his writings were used to undo a form of commonly held ownership rights that had been enjoyed by the citizenry there for *centuries*. The truth, however, never supported his theories, and the fact is that commonly held, mutually managed and freely shared resources continue to thrive today, while admittedly comprising a minor percentage of the world's economic might.

In Mongolia, a study undertaken by the group Environmental and Cultural Conservation in Inner Asia found that land in *shared* pastures degraded in quality by about 9% between 1992 and 1995. By contrast, in China and Russia, where both *state-owned* pastures and *privately* held land were farmed during that interim, degradation ran at 75% and 33%, respectively.

Mongolia is not the only example, but it's staggering if obvious to learn that a shared asset whose modus operandi is to cultivate it in perpetuity— an infinite game—can be *from three to eight times more productive* (and simultaneously less *destructive*) than one in which an entity uses it to squeeze profit and consolidate power, damned be the asset.

That's a finite game of the highest order— one we see play out in rampant deforestation, lakes of carcinogenic glyphosate, monocropping, over-fishing, and wild species destruction.

To be utterly crass, we are less likely to put a bullet in the head of someone we know well or on whom we depend than in that of a stranger whose life has no *obvious* material impact on ours, and whom we therefore don't value. The difference comes down to relationships.

In a relationship economy, connections appear to be deeper, more interdependent, and invested in for the long term. As a result, in a relationship-age company like any of the 96 entities Calvert Impact's website features at the time of this writing, or a town like Mondragón, or a "nation" like the Basque autonomous region, or a sector like Mongolian agriculture, the meaningfulness of our work and our relationships is amplified greatly.

When a group, community, or government commits to support one another and accordingly develops a network of complementary activities, policies, and structures to support the infinite relationships that both contribute to and benefit from the combined energy of the people within it, everybody wins.

Final Thoughts

In an infinite game economy, everybody wins, and nobody loses.

To insist that competition is a necessary or inevitable galvanizing force of progress, as so many advocates of our current paradigm will attest, is to ignore an entire aspect of human capacity, predisposition, and history. Before the advent of permanent settlements, competition assured the *demise* of a community, and therefore wasn't tolerated in any way. Christopher Ryan's book, *Civilized to Death: The Price of Progress* is a powerful treatise on the subject. An important concept regarding people and nations driven by competition is that it is often zealously championed and defended by those who stand to gain the most by it, at the too-frequent expense of large swaths of the human community.

We are on the precipice of a Relationship Age, as Mollner posits, supported by a **Relationship Economy.** Luckily, enough smart, well-capitalized and business-as-usual-weary people are turning more and more attention to this subject and incubating innovations to upend and replace the status quo. Our world, with its accelerating pressures and a pandemic that quickly revealed the stressors of our finite game systems, is desperate for a rewrite that works better for more of our neighbors. The finite game has played its hand, and the price has been our collective wellbeing, as well as that of the planet.

With luck, we won't only live to see this Brave New World, but will be part of the solution in building it.

The next chapter is a deeper dive into an idea we touched on in this chapter: that land and/or resources could once again be a shared, common benefit.

"Among the gods" at 432 Park Avenue, NYC © Anthony Fieldman 2016

11 From Private Goods
To Common Wealth

The Roman-era concept "Res Publica", from which the words "republic" and "commonwealth" originate, once guaranteed the public's welfare with shared ownership of resources. Many centuries later, in just a few generations, the stewards of our common wealth turned the tables, as we saw in the last chapter, and stole then sold our shared inheritance. It may be time for a return to our roots.

The idea that the land on which we live belongs to no one—which is another way of saying, to everyone—is as old as we are. The biosphere is, after all, both ubiquitous and ancient. We were born into its bounty, and simultaneously forced to find our way in a wilderness. That wilderness provided everything we needed, but required us to collaborate with one another in order to survive it, and thrive.

When the Dutch bought Manhattan Island in 1626 for 60 guilders from a group of indigenous Lenape who used it only for hunting and harvesting wood to fashion bows from hickory trees (called "manaháhtaan"), the locals had no idea that they were granting more than access to this shared resource, and would no longer be permitted to continue their practices there.

The Lenape weren't the only ones for whom the concept of "ownership" didn't exist. To most pre-industrial tribes, common wealth was the *primary* way resources were understood, with trade being reserved for "external" communities[71].

Privatization and exclusivity weren't allowed to take root in the world's indigenous cultures because these things undermined the prevailing societal constructs that had led communities to a state of physiological and socio-emotional balance. Equal access and the sharing of resources cemented their stability, chiefly because what was bad for one person was bad for the whole group.

Structured Cooperatives

When roving tribes evolved into fixed villages, we brought what worked with us. That included a commitment to shared prosperity, because there was no better motivation for putting forth one's best efforts than the guarantee of sharing in joint successes from which everyone benefited. There were three reasons for this. First, we are social creatures, and we form bonds over kindnesses, both given and received. Second, there is a unique human pride that stems from enjoying the fruits of one's own labor. And third, we understand intuitively that collective wellbeing produces happy, healthy, balanced communities, and most of us, to no surprise, want to live in one.

The root for the term "cooperative" is cooperation, which is the alignment of group aspiration, interest, effort and reward. Inter-human cooperation is one of the defining traits by which we came to dominate the planet.

Early forays into cooperation were associations in which training, resource-sharing and legal protections strengthened communities. These included the Roman *collegium* and the medieval guild, which laid the groundwork for the world's first universities, including one in Bologna, Italy, and another in Oxford, England. These operated similarly to trade guilds, where members cooperated to control academic standards and living conditions. The concept of *universitas* itself originally meant "a community of teachers and students."[72]

As organizations grew more complex, cooperatives in the 18th and 19th centuries did, as well. These were entities where persons united voluntarily to meet their common economic, social, and cultural needs and aspirations through a jointly-owned enterprise, and where each co-owner held equal and democratically assured voting rights in their shared business.

Many if not most cooperatives follow the **Rochdale Principles**, set out in 1844 England and adopted in 1937 by the International Cooperative Alliance. They are:

- Voluntary and open membership
- Democratic member control, with each member having one vote
- Economic participation by members
- Autonomy and independence

- Education, training, and information
- Cooperation among cooperatives
- Concern for community

The allure of these principles is self-evident. Respectively, they promote inclusivity, impact, equity, self-determination, revitalization, collaboration, and ethics.

And membership is growing.

In 2012, the Worldwatch Institute published research indicating that for the first time, more than *one billion human beings* in 96 countries were members of a co-operative, generating trillions of dollars in economic output[73].

Many of us are likely unaware that even in the United States, worker-owned cooperatives have burgeoned. Today, according to *www.nonprofitquarterly. org*, 47% of new cooperatives are worker-owned, whereas a decade ago, that number was just 1%[74]. They write:

> *"This trend is not surprising, as it fits well with the historical pattern of development. Cooperatives typically emerge when people's needs are not being met by the market—and it would be hard to argue that late-stage capitalism is meeting the needs of most workers in America. From wage stagnation and the emergence of the gig economy to retiring business owners, employee ownership has been identified as a solution to many of our socioeconomic ills."*

It's about time.

As we covered in Chapter 10, Mondragón runs the most profitable business sectors in all of Spain, and has for many decades. Mondragón's drivers—people before things, and relationships for life—are diametrically opposed to the drivers of late-stage, free market capitalism, wherein things (goods and/or profits) come before people, and where relationships are transactional and last only as long as is necessary.

Since the 1980's rise of the Friedman Doctrine, in which shareholder profit became the defining metric of corporate success[75], workers have been treated primarily as mechanisms for maximizing profits. Often, they work for the financial benefit of people they've *never even met*, but for whom they toil regardless without the benefit of guaranteed participation in the success they helped to create. At the same time, rampant inequality, which has resulted in a 281-fold difference (or more, per some studies) between CEO and average worker pay in the United States,[76] just keeps growing.

It's no wonder the cooperative is re-emerging as an alternative to the last century's dominant form of commerce.

Cooperatives cover 98% of rural India, comprising a whopping 854,355 of them, with 290.06 million members.[77] In 2018, Prime Minister Narendra Modi addressed Gujaratis when he announced that cooperatives have "blossomed as **the third economic system**, where neither the government nor the capitalists will have control."

Final Thoughts

Whether or not cooperatives are *the* antidote to late stage, free market capitalism's destructive wake, as they are for the billion-plus people who currently participate in them, *something* will have to eventually replace a system that puts basic resources increasingly out of reach for an increasing number of people.

Beyond the impact to economies, there is the planet itself to consider. The greatest risk of *value extraction,* accelerated by a rigid adherence to quarterly shareholder *growth* (or inflation), is that at some point there will be nothing left. As a strategy for near-term gain, I cannot imagine a higher corollary long-term cost.

So, whether its antidote is a Universal Basic Income to feed a growing "useless class", as championed by Economic Nobel Laureates; a "neo-Georgist" shared land ownership model to ensure all boats are lifted, whose value was acknowledged by Churchill, Einstein, Roosevelt, and even Milton Friedman[78] himself; or the member-owned cooperative structure outlined in this chapter, the enfranchisement and enrichment of the world's people through guaranteed access and equitable participation in the common wealth of the world is the *only* route to true sustainable, long-term prosperity.

Per *Wikipedia*[79]:

> *"Cooperative businesses are typically more productive and economically resilient than many other forms of enterprise, with twice the number of co-operatives (80%) surviving their first five years compared with other business ownership models (41%) according to data from the United Kingdom."*

According to research monograph *Capital and the Debt Trap*, cooperatives' resilience has been attributed to how they share risks and rewards between members, harness the ideas of many, and provide members with tangible ownership stakes. Its authors write:

> *"Cooperatives tend to have a longer life than other types of enterprise, and thus a higher level of entrepreneurial sustainability. [Their] banks build up counter-cyclical buffers that function well in case of a crisis, and are less likely to lead members and clients towards a debt trap. This is explained by their more democratic governance that reduces perverse incentives and subsequent contributions to economic bubbles."*

Given that time-tested and still-thriving systems that focus on the common wealth exist everywhere, and are more resilient and often outperform free market capitalist ones, it certainly feels as though it's time to rein in the "perverse incentives", "economic bubbles", "rampant inequality" and "wage stagnation" referenced in *Capital and the Death Trap*, to which I'd add runaway costs, a focus on the near term, forced inflation (or growth), zero-sum games, and shareholder worship.

As Modi put it, it's time for a *third way*.

In the next chapter, we'll focus on the global economy's Achilles Heel, and what we can do about it.

12   Deflate Everything

"Technology is deflationary, [and] we are entering into an age of deflation unlike any the world has ever seen."

So writes Jeff Booth in his excellent book, *The Price of Tomorrow*.

"Our economic systems were built for a pre-technology era when labour [sic] and capital were inextricably linked—an era that counted on growth and inflation, where we made money from inefficiency. That era is over, but we keep on pretending that those economic systems still work.

"We need to accept deflation and embrace the abundance it can bring. Otherwise, the same technology that has the power to bring abundance to us and our world will instead destroy it."

The book's central point is that the cost of production across industries invariably *lowers* in tandem with advancements in technology, science, and operations, and that for many things human beings need, **costs *should* be approaching *zero***.

Why, instead, are those same goods and services, which include our food, where we live, how we learn, the medicines we take, and the cost of transportation, *rising* instead of lowering, often dramatically, and thus becoming less affordable for the majority whose wages have stagnated?

Consider the following data shared by the Economic Policy Institute, mapping multi-decade economic trends through 2015[80]:

- Middle class incomes have shrunk by 23% relative to overall market growth, since 1979
- Non-executive wages grew just 9% against a productivity increase of 74% overall, since 1973
- CEOs now make 296-350 times what an average worker in their company does, up from 20 times, in 1965

- Wages for college graduates have been falling since 2000, and yet, the cost of an education has increased by 180%
- If home prices grew at the same rate as inflation since 1970, the median home price in the US today would be just $177,788 rather than $408,100

In short, while consumer prices have continued to rise, our incomes have stagnated; and while production costs continue to lower, those benefits are being largely absorbed by those at the top of the economic food chain.

As Chris Rock deadpanned:

"If poor people knew how rich rich people are, there would be riots in the street."

Let's step back for a moment from the house we've built. It was predicated on the false premise that growth *must* exist if we are to compete successfully against other professionals, companies, markets and nations, by shoring up demand that often goes well beyond needs for things like calories and goods. We have done this chiefly to maximize the exchange of capital. But even the slightest perspective would reveal that we are doing so at an unsustainable pace, and cost.

Forbes' review of Booth's book, summarizes it well:

"Booth makes striking and important observations about global debt. He notes that in 2000, the world's cumulative debt was $62 trillion, almost twice its collective GDP of $34 trillion. In early 2020 the numbers rose to $247 trillion and $80 trillion respectively, so debt is now three times GDP. In those two decades, it took $185 trillion of debt to produce $46 trillion of GDP growth."

I shared this 3:1 debt-to-growth ratio in Chapter 1. If present patterns hold, it's only going to get worse. Booth asks of his readers:

"If it takes ever-increasing credit growth to achieve economic growth, how are our economies any different from a Ponzi scheme?"

The global economy we now run is largely predicated on a dangerous concept: that prices *must* increase, when in fact costs naturally *decrease*. Every year, the cost to bring many goods to customers lowers due to real advancements in technology, scientific discovery, data and analysis, and mastery over efficiency (of production, communications, marketing, delivery, waste, etc.) And yet, because we keep increasing prices on those same goods—on housing, education, healthcare, effects and services of all kinds—an ever-increasing percentage of people become unable to participate in any of it. At some point, the end result of these things could plausibly be the collapse of the global economy, because it is being shored up by debt that *outpaces actual gains* and therefore can never be paid back.

The entire problem exists largely because of the pervasive practice of defining "growth" as a driving metric by which success is broadly measured. That mindset often fails to account for the "profoundly deflationary" forces of technology-driven efficiencies and abundance.

Booth's ideas propose that technological deflation, when decoupled from debt-based monetary systems, enables *abundance*.

Booth asks us:

> *"What if, instead of trying to stop deflation at all costs, we embrace it? … Deflation becomes something celebrated because it means that we are getting more for less … We allow ourselves to accept abundance … As technology removes jobs and fewer overall jobs are needed, prices will keep falling, allowing those who lose jobs a way to share in the benefit of technology abundance without massive transfers of wealth."*

What *is* deflation, exactly? An *Investopedia* entry puts it this way:

> *"If, as the common saying goes, inflation is the result of too much money chasing not enough goods in the economy, then conversely deflation can be understood as a growing supply of goods and services being chased by a constant or slower-growing supply of money."*

This last point is consistent with the economic paradigm in which most of us now operate. Or, at least, we *would*, if not for the $185 trillion we have generated in global subsidies (or excess debt) since 2000. *Investopedia* continues:

> *"An increase in the supply of goods and services in an economy typically results from technological progress, the discovery of new resources, or an increase in productivity.*
>
> *"Consumers' purchasing power increases over time and their living standards rise as the increasing value of their wages and business incomes allow them to purchase, use, and consume more and better quality goods and services. This is an unambiguously positive process for the economy and society as a whole."*

The article then concludes:

> *"All in all, it is not deflation, but the* inflationary *period that then leads to debt deflation that is dangerous for a country's economy. Perhaps, unfortunately, consistent and repeated inflation of this kind of debt bubble by central banks has become the norm over the past century or so."*

So, why aren't we passing on real savings to those who need them most?

What To Do?

As we'll see in Chapter 25, some 800 million jobs, or one in four among a 3 billion-strong global workforce, risk being lost to technology in the near term, according to McKinsey[81]. It's no surprise. This could also be a critical catalyst of positive change, *if* we do the right thing with regard to replacing those lost wages.

Why and how? Well, machines, once they're built, work for free, exclusive of the cost of maintenance and repair. They don't need food, housing, healthcare, inspiration, training (apart from software or hardware upgrades) or sleep. They are also typically much more efficient at their "work", whether that's analysis, data-mining, order-taking, welding, farming, dispensing, or anything simple and repetitive, as we're seeing in many employment sectors, already.

Fueled by A.I., machines can also learn, and improve.

In short, they are, as Booth observes, *deflationary*.

Our non-human workforce needs only maintenance, upgrades and/or occasional replacement, which are minor costs relative to the far larger cost burden of a human workforce.

So, what to do about the rising costs of living we artificially face today?

Where Everyone Benefits

We *could* elect to share the savings that we generate from pervasive deflation with the members of companies, communities, markets and/or nations, by making us all beneficiaries in the underlying abundance that Booth references in his treatise, and that the technology boom is only accelerating.

There are multiple forms common benefit could take, all of which exist to one degree or another today.

Shareholding is the pervasive currency of publicly traded companies. Today, we operate in a "buy-in" mode, whereby the more money one has, the more shares one can purchase in any given business who offers them. Most of the time, this limits participation to those with adequate excess capital for the buy-in. Said another way, shareholding is mostly for those who can already afford it.

As the old joke goes: The best way to make one million dollars is to start with ten.

Kidding aside, what if <u>everyone</u> who participated in an enterprise as employees were made a shareholder *by default*?

As we saw in Chapter 10, Mondragón in Spain does exactly that. Every member of its now-84,000-strong community is a beneficiary to its successes. Those who can't cover their initial investment have it loaned to them, and pay it down with their work contributions.

Not dissimilarly, in the start-up world, stock options (as equity grants) are a well-understood means of establishing ownership through sweat equity "invested" and risks shared, rather than relying on outright purchase as a pathway to financial security. In fact, tens of thousands of millionaires (145,000, at last count)[82] have been made in Silicon Valley over the past 30 years, many of these through the provision and exercise of stock options. When compared against the stock market, options often allow for greater participation among those *without the liquidity* to invest.

Sadly, however, the vast majority of startups fail.

Then, there's Universal Basic Income (UBI).

UBI is a government program that provides regular *and unconditional* cash payments to every citizen, regardless of their work status, income, or age.

It's not a new idea. Stanford's Basic Income Lab has mapped more than 190 active and concluded experiments conducted worldwide to date, each providing differing amounts of UBI to varied subject groups, over varying periods of time.

Though no nation has fully implemented a permanent UBI, it may nonetheless point the way toward a true solution to the rise of the Useless Class—a concept we will explore in depth in Chapter 25:

I'll share a few current and concluded examples of UBI here:

Alaska's Permanent Fund Dividend is encoded in State Law and provides every resident $1,000-$2,000/year effectively for being alive.[83]

The Eastern Band of Cherokee Indians Casino Dividend in North Carolina (since renamed the EBCI GenWell Program) shares the profits of its casinos to tribal members, averaging $3,000/year[84], in addition to a whopping payment of up to $130,000 to 18-year old high school graduates, from their Minors Trust Fund[85].

A *Vox* article titled *Everywhere Basic Income has been Tried, in One Map*,[86] states:

> *"Economists found that* [UBI] *doesn't make* [people] *work less. It does*

lead to improved education and mental health, and decreased addiction and crime."

In Germany and Spain, multi-year experiments in UBI have been largely aimed at its poorest citizens. So far, these have resulted in significant self-reported reductions in financial stress *without any measurable negative impacts* on employment-seeking or productivity, just like the Cherokee program.

And since 2010, Iran has "rolled out a nationwide *unconditional* cash transfer program to compensate for the phase-out of subsidies on bread, water, electricity, heating, and fuel, [giving out] sizable monthly payments to each family [equivalent to] 29 percent of the median household income, on average," according to the *Vox* article.

They add that economists found that "[Iran's] program did not affect labor supply in any appreciable way," and added that it is "still running, and it's the only such program in the world to run nationwide."

Critics of UBI will argue often that recipients of income who do not "earn" it through labor will become lazy or disincentivized, when in fact in most places it has been attempted, we've seen that fear has largely failed to materialize. To the contrary, "the evidence so far suggests that getting a basic income tends to boost happiness, health, school attendance, and trust in social institutions, while reducing crime," per *Vox.*

One problem with UBI is that it piggybacks on a conventional economy, because this allows us to ignore the cost of ballooning debt while redistributing growth (via guaranteed income), and thus, in my view, doesn't solve our *underlying problems.*

Whatever we do, we will invariably face the need to do something as more and more people lose jobs to the power of technology, and as an increasing number of us who keep our jobs have to be retrained more and more frequently regardless, because of the inherent and undeniable power of technological advancements. April Rinne warns us about this very thing, in *Flux.*

With debt-fueled inflation rising precipitously and technological deflation exacerbating the divide between the haves and have-nots—pushing even basics like education and shelter ever-farther out of reach for more and more people—something will quite likely *have to give* if we are to avoid the cataclysmic outcome of whole segments of society who can no longer earn a decent enough living to actually survive, let alone thrive.

Final Thoughts

This is where Booth's provocation resonates most with me. His frankly heretical proposal is simple:

> *"Why don't we stop intervening and simply let deflation play out?"*

Said another way, why don't we stop shoring up growth with unsustainable debt and finally take away all the direct subsidies, tax breaks, and legislated (i.e.: forced) growth that boost short-term gains while sowing long-term risk? Why not take the long view of human and environmental wellbeing, and use our faculties and resources to improve outcomes for *the maximum number of participants* possible?

Doesn't (nearly) everyone win at that point?

To "let deflation play out" as Booth proposes would certainly be painful at first, as is any disruption to the status quo. Maybe *seismically* so. With that said, growth and inflation are not natural laws; they are **policy-dependent design choices**. Thus, if deflation were properly governed, and with adequate social scaffolding, we could use our collective intrinsic ingenuity and capacity to implement a new system *before* things collapsed. We saw a corollary and heroic application of human energy in action recently, with the global pandemic.

Invoking financial god Ray Dalio's book, *Principles for Navigating Debt Crises*, Booth lists the four traditional ways by which we deal with debt:

- Austerity
- Debt defaults or restructuring
- Central bank printing and other monetary stimulus

- Transfers of wealth (i.e. higher taxes for the rich) and UBI

Dalio points out that in the end, "Policy makers always print [money]. That is because austerity causes more pain than benefit, big restructurings wipe out too much wealth too fast, and transfers of wealth from haves to have nots don't happen in sufficient size without revolution."

If, by contrast, we were to stop artificially buoying economies and instead let deflation take its natural course, then once a new equilibrium were re-established and stabilized, deflation could take root and the cost of living could conceivably and drastically diminish. Eventually, it could approach zero, once technologies matured adequately, and shouldered a sufficient percentage of economic production.

Heretically, we could even contemplate *hastening it* rather than standing in its way.

With the right governance model and with adequate global collaboration working under conditions of trust, reciprocity, and shared norms, it's conceivable that *all* humans could meet *all* of our basic needs—a home, food, and an education—within a generation. If that came to pass, we could finally channel our "work" energies toward enterprises about which we're passionate.

The idea of **a life spent pursuing meaning** is the core subject of a vision I share in the final chapter of this book.

It's conceivable that A.I. and technology could, at some not-too-future point, create such abundance that no one will have to work anymore to live a reasonable life in full. For some, "enough" may well be enough. They may choose to exit the finite game altogether, and live out their lives modestly, enjoying the fruits of technology's labor in the way that retired people who can afford to, do so today. In a world of technology-fueled abundance, their decisions wouldn't have an excessively deleterious impact on the rest of us.

But others—in my view, a sizable contingent of humans—will want to aim our energies creatively to actively cultivate *purpose*, however each of us defines it. For that group of people, working because (and on what) we *love* to, rather than because (and on things) we *have* to, will only add to the quality of life in our communities.

If and when the cost of life reaches zero, the true creative spirit of human beings will be fully ignited, and I for one can't wait to see what would come from eight billion lives, unshackled.

It may be time to deflate everything.

13 A New Human Paradigm

In 2017, economist and author Umair Haque wrote the following, on *Medium*:

> *"Every age has a paradigm of human organization. A set of defining principles and beliefs about what life is for.*
>
> *"Today's paradigm of human organization — a relic of the industrial age — is economic. Our lives — in fact, all life on the planet — [is] thus oriented around the pursuit of a single end: maximizing short-term income.*
>
> *"In the economic paradigm, well-being, the fullness of life's quest for self-realization — whether or not lives are growing, flourishing, becoming, developing, to what degree, extent, duration, quality — is nonexistent. It's not conceptualized, represented, counted, measured, quite literally valued. Not in GDP, corporate reports, profits, markets, theories, models, prices, costs, benefits, anywhere. Not even in the smallest way — quantitatively, functionally, arithmetically — and so certainly not in the truest way: qualitatively, conceptually, substantively. And so because well-being, life itself, isn't represented or valued* [in the economic paradigm], *it's not worth anything according to* [its] *calculus."*

That's a lot to chew on. As I read his words, they resonated deeply. By one critical measure, economics is the most brutal finite game ever created. While greed and power often directly cause conflict, money acts as a powerful amplifier and proximate cause of savagery when it becomes concentrated. This creates desperate conditions and incentivizes exploitative behaviors within economic systems. In that regard, money, by way of those seeking to expand or consolidate of power and control, or conversely, by way of those fomenting revolution in a bid to reduce inequality or improve their own standing, has directly caused, accelerated, or amplified an outsized share of history's violent conflicts. In the 20th century alone, wars (231 million deaths[87]), famine (70 millon[89]), environmental destruction (40 million[90]) and despotic rulers (168 million[91]) show that the cost of economic fealty is sky high.

And yet: the biting irony of money's power is that for the most part, it's not only no longer a fixed, tangible asset (like gold, cattle, shells, tobacco, or spices), it's also largely no longer even a "specie-backed" currency, or paper money whose value is based on assets like precious metals. Today, the overwhelming majority of money—92% of it[92]— exists only in digital algorithms. That is, it is a "faith-based currency", hidden in computer programs, represented in spreadsheets, or otherwise living in other abstract things called options, equity, debt, e-cash, mortgage, ROI, EBITDA, depreciation and 401k, among hundreds of other imaginary vehicles.

Said another way, money has no true intrinsic value anymore. It is a mere digital promise by banks that may or may not be able to deliver on it. See: 2008.

Stock markets rise and fall, but not necessarily on the backs of production outputs, or even revenues. Rather, they often gyrate based on how financial professionals *feel* on any given day. The roller coaster of our indexes lurch to and fro, inexplicably reversing themselves in minutes or hours due to fleeting panic or optimism-fueled euphoria.

Ultimately, a stock's price reflects the collective agreement between numerous buyers and sellers and is driven by their *perception* of a company's value. This is what often (usually?) sets the real-time price, making it an ever-fluctuating "voting machine" in the short term.

The value of an investment on any given day is largely based on some form of *judgment* rather than *empiricism*; and that value is no longer based on anything tangible (like gold), or fixed (as was the U.S. dollar under Bretton Woods).

In the process of acting the bull or the bear, we too-often wage war on one another over access to resources in pursuit of economic dominance or hegemony, or exploit one another in the name of financial gain or its proxy—power. As a result, people usually find themselves in one of two "finite game" columns: that is, either with an embarrassment of riches, or unable to source even cheap food at the store or pay for a roof under which to sleep.

Haque, who is British, gives a preposterous example of how this works:

"If we break each others' legs, GDP will go up, not down. We'll have to take taxis to work, and pay for more medical care, which are counted as "gains". Does that example strike you as absurd? It is, but it's very real: in the extreme case, you get a society where an economy is growing, but life expectancy is falling—modern day America."

His words made me think of how the United States created, marketed, and distributed the least healthy human diet imaginable. It is frankly guaranteed to make us sick, or die. Concurrently, we see a large contingent of Americans that is antagonistic or even violent toward the notion of "free" health care. Economically, the system—the individuals, companies, and government— stands too much to gain from rampant disease and death to entertain an alternative. Our sickness is *great* for GDP. Food is a $2.58 trillion business in the United States alone[93]. Once we add in healthcare's $5.6 trillion value[94] we begin to understand how sickness is an economic *engine*. That's *before* we fold in the economies of fashion, fitness, dietary supplements, health-oriented services, self-image businesses, and pharmaceuticals, all of which are supercharged by an increasingly unhealthy population.

As I introduced in Chapter 1, and will explore in depth in Chapter 17, more people are now killed from dietary causes, presenting a true economic windfall for those who stand to profit from our illness.

Haque's central point—that **the organizing framework for large groups of humans is economics**—is that this has led to a pervasive paradigm of global suffering and is becoming worse with every passing year as the system continues to "mature".

Haque says:

"The economic paradigm of human organization doesn't care. About life. Yours, mine, our grandkids, our planet's. Its sole end is maximizing immediate income. It doesn't care if you're happy or miserable, if you're fulfilled or hollow, if you're humane and gentle and wise or cruel and brutish and spiteful, if you flourish or wither as a human being, if the oceans dry up and die or teem joyously, if the skies turn to ash, if you, me,

our grandkids, or the planet, dies young or old, or if any of us live or die at all, in fact. It just doesn't care. It wasn't designed to. Thus, all that possibility, all that potential, is never realized: it's used up to maximize immediate income. More and more, maximizing immediate income minimizes life's potential."

Massive Existential Problems (MEPs)

The MEPs we face today are largely the direct result of our economic paradigm. We have created a climate that's become uncorked as the result of an economically ravaged planet. We have created wild and skyrocketing inequality that becomes increasingly extreme at both ends each year as the inevitable outcome of economic obsession. We are seeing the stagnation of entire countries because they have no more to give; no more "game" on the world stage of economic competition. This has incubated extremism in the world, which is really just the most conspicuous expression of a population left in the cold without the means of joining the game of economic access. We produce mass human suffering by playing economic zero-sum games such as physical and resource wars, toxic food systems, and man-made natural disasters. Maybe worst of all, in my view, we have sown widespread *despair*, whether or not any of us is deeply aware of this; a profound disconnect with our own sense of underlying purpose. That's because what governments and companies officially measure no longer has much to do with what actually matters to individual human beings.

Economics, according to Haque, is "the hidden thread that connects today's four Massive Existential Problems." These are: climate change, stagnation, inequality, and extremism. He calls our MEPs "just surface manifestations of the same underlying breakdown—a badly, fatally, irreparably broken paradigm of human organization."

There's a way out.

A New Paradigm

One plausible solution to the problem of mass inequality is the creation of a new, powerful, *unifying* paradigm that rejects manufactured scarcity and competition for control over access to it, and is instead built on the cultivation of "abundance": on the premise that **wellbeing is the *most important* currency** and that human beings are a limitless wellspring of its creation and distribution.

We evolved to thrive together as social beings, to overcome problems with our giant brains and our ability to collaborate on solutions. We are emotional beings, first and foremost, governed by a drive to find *purpose and meaning*, and to aim it toward our individual and collective flourishing. The Ancient Greek philosophers called this Eudaemonia. Its pursuit is the foundation of the related term Eudaemonism: "a theory that the highest ethical goal is happiness and wellbeing."

Bhutan

Bhutan is the world's only nation to include a measure of wellbeing as part of its domestic health assessment. They call it the GNHI: the Gross National Happiness Index.

According to the University of Oxford's Poverty & Human Development Initiative:

> "The phrase 'gross national happiness' was first coined by the 4th King of Bhutan, King Jigme Singye Wangchuck, in 1972 when he declared, "Gross National Happiness is more important than Gross Domestic Product." The concept implies that sustainable development should take a holistic approach towards notions of progress and give equal importance to non-economic aspects of wellbeing.

> "Since then, the idea of Gross National Happiness (GNH) has influenced Bhutan's economic and social policy, and also captured the imagination of others far beyond its borders. In creating the Gross National Happiness Index, Bhutan sought to create a measurement tool that would be useful for policymaking and create policy incentives for the government, NGOs and businesses of Bhutan to increase GNH."

The nine domains of Bhutan's GNH is a great starting point for us to understand what a new, eudaemonia-centered paradigm could begin to look like, in action. As you read them, ask yourself just two questions, without overthinking them *or* measuring them against your current life circumstances. That is, consider them on their own merit. As you read each, ask yourself:

A: "Is this important to me, personally?"
B: "Would its widespread advancement in my community/nation/world make life better for me *and* for others?"

Here they are:

1. Psychological wellbeing
2. Health
3. Education
4. Time use (sufficiently allocated to lead to balance)
5. Cultural diversity and resilience
6. Good governance
7. Community vitality
8. Ecological diversity and resilience
9. Living standards (material and economic security)

I think it's safe to assume that the majority of people would answer my questions with a resounding YES and YES!

Bhutan's system of governance is no doubt influenced by the fact that it is an overwhelmingly Buddhist nation. But regardless, it's a meaningful investment in national wellbeing that is <u>measured</u>. Even so, in recent years as modern technology has crept in there, *economics* has eroded traditional ways, leading the Bhutanese to crises of conscience, and as a result, many of them have become wildly unhappy.

It's ironic. In traditional Buddhism, desire is the chief *obstacle* in life to overcome, as outlined in the Four Noble Truths. Well, in modern Bhutan, burgeoning desire in the form of economic participation has supplanted Buddhism significantly. A 2018 article in *Business Insider* reported about Bhutan's growing malaise[95]:

> *"Advertisements create desires, which cannot be satisfied by people's current economic position. Crimes and corruption are often born out of economic desires.*

"We have an increasing income gap, we have increasing youth unemployment, environmental degradation... We have a lot of things to worry about."

Bhutan has succumbed to the economic paradigm. But that doesn't mean it wasn't onto something.

Burning Man

Burning Man is another exemplar of what happens when economic priorities are supplanted by qualitative ones. It, too, runs on principles corollary to Bhutan's domains. They are:

1. Radical inclusion (everyone is welcome)
2. Gifting (everything is given without exchange or reciprocity)
3. De-commodification (no advertising or sponsorship)
4. Radical self-reliance (on inner resources)
5. Radical self-expression (liberty to express oneself)
6. Communal effort (cooperation and collaboration)
7. Civic responsibility (for public welfare and social fabric)
8. Leaving no trace (respect environment; clean up after oneself)
9. Participation (contribute rather than consume experiences)
10. Immediacy (direct experience over ideas)

If you read these carefully, they could be retitled, in order: acceptance, generosity, trustworthiness, empowerment, authenticity, collaboration, virtue, environmental stewardship, agency, and presence.

You know: the stuff of eudaemonia.

As I shared in the Prologue, Burning Man is the most eye-opening collective experience I've ever had, in 57 years. It is remarkable for the fact that a group of 85,000 strangers can meet, create, and share space, resources, and experiences <u>without a penny changing hands</u> or even being allowed to (with the exception of centralized water and ice), on the basis of no more than a shared goal of manufacturing delight together.

It works.

Yes, there are exceptions. Many go to consume experiences rather than co-create them, and there is plenty of drama, as well as debase and abusive behavior there, as well.

Notwithstanding these critically important things, Burning Man is regardless a paradigm shift, as a major experiment in a higher order of shared human purpose, whether or not the same forces that corrupted Bhutan are closing in on Black Rock City. Of course they are.

Regardless, people are taking note. An article in *Governing.com*[96] recalls a meeting of the U.S. Conference of Mayors:

> *"Most people think of it as some kind of naked bacchanal, and that couldn't be further from the truth," says Columbia, S.C., Mayor Steve Benjamin, who recently completed his term as president of the U.S. Conference of Mayors. Benjamin accompanied half a dozen other local leaders to visit Burning Man last year [2018], and says he was "inspired" by the scale of the infrastructure and the degree of planning involved. "They build a legitimate city. In a very short period of time. It's well planned, well thought out, organized incredibly well. It's amazing."*

He's not alone.

Paul Romer, a Nobel Prize-winning economist, went to study it in 2019 as a potential model for the next stage in our paradigmatic development, as XL communities. *The New York Times* did an article[97] on him afterwards, as I was returning from my first Burn—the same one he attended.

His first reaction was, "it's just like every other city... except in this other way, it's like no city, ever."

Romer is the former chief economist at the World Bank.

The New York Times reported:

> *"Mr. Romer's logic is connected in a roundabout way to the work that won him the Nobel. Macroeconomists used to think about the world by tallying up quantifiable stuff: capital, labor, natural resources. They weren't*

sure how to account for ideas. But Mr. Romer, in a seminal 1990 paper[98], showed that ideas were central to progress. His model of economic growth incorporating them enabled economists to ask entirely new questions about the modern "knowledge economy": Where do ideas come from? How do they spread? Why are cities such hotbeds for creating them?

"To Mr. Romer, the idea was about seeding the right government rules."

The "right government rules". Think about that for a second. He meant *qualitative* ones, not the quantification that drives the current global economy. Burning Man was where it took a man like Romer to "get the paradigm shift" that he intuited 30 years before he *experienced* one.

"By the time he got to Burning Man in August, he was thinking of himself as a University of Chicago-trained economist, once indoctrinated in the almighty free market, now in open revolt against his roots."

In other words, he saw Burning Man as a new paradigm for the growth of cities in an increasingly overcrowded, under-resourced world.

Will Roger, one of Burning Man's founders, sat with Romer just before the 2019 Burn. Speaking about cities in the same *New York Times* article, Roger said:

"All the energy and the helter-skelter and lack of connection to the earth, the energy of all those humans compressed into one space implodes on my own spirit, on my own sense of who I am.

"This is a funny thing to say to an economist. Helter-skelter is a decent description of the force from which economists believe ideas emerge. When people live close to one another, rather than close to the land, they hatch plans, they trade services, they discuss terrible ideas until they eventually arrive at good ones.

"This is more or less what happens at Burning Man, too. But other cities have become symbols of greed and consumption. And that greed is killing our Earth Mother."

Then came Romer's response, as one of the world's pre-eminent economists:

> *"I think I have some of the same anxieties, but I'm coming to the view that it's the market which is the danger, not the city.*

> *"I'm afraid economists have really been serious contributors to this problem. This whole ideology of 'government is bad, government is the problem' has I think provided cover for rich people and rich firms to take advantage of things for their selfish benefit."*

In his Nobel acceptance speech, Romer "implored people to think of cities, especially in the developing world, as places where people get the benefits of interacting with one another. A global economy built on ideas no longer has to be zero-sum," he argued. "Everyone can use ideas at the same time. Someone living in America benefits if someone in India becomes better off and invents a vaccine."

The central discovery Romer made gets at the very heart of Burning Man, even though his acceptance speech and prize pre-dated his visit there. Maybe those things primed him to "get it" once he finally arrived. I know my life followed a similar trajectory, and Burning Man has not only fueled my own reappraisal and social healing, it is the catalyst that precipitated this very book.

As I wrote in the Prologue, writing has all been part of my own "sense-making" journey. And Burning Man cracked open that door.

In contrast to false-notion concepts like "finiteness", non-zero sum ideas are the basis of its opposite: "infiniteness". As in, more for me *doesn't mean* less for you. Romer himself considered this his concluding insight, as he stood in front of the Nobel panel. And then he went to Burning Man—afterwards—and concluded that **the event and place represented a model of things he had theorized**: of infinite, shared resources without losers or conditions, driven by the idea of collective benefit and *delight*.

Lest you think this doesn't pencil out, and that Burning Man is a rich person's bubble, consider this. *The Washington Post* wrote a beautiful article about Burning Man in 2018[99]. In it, they included a graph on the distribution of income of its attendees. I went ahead and compared the *Post's* statistics against the general distribution of income in the United States, which is home to 80% of its attendees[100]. I figured, if the two were similar, then Burning Man is a fair representation of its host nation at large; just one that operates under different principles, as it advertises.

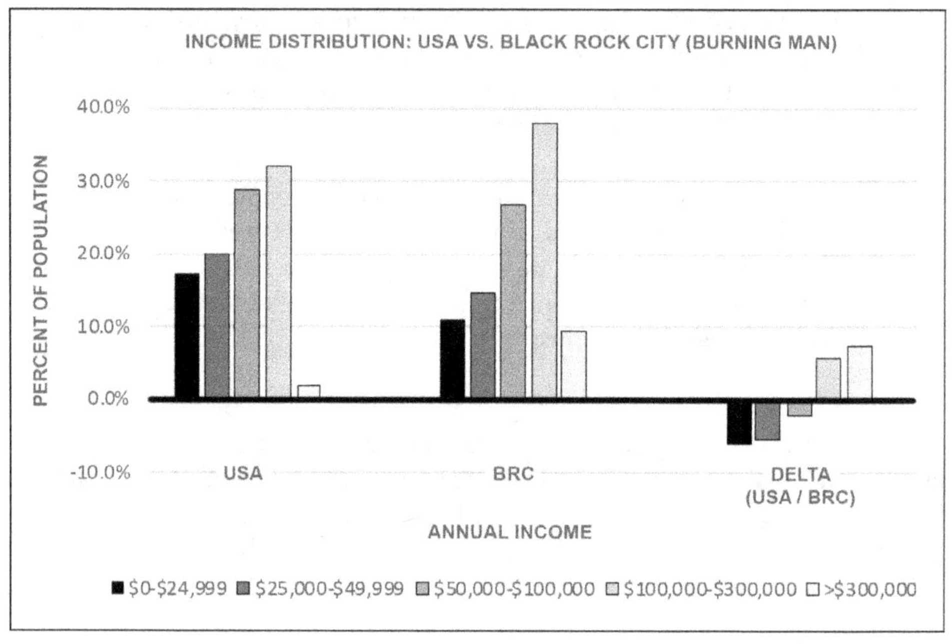

Income Distribution: USA vs. BRC © Anthony Fieldman 2024

In all, Burning Man (represented in the preceding graph as BRC, for Black Rock City—its geographical name) is 13.3% out of step with the rest of the nation. That is, in aggregate, across all income groups, Burning Man skews 13.3% more wealthy than the national average. While that's statistically significant, it's not another animal altogether. Which means, with some tweaking, what works "on Playa" for 85,000 people might just work in other similarly scaled places.

Romer is quick to point out that behind the seeming anarchy of Burning Man's lack of lawmakers, law enforcers, and government lies a group of individuals who act very much like a body politic, with urban planners, fund-raisers, a board of directors, and a host of individuals who spend all year planning, negotiating, organizing, and trouble-shooting the next Burn; and who, once there, spend their Burns ensuring the collective safety, health, and even sewage management of the enterprise. I do the same things myself, for the camp I now run there.

In other words, BRC acts like any other city. Except that it's like no other, as Romer observed, because while Burning Man continues to evolve and face similar problems you find elsewhere, its slate of guiding principles that still guides a majority of behaviors there is decidedly non-zero-sum. It is infinite.

But how does one create a city on infinite values?

Mondragón (Again)

The Basque Spanish corporation/town/cooperative we've now discussed at length is worth a collective €15 billion and has operated successfully for +/-70 years, driven by the foundational principle that "**the common good is given priority over a particular good**".

I won't repeat Chapter 10's lessons here. I will add that a 2013 article on Mondragón in *The Guardian*[101] sought to understand why it was that while "Spain struggles through double-dip recession, fierce austerity and 26% unemployment, [Mondragón's] workforce remains steady at around 84,000 people worldwide (with just a sixth of them outside of Spain)."

The article implied, effectively, that Mondragón had thrived throughout is then-70-year run, through war, fascism, and multiple national economic downturns, that had stress-tested it significantly had nonetheless thrived, and that because of this, *there was something to be studied there*. And that "thing" was Mondragón foundational ethos.

Post-National Societies

Then, there are the Silicon Valley gods. Leaders in the still-glossy Information Economy and armed with infinite cash, many of them are former or present *Burners*. Among these, several are itching to improve upon the paradigm that created their economic success, to incubate new eudaemonia-centric models of human cooperation. Accordingly, they are beta-testing civilizational petri dishes of interaction and community.

Balaji Srinivasan, a former partner at Andreessen Horowitz and CTO at Coinbase, is also the author of *The Network State: How to Start a New Country*, from which platform he created a series of annual conferences named after his book. In his opening address at the 2025 conference, he referred to The Network States of the Internet as a "third kind of thing", suggesting that the Internet itself was the catalyst that could lead to a post-national future. He framed the context as follows:

1. Step 1 was the creation of **Internet companies**, which expanded even micro-scaled commerce across borders;
2. Step 2 was the creation of **Internet currencies**, which created a post-national economic model of exchange; and
3. Step 3, is the opportunity (and current trend) toward the creation of **Internet communities**; that is, a series of post-national social groups whose businesses and exchange are borderless and which—with the right frameworks in place—can evolve into an effective constellation of decentralized, sovereign, micro-states.

Srinivasan refers to the potential that Internet communities hold as being born "cloud first, land last, but not land never". Meaning, the Internet that has hitherto allowed for a massive amount of business and economic freedom can also catalyze our freedom from nationhood. He is convinced that it's just a matter of time, and has created Network States principally to spur these things into existence.

Lest you think this is *exclusively* fringe behavior, 2025's conference included official government representatives from Singapore, Abu Dhabi and Dubai, among other small, ultra-modern nations experimenting with advanced forms of self-organization. It also included a who's who of investors and entrepreneurs in the advancement of post-national human organization.

Among the most interesting presenters at the 2025 conference was Timour Kosters, co-founder of Edge City: a "society incubator" focused on prototyping the future that is currently experimenting[102] with "pop-ups" in existing "edge" cities like Austin, Capetown, Healdsburg, San Martin (Patagonia), and Bhutan.

Kosters thinks of these pop-ups as "accelerators" of human flourishing, and offers applicants scholarships, fellowships, and grant, especially in the area of "D/ACC" or "decentralization acceleration".

Then, there's Jordan Hall (née Greenhall), a former lawyer-turned-music-innovator (MP3.com), DivX founder, Aspen Institute participant, Santa Fe institute trustee, Game B (or Infinite Game) founder, and Neurohacker Collective chairman, who ranks among Silicon Valley's leading thinkers. During COVID-19's lockdown, Hall incubated an initiative called The Civium Project, whose ideas are covered in a compelling series of long-form *YouTube* videos[103].

He said Civium was "hacking the deep code of metaculture." To sum it up, Hall and his co-conspirators (Jim Rutt, John Vervaeke, Gregg Henriques, and my friend Jamie Wheal—the consultant we met in the Prologue)—believe that to prioritize human health and wellbeing *at least as much* as economic prosperity, we must incubate micro-societies of no more than 150 people, consistent with Robin Dunbar's belief in the maximum number of intimate human relationships one could hold and remain a "stable and cohesive group."

These micro-societies, in their view, would invest in one another *personally*, like Mondragón does, and as we all did at one point, within our own tribes.

Unlike pre-modern tribes, Civiums would leverage a global network via digital connectivity—the Internet—which would allow each of these groups to interact and *transact* like the Lenape did with "outsiders." Presumably applying similarly non-zero sum principles of value creation, a planet full of Civiums could collectively generate enough returns to power the whole human enterprise.

Hall and Co.'s primary goal with Civium, which has since re-crafted itself as an incubator of ideas and experimentation named The Voicecraft Network[104], is not dissimilar to Kosters' Edge City, in that both hope to leverage the intimacy of small societies in order to *reframe* what drives our actions, at a scale that naturally favors choosing the common good over personal gain. After all, Mondragón has done this for nearly a century, and has grown organically into an 84,000-person network, without losing or even diluting its moral compass.

And so, whether or not Srinivasan, Kosters, Hall, Rutt, Vervaeke, et al, manage to *directly* author a new post-national model at scale, or simply evolve our thinking so that someone else can pick up their work and advance it to fruition, these rapid innovators at the tip of the Digital Age's spear are framing the conversations that will likely drive the investment countless *others* will make in defining what's next. That's because what's "now" is in countless ways, inherently broken.

Final Thoughts

What is driving all of these experiments, I would propose, is a tacit understanding that Epoch A—the resource-gobbling paradigm we covered in Chapter 3—risks breeding a global society of increasingly adversarial and embattled strangers who share ever-diminishing resources and thus risks the possible collapse of the system itself, in terms of both resources and mental fortitude.

On this last point, the outcomes of Epoch A coexist alongside, and have plausibly influenced, disheartening trends toward rampant increases in self-harm, depression, anxiety, and suicide in the developed world.[105] In the latest data available, fully 29% of American adults, including 34.3% of 18-29 year olds, 36.7% of women, 34.4% of Black adults, and 31.3% of Hispanic adults now suffer from a mental illness, according to Gallup.[106] These are the highest-ever recorded numbers, and have skyrocketed in the last decade alone. Globally, the World Health Organization reports that one billion people now suffer from a mental illness.

The upward trajectories in inequality and mental illness are likely not unrelated. So-called psychosocial stresses (and daily micro-stresses) related to modern life are spurring an increase in the number of peer-reviewed studies and systemic meta-analyses investigating the relationship between the two. These include esteemed journals (*The Lancet*), medical associations (JAMA), hybrid organizations (WPA), and scientific publishers (Frontiers). While these issues remain debated, we would be hard-pressed not to notice that socio-economic life exerts a strong influence on one's sense of wellbeing, and safety.

Attempting to rewrite one of the most powerful organizational structures humankind has ever created seems like an intellectual luxury few of us can afford, but it could also, arguably, have consequential impact on human thriving, including our mental health.

Beyond the experiments cited in this chapter, there are numerous written and web-based treatises we can all familiarize ourselves with, if only to inspire richer thinking on the subject of collective thriving. These include John Vervaeke's "Awakening from the Meaning Crisis" lecture series, Daniel Schmachtenberger's "The War on Sense-Making" videos, Jamie Wheal's "Home Grown Humans" podcast, Tristan Harris' Center for Humane Technology and Downgrading Humans, and of course James Carse's *Finite and Infinite Games.*

And Burning Man itself, while far from perfect, offers participants a firsthand experience that improves upon many aspects of social incubation and exchange.

One worthwhile goal could be to learn from the good and toss the bad, to leverage ideas in service of creating better, more empowering modes of being together.

A mind armed is a mind primed to do something. The more we know that alternative systems exist, allowing us to awaken from our own zero-sum daze, the more we can begin to aim our energies toward what's next. Perhaps that's a large-scale cooperative like Mondragón, or a gift economy like Burning Man. Perhaps it's a Dunbar-sized community connected to the world by the Internet, that shares its abundance freely with its members. Perhaps it's something we haven't yet dreamt of that will *also* prioritize people before things.

As people, we possess all of the ingenuity we need and all of the innate, genetic, and socially predisposed equipment—emotional and social drive— required to recast what it means to live and thrive among other humans in a world comprised of billions of us.

This shouldn't be impossible. We *started* there, in small groups, after all. Epoch A and the tools to exploit it simply supercharged our transformation, and when it did, there really wasn't any choice *not* to participate. Economic life is, right now, dramatically enforced by lawmakers and armed officials. It is the lingua franca of the current paradigm, and most of us have forgotten we weren't put here on Earth to make money—nor to stand on others' heads while doing it.

We evolved as a result of love, manifesting as care, thus leading us to collaboration. These are the things that allowed a physically weak, hairless monkey born in the East African savanna to conquer an entire world in the blink of a universal eye. Sickening and killing one another over scraps *is not* what led to human thriving. It *is* those debase behaviors, however, that have allowed us to create extremely efficient tools for self-destruction and have powered a minority of us to ride the crest of the wave as we head toward the rocks.

Deeper than all of this—more than ROI, EBITDA and GDP—lies the quest for self-realization: of purpose, fulfilled, and shared.

I have long felt that there are only three things *every human*, bar none, ultimately seeks in life, and when we truly have possession of these, fully and without asterisks, then all other desires or needs become secondary. These are:

1. Love
2. Belonging
3. Purpose

This triad is the wellspring of an individual's health, and by extension, a healthy community. Moreover, there's no "magic" to them.

Love given begets love felt, deeply.

Acceptance given begets belonging felt, deeply.

And a sense of purpose arises invariably from the base of the foregoing two pillars, because purpose is borne of strength, aimed at applied creativity.

In the remaining chapters—14 thru 25—we will look in depth at how purpose-fueled creativity is being aimed in the categories of **housing** (shelter and affordability), **health** (food and the environment), **education** (growth and mindset), and **work** (meaning and cities).

HOUSING:

Shelter and Affordability

"In Grand Central", New York City © Anthony Fieldman 2017

14 Our (Real) Homeless Problem

Shelter is broken insofar as the number of unhoused and inadequately housed people is enormous, and increasing.[107] Today, according to the latest UN-Habitat estimates, "318 million people are homeless, while 2.8 billion people lack access to adequate housing."[108]

It doesn't have to be that way.

> *"The only common denominator to the homeless is that they lack a home. This must be the starting point."*

That stunningly simple yet powerful statement was made by Juha Kaakinen during a four-nation symposium I attended on the subject of homelessness. When I asked him, he modestly described himself as a "doer". From 2013 to 2022, when he retired, Kaakinen was the CEO of non-profit housing provider Y-Foundation, in Finland, leading their near-eradication of homelessness. While every country in Europe has seen increases in homelessness since 2008, Finland alone has seen a precipitous drop[109].

The reason? Kaakinen says, "We started on that path [toward ending homelessness] when **we changed our thinking to see housing as a human right**, the foundation of living a good life."

Kaakinen's point of view stands in stark contrast to a common real estate paradigm in which everyone's free to join the melee according to his/her/their own access, capacity, and luck.

Kaakinen is full of clear-eyed statements. Here's a third: "To keep society functioning, you have to keep everyone in [it]."

Taken together, these statements—now Finland's official position—posit that A: homelessness simply means lacking a home; B: access to a home is a human right; and C: unless everyone is not only *in one*, but *thriving*, society stops functioning.

If we were all to act as Finland does, housing would look very different. Rather than play the zero-sum, competitive-bid, win-lose games that define the housing market in many Western nations, we would focus on making sure everyone was *in* one, instead.

Doing the hard work to reintegrate those who have financial or other personal challenges that preclude them from finding safe shelter takes a lot of work. And that work can be at odds with political philosophies prioritizing individual liberty, autonomy, and personal sovereignty, or advocating minimal government intervention in both personal and economic lives.

Y-Foundation, with over 19,000 apartments under management at the time of this writing, is now the Scandinavian nation's fourth largest landlord[110]. A critical factor to its success, the operation goes beyond simply supplying bricks and mortar. Y-Foundation's buildings are staffed by professionals trained in re-integrating marginalized or down-on-their-luck individuals into society.

According to Kaakinen, "There are different kinds of support, from help with daily activities through to detoxification in the home and support for people with recurring psychoses. It's individually tailored but based on free will; you don't have to take support to get the housing. The housing and support services are separate."

And it works. Amazingly, approximately 80% of tenants are able to keep their homes for the long term[111]. What makes this even more incredible is that residents *pay rent*. Yes, it's subsidized; but it is nonetheless rent being earned and paid by formerly homeless people whose support allowed them to reintegrate into society.

A Nordic Mindset

All Scandinavian countries, Finland included, practice a hybrid capitalist-socialist model of collectivism in which market forces allow for competitive aspects of income generation consistent with an economics-driven planet, while social welfare *simultaneously* ensures that the entire population of a country receives the lion's share of governmental focus and funding, to enable it to thrive.

The so-called Nordic Model[112] of socio-economic governance comes closest to proving that it is indeed possible to "have your cake and eat it, too," by ensuring that there's enough cake for everyone.

All five Scandinavian countries, in fact, rank among the world's greatest democracies[113] and, separately, provide the highest quality of life, thereby topping list after list, year after year, as the best places to live[114]. In addition to these accomplishments, they enjoy some of the highest levels of longevity, and rank amongst the highest GDP-per-capita nations on the planet[115].

The data supports the idea that taking care of other people does not necessarily constitute a measurable draw on society, nor does it automatically diminish quality of life for those who don't need the help.

If anything, these powerful statistics suggest the opposite: that the better we care for one another through "socialist" programs, the better our nations fare in terms of metrics like happiness, longevity, economic access, and the true promise of "democracy": having *agency* in one's life.

So, of course, when it comes to homelessness, we can turn to the same quintet of forward-thinking nations, and to Kaakinen's Finland, in particular, to learn strategies that may actually reverse homelessness rather than maintain systems that reinforce the status quo at great cost, and with questionable benefit.

What Socialism *Really* Means

I have spent much the past nine years flying regularly between Canada, where I was raised and where my business is based, and the United States, where I've spent most of my adult life. Before I share what upsets me most about both nations' current mistreatment of the homeless, I feel obligated to address what I see as gross misconceptions about socialism. That's because anti-socialist mindsets in both countries contribute, I believe, to homelessness' persistence, and why attempts to alleviate it through grassroots goodwill and volunteerism are often met with aggressive countermeasures by leaders and citizens who preach inclusivity while simultaneously galvanizing police and lawmakers to limit these things. That includes the repossession or destruction of tents and makeshift homes that lie outside of the system's legal and economic reach; hindered access to public resources like parks, public buildings and transit; and reduced visibility through forced sheltering of people that political constituents don't want to confront in daily life, as long as they remain unshowered, unshaven, unquiet, or ill-clothed.

Socialism's roots lie in ancient Greece, whose custom of *koinonia* encouraged them to voluntarily share their wealth with other citizens, forgive debts, serve in public roles without pay, and allow the poor to access property held in common. It later found a strong voice in Jesus of Nazareth, a philosopher whose teachings were unabashedly socialist[116]. They resurged again under German philosophers Marx and Engels, who advocated for a form of "positive humanism"[117] that Lenin somehow managed to pervert into a bad deal for everyone. Before *that* happened, the German duo primarily championed the agency of human beings, individually and collectively.

The word socialism couldn't be more self-explanatory: a practice, system, and philosophy (the "ism" part) focused primarily on a society's *health* (the "social" part). It is founded on the prioritization of *community*, in that the wellbeing of its members is a societal obligation to meet. These things are based on an understanding that any society is only as strong as its weakest link; and that together, we are stronger.

No Door to Lock

Like others, I have been incredibly dismayed at scenes of makeshift "tent cities" popping up in parks, under overpasses, and urban corners, but not because I find them unsightly. Rather, it is because they speak to our failure to integrate their owners into a safer and more supportive environment.

Far from solving homelessness, Canada and the United States—both among the wealthiest nations on Earth[118]—are actively antagonizing homeless people, in two ways.

First, Canadians and Americans are chasing them away from the public realm and resources to which, in *concept*, they have as much right as you or I do. For example, many American cities have passed "sit-lie" ordinances that prohibit sitting or lying on sidewalks, and "anti-camping" laws that criminalize setting up tents in public spaces. These laws were upheld by the U.S. Supreme

Court in 2024, with *City of Grants Pass, Oregon v. Johnson*[119]. The contested ordinance on which it is based prohibits people who are homeless from using blankets, pillows, or cardboard boxes for protection within city limits. In 2019, the National Homelessness Law Center surveyed 187 cities, and found that 72% of them had at least one enforced public camping bans, representing a 92% increase from 2006.

These laws are essentially telling these people that the soft ground they've found in those parks—nature's beds—is not for them, nor are such creature comforts as pillows or cardboard boxes. The word public, it seems, has asterisks. And so, police, lawyers and elected officials are all putting in long hours to turn the homeless population into a perennially nomadic one, left to wander from one place to another, chased out of each, and into shelters in which these same folks would prefer not to sleep.

This is the second problem. Shelters are dangerous places, full of theft, rape, and abuse. In a 2003 article titled *No Door to Lock*, JAMA Network disclosed that at the time, roughly 33% of women, 27% of men and 38% of transgender people in shelters reported a history of sexual or physical abuse, year over year[120]. That was *before* COVID. Shelters remain, in a very real sense, emblematic of many societies' failure to adequately invest in re-integrating homeless people into society, as the Finns have done, rather than forcing them into dangerous places of convenience.

There's a reason people choose to sleep on the street when there's shelter, heat and a bed to be had for free, thanks to the state. It's called self-preservation.

Back in titularly socialist-leaning Canada, the problem is no better. There, a few sober-minded individuals like Tim Richter, who founded and runs the Canadian Alliance to End Homelessness, are pleading with their government to do something more about the problem than it is. During the height of COVID-19, he was interviewed on the subject by CTV News reported:[121]

> *"Public health tells us that we should be at home, isolating, and wash our hands often, which are all difficult to do when you're experiencing homelessness. Communities around the country have been scrambling to set up isolation shelters* [and] *create* [physical] *distancing. Ultimately, the*

best protection from COVID-19 is a home."

Richter sounds a lot like Kaakinen. It took a mild-mannered Calgarian to point out to the Canadian government that the best protection against COVID and homelessness was *a home* in which to physically distance oneself.

An Architect, Disenfranchised

I am an architect, by trade and by passion, who has spent 30-plus years designing everything from homes to international airports, and most things in between. I have been incredibly fortunate to lead teams within global firms with global reach throughout most of my career. At one memorable point, I even had the eye-opening experience of designing a 450,000 square foot home (not a typo) for the sovereign leader of a Mid-East nation, valued at Allah-knows-how-much.

It is nearly impossible to reconcile the act of designing a twelve-hundred-foot-long palace in a faraway desert—one that requires a fleet of electric vehicles to help its residents traverse it—while living in a city in which I confront homeless human beings daily, laden with snow, sitting on cardboard, and jockeying for access to subway grates for warmth.

And yet, it wasn't until about a year or two ago that I began to wonder what *true value* I contributed to the world beyond winning architectural awards for my colleagues and designing critic-pleasing icons for my clients. After all, what has historically distinguished me from my peers is creativity. And while creativity *can be aimed* at solving existential problems like homelessness, as Kaakinen has shown us, what value is it, *really*, if it's employed to dress up what really amounts to no more than weather-tight containers that anyone *remotely* skillful can piece together, provided they listen carefully enough to their clients to meet the latter group's stated aims? If we strip away the esoteric nature of aesthetic preferences and incremental improvements to existing building typologies, however "cutting edge" they may be, isn't *any* roof that doesn't leak, *any* door that locks, and *any* mechanical system that maintains our thermal comfort *good enough*?

Heretically—for someone in my professional position—I've concluded that it is. That while architecture and urban planning matter deeply, any decent building is better than no building, and that the latter should be our <u>first priority</u> in the investment of our time and energy.

I am not saying that some buildings aren't better than others (they are), or that innovation within each building type doesn't exist, or have meaning (it does). It's just that in my profession, we're largely "gilding the lily" for well-funded clients to meet their business goals, while ignoring other pressing matters in the world wholesale, such as the fact that homelessness, unsafe housing, and lack of access to other built resources if far too common, and receives far too little (if not none) of our energy, because doing so is costly in time and lost fees, and we, too, have businesses to run.

Of course, it's not up to just architects to solve homelessness. When it comes to expertise and capacity, I know plenty of people and companies who would participate eagerly in designing and building shelters, if given the chance. At the same time, execution requires building advocacy and partnerships that lie outside of our "swim lane" as designers. That's because governments and their laws often construct the biggest roadblocks to our collective ability to act quickly and energetically on altruistic instincts.

This is especially true in places like Canada and the United States, where I've collectively spent most of my life and where homelessness is perennially discussed, but politicking unfailingly kills good initiative(s). My two governments typically grind down any attempt to bypass a well-entrenched system seemingly hellbent on maintaining the status quo.

Swimming Upstream

Beyond Scandinavia, some amazing stories—exceptions to the bad news—have emerged out of kindness, volunteerism, resolve, creativity and more than a little "I don't care what's *allowed*; I'm going to do what's *right*."

One of these, a Toronto-based carpenter named Khaleel Seivwright, funded and built 2x6-foot shelters, insulated like homes over COVID's first winter[122]. They were lockable, ventilated, perched *above* the frozen ground, and came complete with a fire extinguisher. They were built in his garage then personally donated to homeless people who had expressed an interest in having one, once he had interviewed them *in person*.

Toronto Police, so-directed by the same government that had been disbanding its "tent cities" religiously, quickly confiscated every single one they could find, upon which Seivwright's work was destroyed.

What had driven Seivwright to make them was the fact that for a period of time, he lived in Vancouver, slept in shelters, and knew just how terrible they were. For him, this was personal.

After enough of his shelters were confiscated and destroyed, he decided, in a bit of marketing genius, to post video footage[123] of his "customers" so that they could explain *in their own words* what these shelters meant to them. One woman shared on camera that for the first time in a decade her chronic pain meds *weren't* being stolen because she finally had a lockable door. Another man said that the homes were the best thing to happen to Toronto and that without them, people would be "dropping left, right and center". In the video, that same man pauses, looks down, and quietly says, "It saved my life, basically." A third person cited the benefit of a real shelter against "the nasty people—the ones who rip your tent in the middle of the night." He added, "It's the best thing that's ever happened."

I could go on. The central point is that Seivwrights' shelters made the difference between life and death for these people, and of feeling *seen*. Moreover, they made great headway toward satisfying what Abraham Maslow famously articulated as the most foundational of human needs: those of **safety, security, warmth and rest** (food and drink being another challenge). All of these things were to be found within a tiny 2x6-foot box, at least until the government came around, and destroyed them.

So why are some legislative bodies seemingly antagonistic to these things?

I have landed on the uneasy conclusion that the true culprits are both legislators and the general public—not the homeless themselves. For one thing, these "eyesores" don't reflect well on our legislators. That is, they are highly visible signs of governments' failure to take care of their neediest citizens, beyond words and politics. For another, it is society itself that pressures their removal and to which politicians react in self-preservation, because tents and shacks are a reminder of *our* failures: they diminish the quality of a bucolic stroll in the park, and it'd be far more palatable to move the homeless "elsewhere", where we assume our governments will deal with them.

There is a third, equally problematic, and perhaps more insidious issue. There is no longer such a thing in the Global West as "shelter without taxation." Our governments have determined that if one is in possession of a shelter of any kind, it is the government's *right* to excise a (real estate) tax, or repossess it. Just try to claim a plot of land and build something *anywhere* within the footprint of a Western nation. You can't: not without the government first electing to map it, zone it, regulate it, establish a tax burden, and legislate every dimension of your privilege to live there.

The shelters that Seivwright and others built were illegal at least in part, I believe, because they weren't *taxable.* Set aside the challenges of building codes and aesthetics, for a moment. In my view, if his shelters met building codes and were deemed "attractive", the government would not suddenly welcome them.

Current development policies in many (most? all?) municipalities incentivize and favor taxable development and profit generation precisely because these things generate municipal and federal revenues, as does the collection of development fees that are often tied to the permission and scale of a development.

And so, I would suggest that taking shelters away that don't fit into the system is easier than figuring out how to house those who cannot pay taxes, beyond relocating them from public land into dangerous shelters that they don't want to live in. And in that paradigm, there is scant incentive to invest in solving the underlying issues of homelessness, especially because the time scale required to do so exceeds election cycles, and because short-term setbacks would risk the re-election prospects of those working on it.

Which leaves the hard work to the fringes, like NGOs and renegades like our carpenter friend.

America the Beautiful

South of the Canadian border, it's a familiar story. In a 2016 *Mashable* article titled "Los Angeles Declares War on Tiny Houses Donated to the

Homeless,"[124] Elvis Summers, the not-for-profit founder of Starting Human/ The Tiny House Project spent months defying police and governments by building and distributing houses to homeless people whom officials often ignored, and more frequently *harassed.* He even created a GoFundMe account called Tiny House, Huge Purpose, to extend his reach. But as in Canada, as fast as he made them, the police took them away.

Summers built and placed 37 of them in one area of Los Angeles, all of which were tagged by the government then removed at the request of a city Councilman named Curren Price[125].

Curren wasn't alone in his actions.

L.A.'s Bureau of Sanitation spokeswoman Elena Stern said, "I don't refer to these as homes or houses because they're really not. They're temporary structures, and while the intent may be noble and good, the structures are not fit for people to stay in them."

And tents are better?! Street grates are better? These were never intended to be permanent solutions. They were acts of empathy and generosity by talented people with the ability to directly improve outcomes in the gross context of *inaction* by the very governments that had publicly sworn to take care of the public.

Like Seivwright, Summers, too, used to be homeless, by the way. Do you see the pattern here? Summers said, "The mayor just threw out two veterans [from the shelters he made for them]. They paid their ticket. They shouldn't be homeless."

He went on:

> *"These guys are a bunch of corrupt bullies. I can think of dozens of ways, and not over a ten-year period, dozens of ways in a month that every single homeless person could be off the streets. There's a lot of ways this could be a win-win for everybody, but they don't want to listen."*

Since then, Summers adapted. He said, of the destroyed shelters:

"These ones were kind of high profile. They haven't found my other ones, and they're not going to."

In both Canada and the U.S., private citizens have voluntarily donated hundreds of thousands of dollars to fund Summers and Seivwright, who in turn supplied the initiative, heart, elbow grease and outreach. It's heartening to see. At the same time, homelessness is not something an individual can solve, however community-minded and selfless they may be. For scalable progress to be made, a government *must lead the effort*, at the very least by enabling it or removing impediments to enable innovators and entrepreneurs to form partnerships built around reach, time, expertise and most importantly, *will*.

The Brutal Numbers

According to the OECD[126], as of 2024, Canada spends just 19.3% of its GDP on social programs—23rd highest of 38 member nations. The U.S. is marginally better, at 19.8% (21st), but not much. By contrast, Finland ranks 2nd highest at 31.4%, just behind Austria, at 31.6%.

According to a 2019 *PressProgress Canada* article[127]:

"Dalhousie University professor Daniel Dutton told PressProgress that social spending includes social assistance payments, housing, and child welfare, which directly drive social determinants of health. Dutton noted social stresses limit people's freedom to remove themselves from harms. 'Lower social spending means we are fine letting people deal with those environments on their own, which means we accept their health will suffer.'"

Final Thoughts

Back to Kaakinen. The economic argument is a plausible deal-killer in many political environments. Housing is one of the economic engines of *any* nation. Real estate and related businesses comprise the biggest contributor to American GDP, at nearly twice the next largest tranche[128]. In Canada, too, it is the largest[129]. Real estate is one reason that Kaakinen and the Finnish government focus so much on homelessness. In the symposium I attended, Kaakinen said:

"You can see what happens when housing is the playground of finance and speculation, rather than seen as a social right, basic social infrastructure that's needed to keep society functioning.

"There is no way you can end homelessness with such a low percentage of affordable social housing. In a [wealthy] country like Finland or Australia, it's not a money issue."

At the time of writing, social housing makes up 13% of Finland's total housing stock, and rising[130]. In Australia, meanwhile, that number stands at 4.1% and is decreasing[131], while simultaneously, 11% of Australians live in structurally deficient homes[132] due to cost barriers. In the United States, it's similar. Just 2.7% of Americans live in subsidized housing[133], while 5.2% of them live in physically deficient homes[134].

Kaakinen says, "It's important to understand that helping the homeless out of homelessness actually saves money. We have studies that show when one homeless person gets permanent housing, with support, it saves our society €15,000 per year."

And so, in human economic terms, ending homelessness is good business. There is another key economic benefit. In addition to reducing the economic burden of homelessness, a human returned to housing and social life, as at least 80% of Finns in Y-Foundation's housing have been, is usually a *contributor to GDP*, in one manner or another.

Lastly, there is a moral imperative to solving homelessness that has nothing to do with economics and everything to do with our values, and the value we place on the wellbeing of *other* members of the human community. Every person is entitled, in my view, to a life that guarantees dignity, safety and belonging. Moreover, for those of us who are lucky enough to be on the #winning side of things, it is our moral obligation to do what we can for those who are not. That includes such unorthodox things as making tiny, senselessly illegal homes for people who might otherwise die, be raped or be beaten, lose toes to frostbite or medicine to thieves, and who might lose all hope *without* these things.

As Summers said, there are a lot of [obvious] ways homelessness can be solved. All we lack is the resolve—the strength and the grit—to do the right thing. Fortunately, there are others acting to solve it, and have shown us the path to doing so, successfully.

In the next chapter, we will look at the broken economics of home ownership itself and emerging innovations that could, with the right framework, lead to a home for everyone, largely free of ownership's current *inaccessibility*.

Urban archeology © Anthony Fieldman 2022

15 A Home for Everyone

Home is broken in the twin senses that there aren't enough of them for those who need one, and the ones we *do* have are increasingly unaffordable or otherwise inadequate to meet even our *basic* needs.

To reiterate what was said in Chapter 6, without one, we are robbed of the means to participate in daily life from a place of stability.

Still, in the United States, we've made home ownership one of the least affordable basic needs with a whopping 75% of Americans being priced out of the market, per a 2025 Bankrate.com analysis[135]. So, if we are truly fix "home"—either the lack thereof, or if we are housed, one that adequately sponsors *reasonable* mental and physical health within the limits of our means—then a number of things must change from the status quo.

The good news is that there are many ready-baked solutions to this issue as well, in different geographic, political and business arenas.

But to fix anything, we have to first understand both *what* is broken, and *how*. With housing, there are a number of culprits. Chief among them are: the **increasing commercialization** of housing as an investment vehicle; accommodative **monetary policies** that have allowed for unhealthy increases in both participation and pricing; **legal barriers** caused by complex or inhibitive regulation; and the relentless **globalization** of the world economy and financial markets, with U.S. monetary policy having an outsize influence on "shaping asset price developments, and in particular, house prices." This last comment was made by editors Rob Nijskens et al[136], of the Central Bank of the Netherlands in an open-source book they wrote on the subject of affordability, called *Hot Property: The Housing Market in Major Cities*.

Deregulation and the New Asset Class

In the United States, the deregulation of the housing market is widely accepted as the de facto trigger event in the meteoric rise in home prices,

which had hitherto been mostly flat since the beginning of the 20th century[137].
That's because establishment of robust government support programs
like 1934's FHA, then later, Fannie Mae, the GI Bill, Freddie Mac, and the
mortgage tax deduction, collectively allowed home ownership to increase
by nearly 50%[138] over a twenty year period, from 1940-1960. It all began to
unravel with 1978's *Marquette v. First of Oklahoma*, as a wave of deregulation
reforms in housing allowed financial markets to become entwined with
housing markets for the very first time, in the United States. As a result, the
government's usual guard rails were weakened, or disappeared entirely. This
allowed bankers to step into the void without government oversight, and the
private label securities market, or PLS, was born[139]. Over the ensuing decades,
bankers created, packaged and traded mortgages and mortgage products
with increasing complexity. This included the expansion of (overleveraged)
mortgage credit, the creation of risky subprime loans, artificially low initial
interest rates that ballooned over time, mortgage pre-payment penalties, CDOs
largely comprised of sub-prime mortgages, and even the ability to repackage
and sell the same assets multiple times[140].

As a direct result, between 1978 and 2008, housing prices skyrocketed,
expanding more than *fourfold*[137], and reached their peak with the 2008
housing crisis.

But it didn't end there. In fact, following the crisis' short-lived correction,
markets once again skyrocketed. Except this time, it wasn't individual home
seekers driving the increase. Rather, for the first time, a significant "market"
comprised of both mom-and-pop and institutional investors turned their
focus to housing, birthing a new asset class for wealth creation. Today, they
are collectively buying up an increasing share of the nation's housing supply.
In 2024, that number stood at 25.7% of that year's total supply, according
to a report by CJ Patrick Co., using numbers from BatchData, a real estate
provider[141].

According to their data, 20% of the nation's 146 million total homes are
owned by people who don't live in them, which both reduces the supply to
aspiring owners and simultaneously puts upward pressure on renters by
way of investors who own them as a means of generating returns on their
investments, like any other business owner.

What all of this has done, in just over a century, is to effectively redefine housing from "a safe haven for raising a family" to "a commodity to be amassed, held, and/or traded", in the name of capital.

Among G7 countries, however, there are two standouts: Japan and Germany. In these two nations, housing prices have remained relatively flat for decades[142] in spite of global trends in housing prices, and they have done so on the basis of one or both of the following two principles:

1.   Build enough homes.
2.   Zone to maximize participation.

Build Enough Homes

In many ways, Japan is the global leader for supplying enough housing to meet the demands of its residents. In Japan, there has been a consistent *surplus* of housing since 1968[143]. That is, there are more homes than people. In the United States, by contrast, there is a shortfall of 3.2 million homes[144]. When we factor in affordability, that number jumps to 6.8 million fewer homes within reach of Americans living below the federal poverty level than there should be[145].

There are several reasons that Japan's housing market is exemplary. First, the Japanese government has centralized control of all housing (unlike the decentralized market system in the United States), thereby removing municipal-level politics from polluting the goal of providing for the people. Second, Japan has overwhelmingly simplified land use codes to include just twelve total zones, as compared against the U.S.'s 30,000-plus[146]. In the U.S., that level of Byzantine complexity leaves "anyone with a stake in land use decisions—including developers, academics, advocates, and the public—[to] struggle to understand and respond to [it],"[147] according to the U.S. HUD's Office of Policy Development and Research. Third, in Japan, a focus on increasing density and infill sites has led to greater efficiencies in resource sharing, and use[148].

Collectively, the result of these initiatives is that fewer homes are torn down, building new ones is simpler and thereby more accessible, and commodification is held at bay since fewer residents find themselves without one and everyone has enough choice to prevent costs from skyrocketing due to lack of supply. Japan's housing market approach is a form of *deflation*, really, because it contravenes the inflationary policy that drives other aspects of its economy. If prices of goods and services are rising there, and GDP continues to drive policy, then a flat real estate market is, *relatively*, deflationary.

Perhaps counterintuitively, Japan's wealth metrics haven't suffered as a result of government intervention. In fact, according to the most recent published OECD statistics, Japan's net financial worth of households stands at more than 12% *higher* than American's[149]. At the same time, among OECD countries, the U.S. leads in income *inequality*, with the top 10% owning 80% of all wealth, while in Japan, they own less than 50%[150].

Economic security, then, isn't negatively impacted by Japan's top-heavy housing policy. This makes sense. In the U.S., the same mechanisms Japan employs fueled its explosive growth of post-war home ownership as well, before free-market capital via PLS stepped in and commoditized the housing market.

It's not shocking, then, that 52.5% of Japanese households' financial assets are held in cash and deposits as of 2024[151], while in the U.S., that number is just 8%[152]. Americans are cash poor and house rich, while at the same time, we are not as rich as the home-owning Japanese.

The impact of American housing policy is that it has effectively resulted in *ninety times* more homelessness[153], 33% more inequality, and 12% less overall wealth than in Japan.

Zone to Maximize Participation

More than half of the world's people live in cities. And yet, if you examine cities like Toronto or Chicago and compare them against ones like Madrid or Berlin (all are roughly similar in population), there is at least one glaring difference. In the second grouping there is a consistent density, while in the first homes spread out in every available direction, without one person's home touching another's.

With *Euclid v. Ambler* (1926), the Unites States Supreme Court ruled that

Euclid, Ohio could ban (minority-dense) apartments in areas of (minority-sparse) single-family housing. Within a few years, racial and economic segregations *increased* by 50 percent, as many cities adopted similar zoning practices. Today, more than 75% of U.S. land zoned for housing *exclusively* allows for private, single-family homes[155].

This is important because, as author M. Nolan Gray lays out in his book, *Arbitrary Lines: How Zoning Broke the American City and How to Fix It*, the current housing crisis in the United States has overtly racist and classist underpinnings; and rethinking (or completely "abolishing", in his view) these regulations is a pre-requisite to solving the current housing crisis, independent of other economic pressures.

Race and income inequality aside, the legal structure of single-family, so-called "exclusionary zoning" exacerbates housing costs in second way: by ignoring the inherent economy of multi-family housing.

Zoning for increased density is one means of increasing affordability, because multi-family apartment buildings are intrinsically more efficient than single family homes are, in a number of ways. Homes within them share engineering systems, walls, stairs, and carrying costs, among other things. They require less heating and cooling per square foot —half, according to the EPA[156]—because more of each home's walls, ceilings and floors are "warm" (by abutting others; think of humans huddling). They are less costly to operate due to economies of scale, since repairs, maintenance, property management, and insurance costs are all shared[157]. They drastically reduce the relative "environmental footprint per family" due to fewer roads, less electro-mechanical and plumbing infrastructure distribution, less destruction to natural systems, fewer cars, and less fossil fuel use.

These are all largely *automatic byproducts* of increased density.

According to the Brookings Institute, exclusionary zoning...

> *"...reduces the supply and drives up the cost of housing, hurting not only individual households looking for a place to live, but also the economy as a whole. It gives people fewer choices over where to live and in what kind of home, often particularly affecting older Americans and people with*

disabilities. It can harm the environment, pushing people from living in climate-friendly apartments or near transit and into longer car commutes and sprawl. And restrictive zoning fuels racial and economic segregation, serving as the mechanism for exclusion and "opportunity hoarding" by wealthy, white communities."

During the 2021-2022 session, the senate in New York State—one of the nation's most punishing exclusionary environments since the 1970's, when white suburbanites vehemently opposed racial integration—weighed some of the country's most progressive proposals[158]. These included Senate Bill S7574, which would **allow duplexes and quadruplexes** in areas of single family zoning and forgive the customary requirements for on-site parking; Bill S4547A, which would **allow existing homeowners to build Accessory Dwelling Units** (ADUs), to not only densify housing but create a new income stream for stretched homeowners, in the process; Bill S7635, which would **allow any affordable housing project in an underserved city to bypass punishing zoning reviews and rules**, which barriers can often double their customary cost; and never-named proposals to **increase NYC's base density** in residential areas and **rezone transit hubs** to grow allowable density where best served by connectivity.

Not one of these initiatives passed, showing just how difficult it is to tackle a century of precedent even with today's runaway housing costs, and shortage.

Manufacture and the "Fordification" of Housing

Even without adequate reforms in supply and regulation, however, there is still one more formidable weapon we could use to lower costs. It owes at least a small debt of gratitude to the man responsible, more than anyone else, for the proliferation of the automobile.

In 1908, Henry Ford's transformation of the assembly line allowed him to reduce the costs of manufacturing a car dramatically. At the time, competing cars cost between $2,000-3,000[159]. That year, Ford sold his Model T for *one third* of that: $850. Sixteen years later, in 1924, the very same vehicle, which was lovingly nicknamed Tin Lizzie, sold for just $240[160], or a 72% *reduction.* How? Why? Ford was not *only* focused on improving production efficiencies and quality control. Of equal importance to him, he chose to *pass the savings onto his customers.*

Five years before the Model T rolled off his assembly line, he famously said:

"I will build a motor car for the great multitude. It will be so low in price that no man will be unable to own one."

His goal—removing barriers to affordability—allowed him to do the unthinkable: he transformed a country: how it lived, worked, and prospered. By 1927, just 19 years after he first manufactured his first true car, he had sold *15,000,000* Model Ts[161]. In a population of 119 million Americans, most of whom had never dreamed of owning a car before, that meant that in less than a generation, one in ten Americans suddenly owned one, for the first time. And it was a Ford Model T.

Today, with all of our advanced manufacture—things Ford could only dream of, a century ago—the cost of a vehicle would be unrecognizable to him. Every year, it goes up, not down.

What changed? Ford's goal was to make cars affordable, and he used technology to do just that, to spectacular and transformational effect. What drives auto prices today? It would be hard to offer any credible answer other than market dominance and profit maximization, in the name of shareholder returns. And so, as we've seen in the preceding chapters, the financial savings that *actually* result from incremental improvements are reserved to enrich the company's owners while the retail price to customers (people we tellingly now call "consumers") continues to increase as much as the public will tolerate. As long as people are buying and the competition plays by the same (unnatural) rules of retail inflation, nothing will change.

When Ford started, it took 12 man-hours on average to assemble a car. By the time he implemented his innovations, it took just 93 *minutes.* That's a labor savings of nearly 90%[162]. But rather than pocket the difference, he passed the majority of savings from cost efficiencies onto his customers.

In spite of Ford's economic heresy, he did just fine, dying with an estimated worth in the billions, in today's dollars[163].

And so, when it comes to housing supply, there is one more principle, along with building enough homes, and separately, zoning to maximize participation, that we can employ to solve housing:

3.   Innovate technologically to keep prices down.

This "tool" is leading to a revolution in home-building while simultaneously repudiating the perceived need for each home to be unique, or even created on site and/or by hand. After a century of experimentation that began with the 1908 Sears, Roebuck and Co. mail order home—a development that emerged at the same time as Ford's Model T and succeeded wildly, selling more than 70,000 units before the Great Depression crippled its "Modern Homes" program, forcing bankruptcy[164]—pre-fabrication is finally, once again, having its day.

In the United States, a number of housing startups are reacting to runaway prices by leveraging new technological tools to begin transforming home-building in ways that would be familiar to Ford.

And it's not just him. Toyota's famed "Toyota Production System", or TPS, is the predecessor of what we now call "lean production". It's TPS that allowed Toyota to become the world's largest car manufacturer by units sold[165], and to "completely [eliminate] all waste in order to deliver quality products at reasonable prices and in a timely manner," according to Toyota Chairman (and former CEO) Akio Toyoda[166].

To both Ford and Toyoda, cost reductions were a driving motive of innovation.

Around the world, the way we construct a home today really hasn't changed much from how we did so a few *thousand* years ago. They are still hand-built, one by one, by skilled laborers, to custom specifications.

As I introduced in Chapter 6, momentum is finally building to move home building from the site to the factory, and/or bring robots to the site itself, so that "lean construction" principles that emerged out of Toyota's TPS can be leveraged, and where resulting cost reductions *can be* passed on to customers, if regulatory policies and reviews don't kill the innovations before they can take root and flourish; and if greed doesn't prevent savings from being passed on to increasingly cash-strapped customers.

Adding to the challenges? While no one I know of will sue you over what kind of car you park in your driveway, a large number of people have strong opinions about both what homes should look like, and what the socio-economic make-up of their potential neighbors should be, as we saw earlier in this chapter. Moreover, many will go out of their way to regulate or litigate their positions, to safeguard their "real estate nest egg". It's called NIMBYism (among other more debase "isms"), and is a major cause of our regulatory woes.

Beyond the single-family housing innovators we met in Chapter 6—companies that are all moving the needle on the affordability of a standalone home—it is the emerging builders of **multi-family, vertical units of housing** who could arguably have the greatest impact on reducing costs and increasing shelter's availability due to the amplifying effects of density and transit-oriented developments, as well as the intrinsic efficiencies of multi-family housing, as we discussed earlier in the chapter. This trend is even more valuable due to the fact that more than half of the world's humans live in urban environments.

If we are to truly meet not only the current 3.2 million home shortfall in the United States, but also the 1.3 *billion* home shortfall, globally—a number that a United Nations report says could increase to *three billion*, by 2030[167]— then we will need to learn to innovate, *at scale*.

Well, it's begun.

The much written about Tahanan Permanent Supportive Housing, a new 145-unit development in San Francisco, was built in half the time (33 months) and at 30%-50% less cost ($382,917 per unit) than comparable projects that can run upwards of $600,000 *per unit*[168].

If $382,917 sounds like a lot for an apartment unit, it is; but remember, this is San Francisco, which at the time Tahanan was built was the nation's second most expensive urban market, with a median price of more than $1 million per home[169].

What makes Tahanan so interesting is fourfold. First, it's *beautiful*. Too often, working class or affordable housing *looks* cheap. Not so with Tahanan. Even if it were market rate, it would be an improvement over the status quo, in my view as an architect. Second, it is staffed in a way that would make Juha Kaakinen proud: with social workers and building maintenance staff who cater to the residents' needs, 24/7. Third, as reported in a 2023 *New York Times* article[170], "Tahanan succeeded because it had the support of city and state officials who streamlined zoning and cut deals to make it possible. But it needed gobs of private money to avoid triggering an avalanche of well-meaning rules and standards that slow public projects in San Francisco, and nationally."

In fact, the majority of the article is an exhaustive (and exhausting) list of regulatory hurdles the project that would have *typically* burdened and slowed the project and thereby inflated its costs and timeline significantly, if not for the will of the political body to waive *all of it*. Which brings us to the fourth and perhaps most salient point about Tahanan: all of the housing units were constructed off-site, as modules—the first such project in the city's history to do so.

Still, in spite of its resounding success, the project's key enabler, a public-private partnership called the Housing Accelerator Fund (or HAF) with $300 million in private and philanthropic donations at the time of this writing, has decided *not* to use modular construction on its next project. Its CEO, Rebecca Foster, has concluded that "it was just too big a political lift."

In view of the fact that the project is a resounding success by most measures, her conclusion is a sad recognition of the many regulatory frictions that stand in the way of innovation's forward march.

Much of the money funding new housing models is coming from private companies who want to do good by solving homelessness and affordability. That includes the $65 million that the Schwabs donated to build the Tahanan; a $1 billion pledge by Google, in 2020[171]; the $2.5 billion that Apple pledged,[172] $50M of which it donated to the HAF following Tahanan's success; a $1 billion pledge by Facebook[173]; and a $500 million pledge by Microsoft[41], whose foundation also spends billions to fight malaria, TB and HIV.

If there is a lesson here, it is that the influx of private money, as demonstrated by Tahanan, may buffer development against regulatory quagmires, *provided* that the politicians, unions, special interest groups, public review boards and NIMBYists agree that *impact* is what matters most.

2011 brought us Syrian and Egyptian revolutions, Osama Bin Laden's demise, NASA's last space shuttle flights, a 9.0 magnitude earthquake that killed thousands in Japan and caused a nuclear catastrophe in Fukushima, and Fidel Castro's retirement in Cuba, after 45 years in power.

Something far less known, but equally consequential, also happened that year. A company in China produced a short time-lapse video of a building being erected, set to a backdrop of melodramatic music. What made the video noteworthy were several facts: that the building was prefabricated; that it was 30-stories tall; that it had 350 rooms, a restaurant, bar, gym, swimming pool and helipad; and that all of these things were constructed on site, in just *fifteen days*[175].

Normally, a project of that size would take *three years* to complete.

In 2015, the same company returned with another time-lapse video. This one went viral. In fact, *The Telegraph*, CNN and other news outlets all carried it in their news cycles, for the astounding fact that it showed viewers a *fifty-seven story* tower going up in just *nineteen days*[176].

In 2021, Broad Group—the company—returned to the web with a *third* time-lapse video. Unlike the other two, in which the buildings still required interior construction such as floor and wall finishes, built-ins, and appliances once the "shell" was up, this one showcased the construction of a "turnkey" tower, interiors and all.

There are two more things that were stunning about this video. The first is that the building's structure was comprised of ultra-thin, high-performance, and *massively expensive* stainless steel structural slabs that weighed just 10% that of similar "conventional" floor plates, while being simultaneously far stronger. The second is that the building went up in just *twenty-eight hours*[177].

They didn't stop there.

In fact, Broad Sustainable Building (or BSB), as the building arm of serial Chinese innovator Broad Group is known, most recently built its 16th generation tower: a 26-story building. This latest construction project is a showcase for *other* dimensions of innovation.

Like its predecessor, the building is in move-in condition. Unlike the others, this new tower requires only bolting on site, no welding. It also includes a high-tech energy recovery ventilation system, which is a key feature of buildings that adhere to the world's leading sustainable standard, Passive House. Just as impressive, and equally unusual amongst its conventional peers, the building's interior walls are not load-bearing, which allows them to be reconfigured later without impact to the integrity of the building's structure, to accommodate changes in occupancy or need with minimal disruption. And lastly, the company says that one of its 40-by-8-foot B-CORE slabs—the structural unit of their buildings—can be produced in just *two minutes*[178].

To expand on that last point, BSB's innovations are no longer limited to streamlining the time it takes to *erect* something made in a factory. Rather, they are taking a page from Toyota's TPS—the lean construction methodologies we discussed earlier—and applying them to a number of building systems in service of building better homes.

At the time of this writing, one "module" comprising a living room and kitchen, or a bedroom and en-suite bathroom, takes BSB just *twenty-one minutes* to produce.

Broad Group has named these modular buildings Holon. And they're going global.

With current projects built or underway in China, the Philippines and the UAE, Jeremy Zimman, Broad USA's Director of Marketing, had this to say:

"The Holon modular system enables the construction of tall residential buildings at great speed, and we look forward to deploying this technology to shorten the construction cycle and alleviate the severe housing shortage in the U.S. and Canada.

"Right now, we've got plans in place for Ohio, Texas, and California. As soon as we can say more, we absolutely will."

Much like Seivwright and Summers, who began building homeless shelters because they had a personal connection to their clients' plight, the Chairman of Broad Group, Zhang Yue, founded his company following a 2008 earthquake near where he worked, in which 87,000 people lost their lives in concrete buildings that fell like dominoes.[179] He was determined to find safer solutions to building technologies by improving access to superior homes.

For his contributions to sustainable living and climate change [buildings produce 37% of the world's GHGs, much of it in the manufacturing[180]], Zhang Yue was awarded the Champions of the Earth Award (Entrepreneurial Vision Category) by the United Nations Environment Programme.

Modular high-rise construction is gaining traction elsewhere, too, albeit often constrained by the general messiness of democratic debate and policy constraints, as we saw in the story of the Tahanan.

To name one of the larger ones, Pennsylvania-based Volumetric Building Companies (VBC) is currently at the forefront of Western modular high-rise construction.

Having built all of the modular (and delightful) Citizen M hotels worldwide, VBC has also recently built a 324-unit student housing facility in Philadelphia, a 149-unit market-rate housing project, also in Philly, New York City's first micro-unit hotel—the 249-unit POD Hotel—and literally thousands of additional market-rate and affordable unit housing projects across the West, from Oakland, CA to Krausnick, Germany.

With its 2022 merger with Polish modular furniture-and-building manufacturer Polcom, the company now has a $1 billion "book of business", 500 employees, and 1.25 million square feet of manufacturing space on two continents[181].

VBC is in good company. According to the Modular Building Institute, as of 2023, 6.64% of all construction starts, with a value of $14.6 billion, are now modular.[182] While it's still a small percentage of the market, this represents a three-fold increase in just eight years. Just as impressive, there are currently 255 modular manufacturing companies in North America alone, *exclusive* of those focused on single-family modular homes, at the time of this writing.

Final Thoughts

Where housing innovation *could* end up, with governmental partners as *enablers* of private enterprise, and with a Ford-like commitment to passing on advancements' inherent savings, is a seismic net reduction in housing costs, as with the Model T, 100 years ago.

If today's innovations are supported and scaled, then it is entirely possible that my $50,000 "dream house" could become a reality, and even, *the norm.*

If that were to happen, we could *similarly* precipitate and end to homelessness, as Kaakinen showed us is possible, when the right people lead with the right goals, and come together to solve what turns out to be not-so-intractable problems.

HEALTH:

Food and the Environment

"The Death of Farming" Rural Ontario © Anthony Fieldman 2022

16 Rebalancing the Earth is Dead Simple

Most of us regularly experience the climatological impacts of how our planet is now broken, and the scientific consensus is that we have ourselves to blame for that inconvenient truth. Over decades of politicized global debate and denial, we have made reversing climate change seem complex, expensive, and nearly insurmountable. In truth, it's dead simple. We are simply looking at the wrong equation.

In 2021, a multi-media Op-Ed I read in *The New York Times* called "Postcards from a World on Fire" illustrated the tangible impacts of climate change in *every* country in the world, one by one. Unsurprisingly, a significant number of nations are mired in climate catastrophe while others face future collapses, as the clouds of early warning signs gather.

Record wildfires, droughts, storms, swarms, erosion, temperatures, floods, collapses, and mass die-offs are the rule now, not the exception. Nearly every nation on Earth is experiencing "unprecedented" everything, and not the good kind. Across the globe, the picture *The New York Times* paints is bleak, indeed.

But there is a glimmer of hope, buried about 150 countries into the piece. A single sentence I read triggered an "aha moment" for me, because it pointed to a possible path out of our existential quagmire.

> *"Most countries are struggling to become carbon neutral. Suriname, 93% of which is covered by forest, is one of three carbon-negative countries in the world."*

After I read that, I quickly Googled the other two. They are Bhutan and Panama. As it turns out, the nations share three common practices that have allowed them to engender long-term national (and by extension, planetary) health without asking their citizens to act in exceptional ways, or accept unreasonable lifestyle burdens.

We can think of the precedent they set as a kind of "'three-step program" that any country could conceivably follow, no matter how big or how populous. It's worth reviewing them here.

Healthy Earth in Three Steps

Step One: Maximize Reforestation

The reason Suriname, Bhutan, and Panama are all carbon-negative is because the carbon that their forests sequester *exceeds the total carbon load produced by human activity.* And so: if we were to do nothing but reforest large swaths of our nations—enough to overcome our respective carbon production—climate change would be powerfully reversed.

Former Kenyan Member of Parliament Wangari Maathai said it beautifully:

"Until you dig a hole, you plant a tree, you water it and make it survive, you haven't done a thing. You are just talking."

In his brilliant book *Collapse,* Jared Diamond brings readers through example after example of historical societies that cratered, then disappeared: the Anasazi. The Rapa Nui. Greenland's Norse. The Maya. The Polynesians. On and on. In each subject population, chosen because it was self-contained and thus scientifically "knowable", the primary driver of collapse was always the same: they cut down too many trees.

As Diamond explains in his book, trees give shade to, and stabilize, the plants and soils beneath them. Once these are cut down, two things happen. First, the trees begin to release the carbon they've sequestered back into the atmosphere, as they decay or are milled. Second, plants that the trees shielded eventually die without cover, and also release *their* carbon. And finally, once trees and plants can no longer stabilize the soil, the Earth itself dries out, and the living things that depended on all of it—the bugs, animals and humans—also die.

The title of a 2011 *Nature* article echoed Diamond's findings: *No Trees… No Humans.*

As I shared in chapter 2, we have cut down *half* of the world's trees—three trillion of them—since we began practicing agriculture 12,000 years ago.[183] Half of that loss, or 1.5 trillion trees, has occurred in just 125 years. The biggest culprit? Deforestation for grazing livestock.[184]

Largely due to our growing understanding of deforestation's impact on human thriving, the International Criminal Court in the Hague, Netherlands, has adopted and added a fifth "new crime" to those it considers to be **the world's gravest offenses**. Those crimes include aggression, war crimes, crimes against humanity, and genocide.

Because the human effects of deforestation are catastrophic, the ICC has put this new crime—**ecocide**—on par with genocide. In fact, in 2021, Brazil's Bolsonaro, who poured accelerant over the practice of deforestation in the Amazon during his 2019-2022 term as their President, was sued for ecocide by indigenous leaders and human rights groups in a case filed with the Hague-based court. At the time of this writing, the case remains pending.

Ecocide was also featured in a 2021 docu-series by NBC called *The Fifth Crime*, which followed ranchers like Jaim Teixeira who illegally set fire to large swaths of the Amazon with the full knowledge of its illegality, because A: it's lucrative, and B: he'd rather eat today than save the world tomorrow.
Those are his words.

Another Brazilian, Sebastião Salgado—the chronicler of war, famine, and genocide we met in Chapter 1—had this to share with his audience during the 2013 talk I attended, on the subject of deforestation:

> *"For all our fighting and wars over nothing, how many seconds do you think we will last once the last tree is gone? 60?"*

You could hear a pin drop in the room as the gravity of his words settled.

Following the completion of GENESIS, Sebastião and his wife, Lélia, established a not-for-profit organization named Instituto Terra to sponsor environmental restoration and sustainable development in rural Brazil. To kick start the initiative, the Salgados returned to their native Brazil to focus on the restoration of the 1,750-acre family farm they had inherited from his father, and which had been wiped out by the same forces of deforestation as so much of the Amazon, in his long absence.

They began by planting *two million trees, comprising* 293 species. Ten years on, the once-barren landscape now sponsors 172 species of bird, 33 types of mammal, and 15 species of reptile/amphibian[185]. The planted trees and ensuing canopy protected the soil and allowed the water table to recharge, further enhancing the ecosystem's ability to maintain itself in perpetuity.

All the Salgados did was plant trees. Nature did the rest.

In addition to restoring forests through planting and cultivation, there are two other steps we can lean on, to restore the Earth's carbon balance.

Step Two: Shrink the Human Footprint

As we learned earlier, more than half of the human population lives in cities. In the United States, that number is 79%. But those numbers don't provide a complete picture because the classification "suburban" is typically lumped together with "urban" and considered "city".

It isn't—not in terms of carbon impact.

In the United States, according to data collected by the Department of Housing and Urban Development and the United States Census Bureau, in 2017, just 27% of households described their neighborhood as urban, while nearly twice that—52%—described it as suburban.

The reason this is important is that on average, urban areas in the Global West fit *three people* for every one person in an equivalent slice of suburbia[186].

Mathematically, then, if everyone who lived in the suburbs relocated to a city or even town, then two thirds of the current U.S. human residential footprint could be returned to its natural state, the way that the Salgados did, and the reparative impact could be immense.

The idea of restoring native landscapes is called "**rewilding**."[187]

In addition to densifying our habitat, we could reconsider our farming practices in pursuit of a smaller human footprint. Consider the following data points:

- 51% of the Earth's habitable land is used for agriculture[7]
- Of this, 77% is used to graze and feed livestock[7]
- In spite of it, animals supply less than 20% of global calories, making animal agriculture not only immensely destructive, but wildly inefficient[7]
- Agriculture uses 92% of the world's annual freshwater[188]
- 41% of that total feeds livestock[189], 52% of which is for cattle[190]
- It takes 1,800 gallons of water to produce one pound of beef[191]
- Livestock cause 40% of global deforestation[192]
- Deforestation alone produces 12-20% of all greenhouse gases (GHGs)[193] *exclusive* of livestock's own contribution to them, which adds another 14.5% related to feed production, cow digestion, and manure decomposition; thus livestock is actually responsible for 26.5-34.5% of *all* global GHGs[194]

Controlled Environment Agriculture (CEA) can reduce all of these things *drastically*. Generally referred to as "indoor agriculture" or "vertical farms", aquaponics, hydroponics, and aeroponics could all make a massive reduction in both water and land use possible.

At a high level, hydroponics saves 70–90% of the water used in conventional farming, while aquaponics saves 90%, and aeroponics saves 98%. These present massive opportunities for cropland, which accounts for more than half of all agricultural water use.

Moreover, vertical farms can produce anywhere from ten times the yield per acre of a conventional farm[195] to *hundreds times more*, depending on the crop, method, and company. To wit: an SF-area startup named Plenty has used A.I.-fueled light, water, and nutrient controls to produce 720 acres' worth of fruit and vegetables on just 2 acres of space[196].

The overarching reason for sharing these data points is as follows: if we urbanized non-animal agriculture and "rewilded" the land we freed up, we could make a sizable dent in GHG production even *without* touching the cars, buildings, energy production, suburban sprawl, waste or anything else we do to harm the Earth.

We will revisit vertical farming in Chapters 18 and 19, in detail.

Step Three: Modernize Energy

Many climate advocates are understandably focused on the *production* of energy—the fuel for our cars, buildings, and industry—as a means of reducing anthropogenic (i.e.: human-induced) climate change. This makes sense because apart from changing how we use the land and what we grow to fuel ourselves, our fuel sources are critical to pretty much everything else we do.

This makes the choices we make in the generation of that power of critical importance.

Luckily, reversing this third category of climate degradation is also straightforward today. The Earth (and our solar system) have always produced infinite energy sources, and we are finally scientifically advanced enough to avail ourselves of this bounty.

And yet, to meet our energy needs, we continue to *primarily* extract and employ fossil fuels to provide for the majority of our energy needs—86.5% of it, that is. As of 2024, oil accounts for 33.6% of global energy consumption, coal for 27.8% and natural gas for 25.1%. As for the rest? Nuclear energy provides 5% of global energy, hydroelectric power just 2.7%, and "other renewables" combined provide the final 5.6%, all according to The Energy Institute's *Statistical Review of World Energy.*[197]

An important, major, difference between fossil fuels and renewables is that the former are *mature* markets, whereas all of the other sources available to us—the Earth's own core heat, wind, water, and solar—are lagging behind in infrastructural investment. This creates a significant roadblock to modernization, since the playing field isn't level.

But that's changing, *fast.*

Between 2010 and 2022, the cost of wind power (onshore and offshore) dropped by 69% and 59%, respectively; concentrating (thermal) solar dropped by 69%; and solar photovoltaics by an eye-popping 89%[198].

Today, the levelized cost of energy (LCOE+) for various power sources is as follows: solar PV: $38-78/MWh; wind (onshore): $37-86/MWh; gas: $48-109/MWh; coal: $71-173/MWh; and nuclear (U.S.): $141-220/MWh [199].

In 2024, IRENA reported that fully 91% of newly commissioned utility-scale renewable projects had lower LCOE than the *cheapest* fossil fuel option, market maturity notwithstanding[200].

That's huge.

My architectural and engineering partners and I are considered experts in sustainable building technologies, and an increasing number of the buildings we design meet the criteria for "net zero energy." That is, they produce as much energy as they consume, thereby making them "zero impact" on the environment from an *operational* standpoint.

This is important because buildings account for approximately 30% of global energy use, which generate 26% of global carbon (GHG) emissions, according to the International Energy Agency (IEA)[201]. With that said, there are hundreds of millions if not billions of buildings on Earth (it's impossible to properly count), and countless families and businesses that draw on energy to operate them. Converting each of these to net-zero energy is not only a highly unlikely prospect, it is not *incontrovertibly* necessary because there is a far easier path to meeting most of our GHG reduction goals, within that energy category.

If the **energy grids** on which all of our cities and industries rely were clean—meaning, if the energy they generated came from renewable sources, rather than ones that generate greenhouse gases—and if we further did *nothing* to the buildings themselves, then roughly 69% of buildings' operational energy GHGs would *still* go away.

How?

Here's the clean way to explain it, using that same report:

- The 26% of global energy-related emissions that buildings contribute are 18% "indirect" (from producing the electricity and heat used) and 8% "direct" (emitted on-site, e.g., burning gas/oil for space/water heating, cooling and cooking)
- If the grid-supplied energy becomes net-zero, the indirect portion of GHGs goes away, resulting in a fractional reduction in operational energy emissions of 18/26, which is 69% of total building energy. That's without touching the 8% direct energy in buildings themselves

This matters because utilities are generally larger and better capitalized as businesses than most individuals are. Furthermore, many receive direct and indirect subsidies from governments.[202]

A two-thirds reduction in building energy at the scale of the grid is huge, and would get us most the way to our goal of eliminating operational building carbon.

Eventually, remaining building carbon would plausibly diminish over time *naturally*, as the forced replacement of building owners' own equipment was accomplished in the natural course of their failure; especially if the market only sold renewable systems.

Well, that very energy transition has already begun, in some countries. Iceland already produces nearly 100% of its energy from hydroelectric and geothermal sources. Nine other countries' grids are also 100% net-zero, representing 300M humans. Norway's grid is 99% renewable, and 50% of that is heat energy produced by our waste. Thus, Norway has solved two problems with one solution.

In all, 20 countries produce over 90% of their power renewably, and 66 of them at 50% or greater.[203]

It's not all good news. Ranked 118th out of 212 nations, the U.S. produces just 23% of energy renewably, yet is the world's second biggest emitter, at 12.6% of total CO_2. That puts them behind only China, whose 30% renewable grid offset just a portion of its 32.88% share of global CO_2.[204]

Once we green our grids, none more critically than those of China and the United States, the need to green individual buildings will become far less critical. At that point, GHGs generated from the energy sector—energy that powers utilities, industry and buildings—will cease to drive anthropogenic climate change.

Final Thoughts

There is an old joke about a lion who starts charging toward two safari tourists. One bends down to tie his shoe. The other screams, "You idiot! You'll never outrun a lion," to which his friend turns to him deadpan, and says, "I just need to outrun *you*."

The climate is a little bit like that, in reverse. We don't need to stop polluting it wholesale, or change everything about how humans live. We just need to do enough to slow ourselves down to let the Earth outrun us. That means acting more like Bhutan, Panama, and Suriname—the carbon negative countries with which we started this chapter. Their cars aren't all electric; their buildings aren't particularly renewable; their food doesn't all come from vertical farms; and the nation isn't vegan. In fact, probably little of what each nation does, apart from preserving or planting trees, is different from what richer nations are capable of doing much better.

What all three countries are is *balanced*.

In each, more carbon is sequestered than is produced.

For this, they can thank the trees and the rich ecosystems that invariably follow. Just look at what the Salgados did.

The formula is straightforward: Shrink the human footprint (due to farming, livestock, and sprawl). Take that land and restore it (as much as possible). Modernize energy (by greening our grids, more critically than anything else).

- Shrink our footprint
- Rewild the land
- Modernize energy

All three of these things are not only doable, they are being done in various parts of the world that have determined that collective, long-term sustainability is worth the investment, and have begun to fix what's broken.

Enough of us have the technological and economic means at our disposal today to do far more than what Panama, Bhutan and Suriname have managed to eke out, in terms of creating a carbon balance. All we lack is the *will* to make choices that put some kind of limit on business as usual: what we eat; how we grow it; where we live, and in what form of home; whether or not we protect our natural resources; and how we power our daily lives.

The true costs of anthropogenic climate change dwarf the investment dollars it would take to *prevent* the damage we have caused in the first place: to our infrastructure, real property, agriculture, the health of the macrobiome, and human health, including catastrophic loss of life. A 2023 article titled "Climate change is costing the world $16 million per hour," posted to the World Economic Forum's website, cites a study that estimates we have spent $2.8 trillion over the past 20 years to repair damages from extreme weather; and that by 2050, we will be spending that amount *annually*.[205] That's even without accounting for the *millions of lives lost each year* to a broken food system—a topic we will revisit in the next chapter.

Doing nothing is an incredibly expensive strategy.

Chapter 7's rallying cry, "Do No Harm", was an appeal for us to rise to the better angels of our nature. In the context of climate catastrophe, it wouldn't be wrong to repurpose and rename it *Do No Harm (That the Earth can't Absorb)*.

All we need to do is *no more harm* than the land itself can sustain, and counter-balance. This is the true genius of *The New York Times*' Suriname example.

17 The Case for Plant-Based Diets

The so-called "western diet" is broken principally because the global success of "Big Ag", as industrialized food is often nicknamed, has led to weakened bodies that bear little resemblance, inside and out, to what they did for the majority of our existence.

The case for a plant-based diet, by which I mean the *prioritization* of non-animal foods over animal sources, not their wholesale replacement, can be made on the basis of three topics:

- Human (both physiological and psychological) health
- Environmental stewardship
- Animal welfare

The stakes are higher than most of us realize in all three areas. That's because in the context of 21st century living, gaining a true understanding of our actions' costs requires us to trade fads for facts, convenience for consequence, and image for impact.

Fast Facts

Let's start with the most consequential data point—one I've shared twice already in earlier chapters, but is worth repeating because it's utterly stunning:

The ubiquitous industrial-era diet, born in America, and exported around the world, now **kills more people than *anything else* on Earth**.

Fully one in five global annual deaths—11 out of 55 million of them—are now attributable to what we eat[6]. And counterintuitively, three times as many people die from *overeating* as from malnourishment.[206]

That means that 3x as many of us die from eating *too much* unhealthy food as from not having *enough* food at all.

Beyond its specific impacts on the environment, which statistics I shared in the last chapter, increased consumption of red meat in particular significantly increases one's risk of myriad chronic diseases, cancers, and overall mortality.

More on this shortly.

Science suggests that our human ancestors were majority vegetarian, eating far more plants than anything else, contrary to what you may have heard, read, or seen in social media and marketing literature. The archaeological record[208] and our primate ancestors[208] strongly support that conclusion.

Until the 20th century, meat was not even a central component of most people's diets, and likely comprised roughly 20% of overall caloric intake.[209] Meat itself ("mete", in Old English), was originally just a general term for "food".

As we saw in the last chapter, livestock now represents one of the biggest environmental threats to global homeostasis, and cattle are the main culprit in global water use and deforestation.

Livestock also now make up 67% of *all* land vertebrate biomass, while the wild ones we mostly read about in books these days—animals we *imagine* filling the planet's savannas, forests and mountain ranges—comprise just 1% of those living and breathing today.[210] That's a shocking reversal of pre-modern times, when wild animals constituted 99% of biomass, and livestock was nonexistent.

Beyond our landmasses, the overfishing of the world's oceans has reached an inflection point from which recovery may frankly no longer be possible.[211]

Your Body on Plants

"You are what you eat."

The first reason we should care deeply about what we consume—and the one dimension of diet that seems to grab our attention—is that the foods we eat determine our physical and mental fitness, or its flip side, illness. While nutrition is a complex subject, learning just two things can make all the difference:

1. **Complete diets require 33 essential nutrients**, not only the "big three" macros [proteins, carbohydrates and fats] that largely dominate our dietary focus and dollars, and an adequate deficiency of *any* of these leads to illness.
2. **Plant foods are anti-inflammatory**, while meat products are *inflammatory;* and chronic inflammation is a leading cause of human mortality: heart disease (45% of which is attributed to diet); cancer (33%); stroke (45%); Alzheimer's (50%); and diabetes (45%).[212]

Essential Nutrients

Basing one's diet on the three **macronutrients** ("macros"), or carbohydrates (fiber, starch and sugar), amino acids (proteins), and fatty acids (saturated and unsaturated), is like looking for elephants, lions and rhinos while ignoring the rest of the biome, in spite of the fact that the "other things" make up the *majority* of it.

To wit: in addition to macronutrients, our bodies contain **thirty micronutrients**: 14 vitamins, 7 macro-minerals, and 9 micro- (or trace) minerals. When any of these corporeal building blocks is sufficiently depleted in our bodies, it can result in illness.

Because micronutrient deficiencies are not always acutely visible, they are sometimes referred to as "hidden hunger".

Here are just a few such health risks:

- lack of vitamin A can lead to visual problems, such as blindness, acne, dry skin, infertility and ENT infections
- lack of vitamin B2 can lead to fatigue and blurred vision
- lack of vitamin B6 can lead to dermatitis and skin rashes
- lack of vitamin B9 can lead to fetal defects and miscarriage
- lack of vitamin D can lead to high blood sugar, bone pain, hair loss, and (seasonal) depression
- lack of vitamin E can lead to cardiovascular disease, nerve damage, and even dementia

In addition:

- lack of calcium can lead to bone disorders and dental issues
- lack of iron can lead to anemia and pregnancy complications
- lack of iodine can lead to hypothyroidism and—in pregnancy—may be associated with increased ADHD symptoms in children
- lack of zinc can lead to impaired immune function low insulin levels, low bone mineral density, and reproductive problems

According to the World Health Organization, "More than 2 billion people in the world today are estimated to be deficient in key vitamins and minerals, particularly vitamin A, iodine, iron and zinc."[10]

Plant foods are rich in *all* vitamins and minerals with the sole exception of vitamin B12, which is used in the development of red blood cells, maintenance of nerves, and normal brain function, and which primarily exist in animal products. With that said, supplements and fortified foods containing vitamin B12 are easy ways to meet that need without requiring us to consume animals, per se.

In addition to micronutrients, plants teem with **phytonutrients**—over *10,000* of them. While these compounds have traditionally been less studied than macro- and micro-nutrients, they nonetheless exert a major impact on our health, essentially protecting our bodies from a near-constant barrage of oxidative stress (cell damage) and damage caused by environmental toxicity.

In fact, adequate intake of phytonutrients—nature's "armor"—has been shown to help reduce the risk of cancer, heart disease, stroke, Alzheimer's and Parkinson's disease.

But the truth is, we don't need to remember *any* of this.

Nature designed us to thrive amid the things we found and foraged whether or not we knew about what ingesting them did for us. Our ancestors didn't. When they foraged for nuts, beans, bananas, berries, and peppers, or they ate barley, lentils, corn, oats, and carrots, their bodies' needs were mostly met *by default* because plant foods contain constellations of nutrients, and because over the course of a month we invariably consumed *enough of each* to maintain our overall health.

"Eat the rainbow" is an excellent adage, and will get you close to an optimal diet without needing to know much more, but for a few things.

By contrast, animal products—which include fish, poultry, mammals and their byproducts—can supply only *some* of the vitamins, minerals, carbohydrates and phytonutrients, and *none* of the healthy fiber that plants provide[213].

There's a second key reason a plant-based diet is important.

Inflammation

One of the prime reasons plant foods are so healthy is that they are anti-inflammatory. The only exceptions to this rule are highly processed "plants" like industrial seed oils, refined carbohydrates, and junk food. Ignoring those for a moment, "anti-inflammatory" means they are well-tolerated by the body without triggering its self-defense mechanisms, provided you don't *clinically* suffer from modern sensitivities such as celiac, nut allergies, or similar health issues.

Animal products do the opposite. Meats and meat by-products *cause* inflammation. This matters because while short-term inflammation is an important part of the immune response, *chronic* inflammation—the kind that daily intake of inflammatory foods like animal products [and ultra-processed foods aka UPFs] catalyze—is a major contributor to many of the leading causes of death today, as reflected in the statistics I shared earlier this chapter.[214]

The exception to the animal product rule is that cold-water fatty fish like salmon, anchovies, herring, and sardines, among others, are high in omega-3 fatty acids, which reduce inflammation, overall.

Think of inflammation this way. When our bodies are under constant attack, our defenses (the immune response) exact a price. Each battle wears us down, and we can't fight forever. At some point, our body's auto-reparative reserves become depleted, which is when our tireless cellular attackers overwhelm us. At the same time, our bodies' inflammatory response can eventually start damaging healthy cells, tissues, and organs, directly. This can lead—over time—to DNA damage, tissue death, and internal scarring.[215]

And it's not just our bodies that are under attack.

Environment

The planet that hosts us is *also* under chronic assault, in the form of trawled and emptied oceans, clear-cut forests, polluted air and contaminated waterways, all in the name of gathering, growing and processing animal sources of human fuel.

In spite of the truly global scale of our food footprint, it is—incomprehensibly—both inefficient and *unprofitable.*

Here are a few facts:

- Per the COP, "a staggering 153 million tonnes of meat are wasted at the farm level every year."[216] That's of an estimated total global meat production of 350 million tonnes—a near 50% loss
- Global meat consumption has increased threefold in just 50 years as more humans can afford the "luxury", resulting in 80 billion land animals slaughtered annually[217]
- Producing 1kg of beef requires roughly 8kg of feed. That is to say that fully 88% of food calories grown in fields *never even make it into human bodies*
- It takes 50 calories of cow feed to return 1 calories of beef. That means beef is 2% efficient—or 98% *inefficient.* For pork, it's 12 calories per calorie of meat. For poultry, livestock's most efficient conversion, it still requires 8 calories of feed per calorie of poultry[218]
- As we saw earlier, it takes 1,800 gallons of water to produce just one pound of beef

The environmental case for a plant-based diet is straightforward, and urgent:

- If we do not stop trawling the oceans, which cover 71% of the Earth's

surface, the world (and its humans) could run out of fish by 2047[219]
- If we do not stop raising cattle, more and more humans will run out of water; four billion people already experience severe water scarcity for at least one month per year, today[220]
- If we were to stop clear-cutting forests, and razing natural biomes to raise livestock, and to do so by eliminating meat and dairy consumption altogether, that alone could "pause" the growth of greenhouse gas emissions for 30 years, a 2022 study suggests[221]

Animal Welfare

As I mentioned above, we slaughter 80 billion land animals per year, globally, nearly 50% of which never even reach our stomachs. In the U.S., we dispatch over 50 billion of those. There's even a uniquely American "animal kill clock" you can watch, at https://animalclock.org/

That total *excludes* the 1.1–2.2 trillion fish that are caught in the oceans every year, of which 17–22% (or between 187 and 484 billion) are bycatch that we discard.[222] That is, sea creatures that were simply in the wrong net at the wrong time—something the industry calls "the cost of business."

And lastly, all of the above statistics represent only those animals we consume as *food.* Our impact as a species on the natural order—the ecosystems we inherited, that birthed and multiplied us, and which we have disfigured irreversibly—is far greater. In fact, we are now in the midst of a sixth mass extinction: the planet's first-ever one caused by living creatures. It goes by "Holocene," or "Anthropocene."[223]

In my lifetime alone, since 1969, we have obliterated some 60% of the planet's fauna: the mammals, birds, fish and reptiles we read about in our idyllic textbooks. This is between "1,000 and 10,000 times higher than natural extinction rates."[224]

Final Thoughts

Why should we care? Well, apart from the obvious biblical imperative "Thou shalt not kill", animals—from bacteria and insects to phytoplankton and megafauna—are not only a stabilizing force in nature, they *are* nature, insofar as without them, all of our ecosystems would collapse, bringing ruin upon our own heads.

How do you like the weather?

It's hard for me these days *not* to envision humans standing on a footprint-sized patch of land surrounded by a field of bubbling lava, swinging away with a hammer at the ground underfoot, in order to sell it.

It doesn't take a rocket scientist to see that destruction of animals is not only cruel and unnecessary, it is masochistic, since we are destroying that which gives *us* life.

The mathematicians and economists among us will recognize the inefficiencies of conversion and income related to livestock. In Brazil, whose Amazon is being wiped out for cattle farming, ranchers earn $250 per hectare. Meanwhile, soy, rice and bean farmers can earn four-to-seven-fold that amount, or $1,000–1,700 per hectare. Most profitable? Fruit and horticulture farmers in Brazil earn *twelve-fold* what ranchers do, at $3,300 per hectare.[225]

And yet, most farmers opt to raise cattle largely due to lack of infrastructure, refrigeration trucks, and supply chains that fruit and horticulture demand, and due to the high start-up (i.e.: short-term) costs attendant to the more lucrative farming options.

Beyond the damage we cause to the planet, there are other costs our food choices levy on our bodies. In the U.S. alone, a 2018 report by the Milken Institute estimated that the total economic cost of *obesity* was $1.72 trillion per year, or 9.3 percent of gross domestic product.[226]

In summary, *not* trawling, raising, and slaughtering animals would both slow down climate change by a generation and also produce healthier and wealthier humans—humans whose caloric needs could be more easily met. To wit: if we were to *eat* what we feed to our livestock, COP26 concluded, "the greater cultivation of non-animal crops would result in up to a 70% increase in available food calories, serving an additional four billion people."[216]

And so, if we care about our own physiological health—which is the direct result of the foods we choose to eat, the air we breathe, the water we drink, the climate that supports (or kills) us, the food calories we have available, the quality of however many years we have on Earth, and even the economic power we wield as productive humans—then we would do very, very well to ease up on animal foods and embrace a predominantly plant-based diet to seed our collective thriving: in healthy bodies hosted by a planet that can sustain not only us, but the generations that we *hope* will come after us, if we stop squandering our inheritance.

As Michael Pollan famously said:

"Eat [real] food. Not too much. Mostly plants." [227]

My favorite vegetable: Romanesco © Anthony Fieldman 2015

18 The Case for the Vertical Farm–
Part I

Bill Reed is the co-founder of the LEED green building rating system and one of the world's leading experts on the environment. Several years ago, I invited him to speak at an event I hosted. Chatting privately, he said two things that changed my perspective on sustainability.

First: "There is no such thing as sustainability at a scale smaller than the watershed."

What he meant by this was that nature is comprised of ecosystems: dynamic, complex, and comprised of all living organisms and the physical environment in which they interact, and interdepend. So, while photosynthesis a ubiquitous resource by which energy enters and drives any ecosystem, water, without which the ecosystem would die, is notoriously local, finite, and as much as anything else, gives the ecosystem its specific biological character.

Second: "The true definition of 'sustainable' is that something can thrive in perpetuity *without* human intervention."

With this stunning statement, Bill was illustrating that the way we use the word sustainable is wrong, in that we apply it to *components* instead of *systems*.

Doing so is a common over-simplification spurred by 150 years of Industrialism aimed at maximizing gains by parsing interconnected networks, which has enabled us to study, harness and *monetize* each of them independently. The *reality* is that no single part of an ecosystem—including its energy production, distribution, consumption and regeneration—can be isolated *without* risk to the collapse of the whole.

Said another way, nature is incredibly resilient, and at the same time, incredibly fragile.

Bill's twin statements led me to appreciate for the first time that the way we think of sustainability is far too granular.

Put simply: Buildings cannot be sustainable, per se.

So what can humans do to reverse the damage we continue to do to the planet in the name of long-term survival, i.e.: sustainability?

Technological Band-aids

So far, we have spent untold human and financial resources to come up with solutions to human-exacerbated ecological collapse. The electric car. Geothermal energy. Solar. Wind. Biomass. They are all amazing inventions. But each of them would have to be deployed at such a vast scale to *replace* every carbon-emitting version of the same, that the task would be daunting, if at all plausible.

I don't think it is.

The electric car still uses energy. Less, for sure. But there's no such thing as a free lunch. It still needs to be produced to run them [*and* our buildings], to say nothing of the human rights abuses related to the mining cobalt, lithium, and rare earth metals[228]. Geothermal must be recharged because equilibrium must be maintained underground. Solar and wind gobble up resources, too: not just in the building and maintaining of a planetary array of ever-aging devices, but to move that energy from source to point of consumption, dynamically, according to need. Biomass, too, produces waste that must go somewhere. And tidal turbines disrupt the natural ecosystems of fish and aquatic organisms, alike.

In short, all technological systems will still require being created and maintained and thus cannot be called "sustainable" by Bill Reed's definition; moreover, they all cause other forms of disruption to the ecosystems in which they sit.

Are they better than the status quo? The answer is a resounding yes. But as Bill also said to me that day:

> *"Doing less bad is not the same as doing good."*

So what to do?

The answer, like everything else, is found in nature—unsurprisingly, at the scale of the ecosystem.

By the Numbers

Consider three facts:

- The world emits 37.8 billion metric tons of energy-related carbon dioxide per year. The U.S. total is 5.13 billion metric tons.[229]
- Globally, cropland consumes up to 4.62 billion acres[230] of land, or 11.86 billion acres, if we include livestock.[231]
- Between 1 and 15 tons of carbon dioxide is sequestered per acre of *healthy* forest ecosystem in the United States annually, depending on the species, age, and forest management.[232]

Playing with the metrics above, mathematically, the United States could theoretically offset 100% of its annual CO_2 emissions with as little as 342,000,000 additional acres of well-managed southern pine woodland[233] added to its existing 866,000,000 acres of national forest.[234] It's unlikely, because those numbers are at the upper end of sequestration limits and are species-dependent; but still, it's *possible.*

If we used the same logic to calculate offsetting the world's 37.8 billion metric tons of annual carbon dioxide, at the maximum forest capture capacity of 15 metric tons/acre, we would need 2.5 billion acres of new forest to offset it.

That equates to just 22% of existing agriculture acres, globally.

Even if we halved the potential carbon capture of forests and more than doubled the amount of acres to be restored, we could still *offset 100% of human carbon dioxide,* each and every year, just by rewilding lands equivalent to the majority of livestock production, while still eating fish and poultry, and *without changing a single thing* about how we fuel our cars, heat and cool our buildings, and run our commerce and lives.

It's an academic exercise, of course, and I'm not suggesting we continue business as usual. We do a lot of damage to the Earth that needs to be addressed. But I *am* pointing out that rewilding nature in some realistic measure could plausibly result in a carbon-balancing ecosystem that requires zero maintenance from human beings in order for it to thrive and sustain itself, *in perpetuity*, as Bill intuited, and as Suriname, Panama and Bhutan have all discovered.

But how would we eat?

The Vertical Farm

First, the bad news, and it's very, very bad:

- In just 40 years, we have "used up" one third of the world's arable land.[235]
- By 2050, it is expected that the arable land available per person will further drop by 66%.[236]
- One third of the world's soil [that remains] has been "moderately to highly degraded" by modern farming techniques, in particular pesticides, mono-cropping, tilling, modern farm equipment and food cultivation techniques.[237]
- We have burst through the "planetary boundary" (i.e.: sustainable limit) of 4,000 cubic km of freshwater consumption per annum, and now consume 10,800 cu. km.—or 2.5x the maximum threshold. Just look at Lake Mead. It has lost 70% of its capacity in 39 years, dropping 170 vertical feet.[238]
- The title of a *Scientific American* article that reads "Only 60 Years of Farming Left If Soil Degradation Continues" highlights the fact that it takes 1,000 years to produce just 3 cm of topsoil.[239]

Now for some good news, some of which I'm repeating:

- Hydroponics, aquaponics, and aeroponics save 70–90%, 90%, and 98% of conventional farming water, respectively.[240]
- Vertical Farms can produce at least ten times the yield per acre as that of a traditional farm.[240]
- With the appropriate density and tech, we could glean 360 *or more* times the yield per acre of a traditional farm, as San Fransisco startup Plenty proved, by converging technologies in holistic fashion.[241]
- Conventional farms lose 20–40% of outdoor crops to disease, pests and

- weeds, none of which occurs in a vertical farm.[242]
- U.S. grocers, restaurants and homes throw out roughly 31% of all produce, partly due to shelf life. That's 1.2 lbs. of food per person per day.[243]
- Vertical farms can grow food anywhere, any time of the year closer to the point of consumption because they are weather- and climate-independent, with a smaller relative footprint.[244]

Vertical farms are popping up everywhere right now, though the technologies that drive them—the light energy, nutrient provision and growth optimization—are still emerging. Still, there have been market successes, the industry has grown every year, and is expected to achieve a 25.5% compound annual growth rate (CAGR), through 2030.[245]

And yet: there are just over 500 acres of vertical farms operating in the world today,[246] at the time of this writing.

There are three things I hear again and again when I propose to people that vertical farming is the solution to climate change, when paired with the rewilding of decanted farms.

First: "Is food grown in buildings, rather than soil, as nutritious?"

Second: "Can't we simply farm more sustainably—notably, with 'regenerative farming'?"

And third: "The amount of energy required to run a vertical farm is unsustainable, and erases all the gains."

Let's examine them one by one.

Nutrition and The Vertical Farm

Marion Nestle, a nine-time author and one of the world's experts and champions on the subject of nutritional health, had this to say:

> "Much as I think that soil is just great for growing plants, hydroponics has come a long way. I've seen hydroponic producers who have tested their

leafy greens for key nutrients, and the amounts fall well within normal limits for their crop, and are sometimes even higher.[247]

She goes on to point out that plants create their own vitamins, not the soil, and that while mineral content is highly affected by the choice of fertilizer, as it is with conventional farming, these can be supplemented in the growth medium chosen in vertical farms, and in some cases, can lead to improvements over what's grown in open fields.

She added:

"Keep in mind that nutrient content varies for produce in general, regardless of the growing method. The differences relate to the type of fruit or vegetable, the time of year it is harvested, how long after harvesting the crop gets eaten, and how it is handled and stored from farm to fork."

And lastly, as I'm fond of pointing out: even plant foods with sub-optimal levels of zinc or copper, for example, would still be leaps and bounds more nutritious than a happy meal or a bag of potato chips.

In the end, it's what we choose to eat, how much of it, and how fresh it all is that determines its nutritional value to us.

Regenerative Farming

When it comes to measuring the sustainability of conventional vs. regenerative farming, regenerative comes out on top every time. It trades on ecosystems thinking, insofar as the practice requires the planting of cover crops, animal grazing, and "natural fertilizers" (i.e.: poop) to recharge the land and reduce soil degradation.

And so: if I were made to choose between the two, I'd pick regenerative all day long, and pay the sticker price. Still, there are two glaring problems with adopting this practice as a one-size-fits-all approach.

First, the soil and water footprints of conventional and regenerative farming aren't much different. Said another way, farming regeneratively *still displaces* vast swaths of natural ecosystems and gobbles up unsustainable amounts of water, as we saw earlier in this chapter.

Second, David Montgomery, a geologist at the University of Washington and author of *Dirt: The Erosion of Civilizations* and *Growing a Revolution: Bringing Our Soil Back to Life*, said there's no question that regenerative agriculture can sequester carbon, but the amount of carbon that can be added to the soil is finite[248].

He adds, "The claims that you can reverse climate change with regenerative agriculture, that's a real stretch. The more credible estimates are a good down payment on reducing atmospheric carbon dioxide."

Perhaps the biggest problem with conventional farming, regenerative or not, is what Montgomery highlights next:

"If we invest in regenerative agriculture and 50 years later we plow it up, we undo all the benefits. We have to find a way to help maintain it there. To do that, we need policies in place to ensure that the regenerative work that's done today is beneficial in the future."

In other words, without policies, laws, oversight and adherence to practice—at a global scale, ad infinitum—regenerative farms would release their carbon the moment they were tilled, or the moment a human being elected to ignore the required orthodoxy to do so.

Forests, wetlands, and other major carbon sinks, on the other hand, require no humans but for the commitment to leave them alone. Thus, they are *truly* sustainable, as Bill Reed and others would define it.

And so, to sustain human prosperity over the long term in ways that improve human and environmental outcomes symbiotically, I believe there are few approaches that could be more impactful than to forego conventional farming practices we've clung onto for 12,000 years, and to modernize our approach to meeting our food needs.

Ergo: the vertical farm.

Vertical Farms: Energy Hogs

The last point raised by vertical farming skeptics is an admittedly important one. The sun is free when it hits plants, but in a warehouse full of them stacked on top of one another, artificial lighting must counter the loss of this free resource. Vertical farms are massive employers of LED light energy. By some estimates, they comprise 65%-85% of total energy used by these structures.[249]

People rightly point out that if non-renewable energy is used to meet these demands, vertical farms could produce *more* pollution than traditional farms or greenhouses do.

In my architectural practice, I have assembled a wide-ranging team of architects, engineers, ag-tech leaders, real estate and finance experts, and construction professionals to undertake a research effort to understand the viability of creating vertical farms *at scale*. By studying the intersection and cross-impacts of technology, building systems, the business case, regulation, incentives, market forces, the moral imperative, and nutritional health, we can assess the potential of adding this particularly powerful sustainability arrow to our "sustainability quiver".

More on this in the next chapter.

For any vertical farming scheme to work and be sustainable in the sense we use the word today, it would have to generate as much energy as it uses or draw it from a truly sustainable grid, and separately, handle its own waste in a closed-loop system.

It would be required of all key inputs to growing food indoors: energy production (primarily lighting), water use and management, food and animal waste (in the case of aquaponics, which relies on fish for fertilizer), and the general operational energy requirements of an enclosed building.

The good news that a growing number of architecture and engineering (A&E) firms worldwide are already experts in designing net-zero energy buildings, and the use of green energy technologies is, as we saw earlier, far less destructive to the environment than the use of conventional fossil fuel sources.

It's been several years since I designed a building that *wasn't* net-zero energy. That, in my view, is the easy part.

The energy requirements of creating and maintaining a zero-impact vertical farm would be somewhat tempered by positive impacts of a healthy forest or wetland, once the conventional farm it conceptually replaced was restored as a carbon-sequestering biome.

In all, if done correctly, vertical farming can be a real force that helps us transition from "doing less bad" to "doing good", with the contributions of new sustainable carbon sinks, nutrition-optimized food, transport carbon reductions, water and soil conservation, *and* the health benefits that come with nutritious and longer-lasting produce, due to its being closer to the point of consumption, and thus less "rotten" by the time it reaches our mouths.

Final Thoughts

The race to electrify all cars, the energy grid and every building in the world is a daunting one. While there's no official count, there are at least hundreds of millions of buildings dispersed around the world—likely billions—and over one billion motor vehicles ferrying between them.

Equally problematic, there are 195 nations with wildly varying political ideologies, priorities, purchasing power, economic distribution models and organizational infrastructure.

Getting all of them to modernize the built world ethically is, in my view, a specious pursuit. Humans—chiefly politicians and corporate leaders, but also individual beings—are simply not equally consistent, mature, generous, rigorous, nurturing, far-sighted, energetic, clear-headed, informed and brave enough for us to do so consistently, and *stay* the course over generations.

The best, then, that we can do is to incrementally design and build better buildings where and when the audience allows it, and sell more and more electric cars to those who elect to build, sell and/or buy them.

But we would do well to realize that there is only one proven means of guaranteeing that the planet can handle whatever abuse we throw at it from a carbon standpoint, and that is by restoring an adequate quantum of the planet's biomes, so that nature can do what it has always done so incredibly well, which is sustain itself within complex and effective, human-free ecosystems.

Specifically, we need to rewild an adequate amount cropland and livestock pasture to counter our transgressions, then leave nature alone, unmolested, in perpetuity.

This central idea—rewilding nature, then leaving it alone—came to me after reading about Suriname's carbon negativity, as we explored in Chapter 16. It is how I came to the conclusion that as long as nature can handle our abuse, it, and we, will be just fine.

A simple, quantifiable question is all that really matters here: Can we restore and safeguard enough natural, perpetually sustainable biomes on Earth to counter deleterious human activity?
And to that I say: there is a clear path forward.

Using the statistics supplied throughout this chapter, it's *conceivable* that turning between 22% and 50% of global agriculture acres into high-sequestration biomes can offset 100% of the global annual production of atmospheric carbon dioxide.

It comes back to what Bill said to me: "sustainable is the ability to thrive in perpetuity without human intervention." And there's only one thing on Earth that does that.

That thing is a natural ecosystem.

Our chief means of achieving a carbon balance, in my view, is through the creation of new (or even better, existing/converted) buildings into sources of food production at scale. Better still, we could do so in city centers to further offset the carbon emissions that *transporting* foods generates, where most of the humans live.

There are two more serendipitous byproducts of the scenario I just posited. The first is that growing foods in city centers would *increase their nutrient density*, because as nutritionists know well, nutrition decreases with time as food decays, and buying something that was growing hours before you purchased it would last far longer and be far more nutritious than something that had spent a week or two effectively rotting slowly on its way from Mexico, Peru, or New Zealand. The second is that vertical farms' prodigious increase in yield per acre over open-field farming, multiplied by the preservation of all the food currently lost to climate, pestilence and disease, means that it's conceivable that *even fewer* acres of vertical farm than I've provoked in these pages could replace swaths of conventional cropland, since vertical farms are *effectively* loss-free.

Specifically, the 20–40% of outdoor crops we lose to disease, pests and weeds; and a portion of the 31% of additional food grocers toss, some of which is due to its advanced decay.

So, while vertical farms aren't sustainable, per se, modernizing (and potentially urbanizing) our food production could free up the land resources required to rewild erstwhile farmland into biologically rich, thriving, long-term, carbon-sequestering biomes, and put the richest and most sustainable foods where the greatest number of people live, to benefit from them.

If we allowed a big enough chunk of agricultural land to rewild and mature, while satisfying our food needs in a modern manner befitting the era of incredible technological prowess in which we live, then we might just be here long enough to meet our other sticky challenges, and overcome them, too.

Let's take just one more look at the vertical farm "in situ", before moving onto other broken things.

"SEED" NYC — a truly vertical farm © Anthony Fieldman 2026, with help from DALL-E

19 The Case for the Vertical Farm—Part II

We now know that food—its production, processing and resale—takes an unparalleled toll on the planet and our bodies, giving it an outsize influence over our wellbeing.

We also know that in the 21st century, controlled environment agriculture (CEA) has begun to move food production indoors by optimizing some or all of plant foods' five primary production inputs, to create predictable outcomes and yields. Those inputs are light, air, water, nutrients, and humidity.

So-called "vertical farm" startups seem to be founded daily, with over 2,000 of them now operating in the United States alone, as of 2023.[24] While they take different forms, all of them aim to achieve similar ends: independence from the climate on which we have relied throughout history to grow (or catch) the foods we eat.

But with any shift in prevailing paradigms—in this case, growing food as we've done for 12,000 years: in open fields driven by ever-shifting qualities of sun, rain, soil, air and seasonality—comes rapid failure, as scientists and investors who fund them test different ways of achieving their goals while bumping up against the punishing demands of market capitalism.

That's because while science drives progress, capital too-often kills it in the absence of adequate short-term yields. And so, vertical farming is still struggling to get an economically competitive toehold in the heavily subsidized, capital-focused and planet-depleting context of "Big Ag", which has led in large part to our current climate catastrophe.

Counterintuitively, a parallel catastrophe may play a key role in stabilizing CEA, but only if elected officials and capital markets are willing to *adequately* invest in their paradigm-busting success.

The stakes couldn't be higher.

Urban Renewal

The last chapter focused on a simple idea: decant farms into buildings to enable returning that land to a natural, carbon-absorbing state, thereby spurring the re-emergence of complex and powerful biomes that re-balance a planet that sustained itself until we sufficiently weakened it.

Well, there is another opportunity staring us in the face. It is this: that the industrial-era definition of "the office"—the ubiquitous factory-like environments in which humans have been required to sit for half of their waking lives, often in silence—is in sore need of an upgrade; and that their pandemic-era forced closure showed us that the business world didn't collapse while we worked from home, the local café, or for the lucky few, a faraway beach.

We will do a deep dive into work and the office in Chapters 23 and 24. In this one, I'd like to share an idea about what to do with all those empty—and I'd argue, never-to-refill—commercial buildings.

We are talking about more than one billion *abandoned* square feet in the United States alone, where more than 20% of *all* office space, nationally, is now vacant.[250]

Over the past few years, I have read story after story championing the conversion of office buildings into residences. The idea's proponents are well-intended, but there are two major challenges in doing so. The first of these is that just 3% and 15% of office buildings are "suitable candidates" for conversion to apartments.[251] The rest have the wrong shape and/or systems to support urban living; or are too costly to convert because of those limits. The second is, the slavish adherence to one idea evidences, in my view, a lack of imagination.

Consider the following two statistics:

- 25% of commercial office buildings are now functionally obsolete[252]
- Commercial office property taxes comprise at least 10% of municipal revenues[253]

While a 10% loss in municipal revenues may not seem like much, a 2023 article in *The Atlantic*[254] shone a light on an underreported problem:

> *"The* [commercial real estate] *focus on glittering superstar cities is misguided, because many more fragile downtowns—the likes of Dayton, Ohio; Birmingham, Alabama; and St. Louis—entered the pandemic with little margin for failure.*

> *"If office rents in the Rust Belt or the Mississippi River Valley drop by anything close to half, downtowns in those regions face abandonment—not only by white-collar businesses and the shops and restaurants that once served their employees but also by the owners of entire buildings."*

Citing cities like Detroit, Buffalo or Flint, whose downtowns were historically decimated after owners stopped paying rent and abandoned their buildings, the article concludes:

> *"National policy makers and urbanists should be worrying about the already-cheap downtowns of cities that cannot survive any more rent cuts."*

So what to do with all those buildings?

The *Truly* Vertical Farm

We know that vertical farm output varies widely, but in any form it is far more efficient than conventional farming, from as "little" as 10x the yield per acre to as much as 360x, as we saw in prior chapters.

Moreover, we know that if these are located near the point of consumption, CEAs can significantly reduce the enormous amount of food that our grocers (and we) toss out daily due to rot, by minimizing the time it takes to bring produce from harvest to plate.

Food security—and potentially, affordability—are two more important considerations that CEAs could help bolster. That's because capitalism has led to the increasing consolidation of the world's food products into the hands of just ten mega-companies,[255] while half of the world's seeds are now produced by just four others.[256] The small farmer is all but gone, which not only affords conglomerates total control over pricing and quality (the oil industry is a good corollary), but also means that cyberattacks could disrupt the global food supply far more efficiently.

Food sector cyberattacks are on a steep rise.[257] And even on conventional farms, farming is increasingly technological.

Decentralizing food could be achieved by putting nutrition in the hands of thousands of local enterprises if they were to pool investment dollars to purchase farm towers, not unlike how REITs and pension funds invest in real estate, today. This could become one of our best tools for achieving food security (from climate and cyberattacks), affordability (from price fixing and controls) and urban renewal (with the creation of food ecosystems that include restaurants, grocers, the burgeoning nutraceutical and bio-pharma industries, health and wellness-focused businesses, etc.) thereby solving the problem of empty office buildings and a diminishing municipal tax base, all at once.

Further, if these farms generated as much energy as they needed as proposed in the last chapter—what we call "net-zero energy in operation"— it would further bolster the security of not only the food system but the businesses that operate them. A large share of startups in the industry have failed in recent years due to the vagaries of the energy market, given the majority of energy needs for farms is to power the LED lights that feed the plants, and LED energy isn't free, unlike sunlight. A net-zero CEA that bakes the capital and operational costs of these systems into its pro forma would be independent from one more major influence over the cost of our food, and the stability of its emerging market.

All it takes is the right financial formula. And the right financial formula has to look through a bigger lens than just that of produce.

A New Recipe

While late-stage capitalism has largely fueled the consolidation of the world's conglomerates, it has simultaneously fragmented skill sets into ever-more specializing subsets of knowledge in order to supercharge growth.

As we will see in the next chapter, the Industrial Revolution killed the generalist.

As a result, not only does a decreasing number of individuals control ever-increasing amounts of things we need, but an ever-shrinking number of us understands enough about adjacent businesses to leverage one against the other and unlock synergies that could spur virtuous cycles of cost-reducing, revenue-enhancing stability. The M&A industry knows this well.

To illustrate the idea I'm championing here, ask yourself, "What happens when you create a farm in the middle of the city?"

Does it *not* draw people who want to see food grow and learn how that happens, and would they not pay for experiences built around this idea, as they do for other events? Does everyone *not* benefit from the oxygen food produces where it's needed most, since 70% of global CO2 is generated in cities? Do we *not* all want to purchase food at its maximum, just-picked freshness the way we do at farmers' markets and CSAs? Do we *not* want to learn how to prepare it and/or enjoy the fruits of others' labor, by patronizing restaurants or cooking classes? Are we *not* interested in using it to study (and in some cases, re-learn) how nature's bounty can help heal the body, both scientifically and pseudo-scientifically, in businesses that need and benefit from their co-location to "source material" (think bio-pharma and nutraceuticals, or nutritional science)? And do many of us *not* simply want to live near and patronize urban farming towers, so that our "spend" supports the planet and the people in it?

I believe the answer to all these things is a resounding *yes*, certainly for enough of us. Food and its production support an obvious ecosystem of related businesses and activities, well beyond those I just listed.

When we build a vertical farm in a city center, micro-grids and/ or municipal-scaled power can be leveraged to reduce the cost of food production. Transportation costs for its sale and distribution either lower or disappear altogether. Freshness peaks, reducing waste and associated costs, both at point of sale and in one's own home. Multi-industry, synergistic building tenancies can stabilize vagaries in one market like a diversified portfolio does, where strength in one area can offset challenges in another for building owners, helping it to weather capital demands. Countless urbanites who live and/or work near them can easily support and steady its business ecosystem, which is more difficult (and carbon intensive) in a rural or ex-urban milieu. And the real estate itself—a fairly resistant class of asset over the long term, in *most* cases (sorry, workplace)—can act as a bulwark against the changing nature of demand and opportunity inside of the building.

Simply put, a farm ecosystem that owns its real estate, generates its own power and acts as a landlord for related businesses can stabilize itself and the things around it, allowing for a level of resilience in the city that escapes it in single-focus corners of the rural landscape: the things we call "farms".

Calories Count

So, we know that moving farms into towers would be good for the land, the city, and for everyone in it. But what about all those calories we need to survive?

Not everyone loves fruits and vegetables, and those with reasonable knowledge of calories knows that grains are the largest source of global daily calories (more than 50% of them) and that animal proteins are the third biggest tranche.[258]

Most of us also know that it takes giants swaths of land to grow wheat and soy, and nation-sized fields to graze animals.

Well, both of these things may soon change.

At the time of this writing, several entrepreneurs are blazing new trails in large-footprint farming areas that were recently thought to be impossible to replicate in a lab. At the time of this writing:

- Germany's Infarm is now growing wheat in vertical farms, enjoying 26x the yield per acre of its conventional counterparts[259]
- Singapore's Temasek has been growing semi-dwarf rice indoors with higher yields in less time, and using 70% less water over conventional[260]
- America's Air Protein grows "meat" from airborne carbon molecules, delivering field-, deforestation-, and animal-free nutrients to hungry mouths (a friend has tried it, and said it was indistinguishable from chicken)[261]

- Finland's Onego Bio produces actual eggs without chickens, using their DNA and proprietary processes; one of the world's most celebrated restaurants is already using them[262]
- And US-based Quorn is cultivating then fermenting mycoproteins—fungi—to create protein alternatives that deliver the same nutrients as meat, without the animals[263]

There are many, many others.

It's early days yet. But taken in sum, these things harken to a critical investment in food industry innovation, produce, grains, and animal proteins included, using technology and scientific ingenuity to bring all of it indoors… potentially to a tower near you.

In pioneering these early experiments, startups are doing no less than charting a paradigm-busting path that could lead us toward decentralized, climate-independent, land- and climate-restoring, affordable, secure and revenue-generating food.

If you recall Everett Rogers' Diffusion of Innovations chart from Chapter 1, you will now see that each of the companies I mentioned are at the "tip of the curve" awaiting enough early adopters to test and de-risk their businesses *adequately* to stabilize it, so that the early and late majorities can come along for the ride, and complete food's transformation from the old paradigm to a new one.

So, while the last chapter focused on farming's environmental impact, this one is about the cultivation (creation, really) of a new asset class of buildings.

Said differently, it identifies *new uses for an old and increasingly obsolete* asset class.

A 2023 *Wall Street Journal* analysis found that roughly 20% of all bank investments ($3.6 trillion) are currently held in commercial real estate; and that more than $900 billion (25%) of it is coming due in the near term.[264] The asset class itself has plummeted in value for years on end as offices remain empty due to changing work habits that were spurred by the pandemic and empowered by the Internet. We *continue* to resist the pull back to full-time office work.

As I'll argue in chapters 23 and 24, the office always sucked.

So, while we still need places to work, and while the benefits of "going to work" are obvious and include **efficiency** in the presence of a dynamic and collaborative environment, **knowledge gains** made with exposure to other workers, in-person training, and mentorship, and **social cohesion** forged in the pantry, at lunch, or at drinks, and over late nights at work, I would wager that the genie isn't going back in the bottle.

That's because what *doesn't* suck about *not* going to the office includes **reduced commutes** and **associated savings**, both of which can be significant; **flexibility** that allows us to better manage non-work life organically; and for some, **increases in productivity**, because that's what happens when we have agency to work when and where we are most inspired, energetic and/or focused, and for some, when we don't feel micromanaged.

Final Thoughts

On this last point about productivity, most of us work better in environments that aren't fluorescent-lit, filled with sterile, commercial-grade furniture and fixtures, or are hermetically sealed and therefore always too stuffy or cold or hot or noisy or quiet, or bright for *some of us* to do our best work.

The reality is, something will have to replace all those empty office buildings. Something will have to provide cities with the revenues they need to pay firemen and teachers and trash collectors. Something has to begin reversing industrial era-fueled planetary destruction. Something has to prioritize human health and thriving over market share and addiction. Something has to markedly improve the affordability of basic needs in an increasingly unaffordable capitalist landscape. And something has to begin leveraging the connections between related needs and business opportunities, that once combined can *improve access and outcomes* for all of us.

That thing, I would suggest, could just as easily be the creation of vertical farm ecosystems in the middle of our cities, as *not*.

EDUCATION:

Growth and Mindset

"The Polymath" © Anthony Fieldman 2024, with help from DALL-E

20 How Amateurs Created Our World

We have revered the idea of expertise for as long as any of us has lived. Generally, the more credentials one has, the more their ideas are valued. The schools in which nearly all of us are inculcated were created to institutionalize this. Countless fields of ever-more-specialized professional study and post-instructional enterprise have been conceived and organized to "divide and conquer" the world of knowledge, applied. As a result, our receptiveness and adulation have been largely, near-automatically, reserved for those who are considered the sanctioned authorities on any given subject: the chroniclers of written lore and the talking heads of recorded media upon whom most of us rely helps us understand the complexity of our world.

These are paper truths.

In reality, experts are more often the implementers and defenders of what others created when they *ignored the rules.*

One of language's most sardonic and indicting quips goes, "An expert is someone who knows more and more about less and less, until they know absolutely *everything* about *nothing.*" While its author remains unknown, the witticism shines a light on a key insight: that by narrowing our focus, we effectively "lose the forest for the trees", to explain one idiom with another.

In plain English, when we are deeply invested in one thing to the exclusion of others, three things happen: first, we miss out on a broader understanding of how the things over which we have mastery are influenced by—and influence—the things to which they are adjacently connected. Second, we become vested in certain truths because our self-worth—a large chunk of our identity—becomes wrapped up in whether or not we are *right* about the elements of our mastery, and the moment we begin defending central pillars of our self-narrative we lose our objectivity. And third, we lose out on the opportunity to see the world from an *outsider's* perspective; that is, with fresh eyes.

In our zeal, we often forget that the world in which we live and operate was largely conceived by the minds and efforts of *amateurs*. Medicine, philosophy, psychology, science and the built environment: all of these were advanced, if not outright created, by people with no formal training, but who regardless held a passion for a specific avenue—or twenty—of experimentation, inquiry, and observation; a rich soup from which to draw inspiration, and make new connections.

Amateurs—people who pursue "a particular activity or field of study independently from their source of income," as one definition puts it—are "considered to be the ideal balance between pure intent, open mind, and the interest or passion for a subject."

There is indeed something pure about a passion, pursued, when it lies beyond the direct influence of something that could contaminate our unbridled curiosity and interest, and that thing is, more often than not, the economic motive. And yet, when we hear someone opine on a subject or offer up an idea, most of us look for third-party qualifications to prejudice—i.e.: inform—how closely, or openly, we will listen to them.

Said another way, experience shows that whether or not we are willing to listen to *or accept* someone's ideas rests largely on the quantum and prestige of their professional qualifications, accolades, and "signature line" acronyms. These tend to exert a big influence on our interest in their ideas, regardless of the quality of their thoughts.

We are a judgmental lot.

A perfunctory, incomplete look into our own history betrays the shortcomings of this tendency and bias.

A Brief History Lesson

The educational paradigm of Ancient Greece, one could argue, began and ended with Aristotle, a proto-polymath. Aristotle founded the Lyceum and its famed Peripatetic School, which was a place of empirical philosophy that favored *experience* over *theory*. Aristotle didn't recognize the difference between philosophy and science. His aim was to uncover what many of us currently call the "why" of things.

Because of this, and the fact that Aristotle didn't recognize boundaries to his curiosity, his writings covered the modern fields of biology, zoology, physics, metaphysics, logic, ethics, theology, music, poetry, economics, theater, politics and government—almost *none of which existed* as such, before he wrote about them.

By today's standards, he had no business looking into any of it.

He had no qualifications!

And yet: Aristotle's contributions to our understanding of the world cannot be overstated. He is considered to have "exerted a unique influence on almost every form of knowledge in the West", one that "continues to be a subject of contemporary philosophical discussion," according to *Wikipedia*.[265]

That is, everything he thought about in his amateur way still holds sway over our lives, some *two thousand four hundred years* after his death.

All Aristotle had was his mind and his powers of observation, and he fed on everything that came across his path. As a result, we continue to live in a world he largely created for us.

He was an amateur.

And he wasn't alone.

A poor Londoner named Michael Faraday without a formal education was working as a servant to famed English chemist Humphry Davy, who inspired him to experiment on his own. Before long, Faraday would become the world's foremost authority on electromagnetism, establishing the basis for magnetic fields and leading to the existence of the electric motor upon which we have relied for centuries. In the process, he created the "science of experimentation". Before Faraday, science had been viewed as a "philosophical" undertaking.

An Augustinian priest named Gregor Mendel passed the time in the Czech abbey he inhabited conducting experiments with pea plants, leading to his observation-based theory of dominant and recessive genes, and laying the foundations for the science of genetics. While summarily ignored by the Establishment, his published discoveries, which were picked up by scientists long after his death and earlier *discreditation*, ultimately paved the way for his posthumous recognition as the founder of modern genetics.

An American "computer"—as women who sorted and classified thousands of photographic plates were called, nearly a century before what is now done by their silicon replacements—named Henrietta Swan Leavitt devised a system to measure the brightness of stars, and had an epiphany that led her to use their "twinkle" to determine, for the first time, the distance between celestial objects, and in the process, birthed the field of astronomical measurement. Edwin Hubble, whose namesake telescope we now use to understand the world, used Leavitt's "period-lumosity relation" to establish his namesake Law, allowing us to understand, finally, that the universe is expanding, and to measure its age.

And a home-schooled tinkerer named Thomas Edison conducted experiments at home during breaks from his late-night job at the AP Wire Service. Along the way, he became "America's Greatest Inventor", birthing the phonograph, the motion picture (movie) camera, and the electric light bulb. He held 1,093 patents in the United States alone, by the time he died. And along the way, he established the world's first industrial research laboratory, in Menlo Park, where he scratched his tinkering itch.

There are countless amateurs beyond those I listed.

People like Leonardo da Vinci, who without a formal education was one of history's greatest painters, architects, engineers, scientists, anatomists, geologists, astronomers, botanists, paleontologists and cartographers, who invented things like the helicopter, the scuba tank, armored vehicles, the parachute, solar power, an adding machine and the double hulled ship, some of which took hundreds of years to mature or be realized after his fertile imagination conceived of them.

Or like Nikola Tesla, a university dropout whose work is being revived a century after his greatest contributions were buried by capitalist titans who couldn't find a way to monetize the things he had invented to fuel all of mankind, for *free*. Tesla's inventions included the induction motor, x-rays, radio-controlled vehicles, hydroelectric power turbines, wireless transmission stations, and AC power (which he didn't invent, but advanced and perfected, before Edison "stole" it back from him). He also discovered the electron, radioactivity, cosmic rays, terrestrial resonance, and standing waves, and he pioneered the fluorescent light bulb.

Tesla's eponymous coil could wirelessly power *entire cities*, much in the way that the radio that he at least partly invented, via his patented inventions that Marconi drew on, sent sound into our homes through the ether, *magically*.

I am simply making the point that formal training in a specific area of inquiry is not the *only* path to knowledge and invention. In fact, there is an inherent advantage to self-initiated inquiry that lies apart from one's degrees or training, in that being "ignorant" about any given thing allows some of us make leaps of *illogic* that seem utterly nonsensical to established orthodoxy, but which regardless, by their very irreverence for (or disinterest in) the status quo, allow their authors to pursue understanding without bias, or corruptible influence.

Said another way, when one is not vested in any particular outcome, we are free to experiment, ask crazy questions, and see where they lead us. In that way, if expertise follows the beautiful but rigid structure of a classical symphony, amateurism follows the syncopated, often faltering yet ever-dynamic path of jazz.

Polymathy

What all the great thinkers of history had in common is that they are what are referred to as polymaths: people described somewhat mundanely as being "of great learning in several fields of study."

There are other terms we now use freely to describe what is meant by a polymath: jack of all trades; renaissance man; genius; generalist; and my favorite, *amateur*. While we use these terms to imply very different things from one another, they all have polymathic origins in common, describing those given to serious experimentation and reflection but with minimal bias and maximal curiosity, without regard to the prevailing state of things.

They describe, above all, people with a specific interest in the *intersection* of things—that is, how one sphere of our world might relate to others, outside of itself.

To be labeled a polymath, one's learning must span a substantial number of oft-unrelated subjects by which one can draw on diverse bodies of knowledge to solve specific problems.

Karl Kraus, the 19th century Austrian satirist, famously quipped, "I had a terrible vision: I saw an encyclopaedia walk up to a polymath and open him up."

It's one of the funniest things I've read, because it's one of the truest. What would possess a satirist to suggest an encyclopaedia has something to learn from a lifelong tinkerer who resists the call to specialize, or absorb and accept dogma as facts? Polymaths are, first and foremost, the world's great amateurs. They resist all attempts to box and limit inquiry, and instead service a healthy appetite for curiosity, and to trust themselves to explore their urges.

Polymaths go by another forgotten moniker: autodidacts, or "self-taught persons." You know these people by their names and reputations. Beyond the polymaths I already named, we can add Franklin, Khayyam, Copernicus, Newton (the "father of the scientific method"), al-Jazari, Ptolemy, Archimedes, Darwin (the "father of evolution"), Michelangelo, and Russell to the list.

Amateurs, all.

Education and the Economy

Well, the global education system is now organized to feed our commercial tunnel vision—our intensive education. That's because organized learning's chief goal is to increase global GDP in order to create and move goods, to conceive and build services and to optimize specialized tasks within increasingly complex networks of production: in finance, infrastructure, development, technology, agribusiness, government, the military-industrial complex, and scientific advancement.

Our laser focus on human commercial value has accordingly bled *extensive*—what we now call multi-disciplinary—learning. We have traded self-initiated open inquiry for controlled specialization. And in the process, we have lost the "leaps of logic" that historically arose from minds who thought about problems differently precisely because they had broad and seemingly unrelated knowledge sets to draw on, so they could see old problems through new eyes.

And yet: human cognition evolved for broad skill acquisition before specialization became economically dominant.

Regardless, the holy grail of advancement is still insight. And insight lies squarely in the intersection of things at the surface, not at the bottom of an ever-deepening line of inquiry.

Said another way, while expertise provides us with horsepower on the battlefield, polymathy aims it from central command.

We need look no further than quixotic, contrarian or unsanctioned thinking to see the different archetypes at play. To an expert, thoughts that lie outside of accepted dogma—that question things an expert has studied deeply, and concluded represent "best practices" or "truth"—are labeled *unscientific.* Well, to a polymath, those same outlier thoughts go by another name: *stimulation.*

The two couldn't conceive of "left field" thinking differently. An expert relies on accumulated learning to focus action and arrive at conclusions. A polymath relies on skepticism and unencumbered riffing to broaden thinking, without prejudice as to where it takes them.

Fresh Insights

I have devoted over thirty years to a specific creative profession— architecture—in which, unlike the polymaths, I was officially schooled. Like my peers, my decision was heavily informed by my desire to earn a secure living (note to self: do research first, next time!).

Since I was a child, I have dabbled in a number of things I still do, "on the side". I'm extremely passionate about them, and take my amateur activities very seriously. But because of our prevailing predilection for expertise, it still feels awkward for me to sheepishly aver, out loud, that I am a writer, photographer, graphic designer, poet, furniture-maker, philosopher, or installation artist, because I don't have professional degrees or even "real" critical acclaim in any of these. Every time I share one of my passions with others I am reflexively cowed by my own lack of bonafides and am thus tentative about admitting I do all of these things, lest I be dismissed, or my talents rejected as *amateurish*.

And yet, the truth of the matter is that even in my profession, some of the greatest buildings and processes have come from people who had no business authoring them because they approached their creative process from the *outside*, without the earned expertise to endow their investigations with the aura of expert knowledge.

Which is a fancy way of saying, sometimes you need to be ignorant enough *not to know* what you're *not supposed to do*, in order to discover a *truth*.

In the process of indulging one's ignorance, sometimes radical insights and fresh perspectives result.

One of my favorite moments in film is the concluding scene in the movie *Being There*. Chance the gardener, played by Peter Sellars, is a simple-minded man who has never ventured outside of the Washington, D.C. townhouse in which he tended a garden since youth. Suddenly, a complex turn of events results in his inheritance of the estate in which he's spent his life. Chance finds himself thrust into the company of intellectuals who, not realizing Chance was ever anything other than an eccentric aristocratic recluse, *assume* by his idiotic musings that these are the deep thoughts of a successful colleague. In the closing scene, we watch from behind as Chance—a certifiable "moron" or "imbecile" on the Stanford-Binet Intelligence Scale—walks across the surface of a lake, ignorant enough *not to know* that one cannot do that without falling in, and because he doesn't know any better, strolls across it without getting wet. At one point he even stops, and indulging his dim curiosity, sticks his umbrella into the water far below his feet. Unable to connect the dots because of his limited mind, he shrugs and keeps walking on the lake, out of view.

The moral of the fable, in my view, is that ignorance can lead to the extraordinary.

Expertise

Expertise is a dangerous thing. It dulls the mind, if truth be told. I am fully aware this is institutional heresy, and that my own profession lives and dies by its ability to convince clients of our peace-of-mind-conferring deep expertise: the kind that makes their multi-million or multi-billion dollar financial investments weigh less heavily on their choice of a dance partner. The term "safe bet" comes to mind.

And yet, safe never stirred the soul.

This is not in any way to suggest that deep knowledge of a particular thing is anything other than noble, and valuable. I personally know many experts whose particular expertise I seek to expand my own understanding. Expertise is valuable. *Someone* has to dive deep, to ask the nuanced questions that come from devotion to a particular thing. None of the scientists I listed doggy-paddled. They plunged. I am not proposing a thesis that resists deep knowledge or learning. Any skill, exercised enough, confers increasing benefits and capacity. You can't become a world-class athlete by dabbling, just as you can't solve deep scientific or social issues without first building a reservoir of knowledge.

When it comes to *applying* knowledge, you want an expert, every time. Knowing what meds to prescribe can make the difference between living and dying. I am suggesting, however, that it is as likely as not that the person who *discovered* them in the first place was an *amateur*.

In this chapter, I am advocating that the pursuit of great and varied learning—polymathy—is like a tidal pool in the sense that one needs to continually recharge the waters of knowledge with something external if one is interested in creating vibrant feeding grounds, and avoiding stagnation.

And today's world's problems frankly *demand* it.

Outside Influences

Well-founded, reliable, replicable products and productivity may well garner market share, robust ROIs and huzzahs from esteemed critics and uninitiated whisperers alike. But these things have no relationship whatsoever to *innovation*, which I would go as far as to posit is the rightful domain of those unencumbered by prevailing "truths", like our water-walking friend, Chance. Even in my own profession, a list of architecture's most revered practitioners—the ones we 'experts' count on our fingers—include a career glassblower (Carlo Scarpa), a brick layer (Louis Kahn), and a cabinet maker (Peter Zumthor). All had a "side interest" in the built environment, and decided at one point late in their *other* careers to throw in and dabble with architecture. Zumthor is, in my view, the single greatest architect alive. The cabinet maker—the lover of material specificity, and craft—is on dazzling display in every one of his innovative buildings.

The most innovative works of any kind have *always* emerged from the outside, from the minds of those who approach any given problem with fresh eyes, curiosity, passion and innocence. The world of science has proven this dozens of times over. My chosen avocation is no different, even if few clients trust themselves enough to invest in the concept of open-ended inquiry, without guaranteed returns.

Some do. But risk and innovation face off against the balance sheet every single time.

Micromastery

And yet: the root source of ingenuity and inventiveness remains unchanged from what they were during Ancient Greece, the Renaissance, the Scientific Revolution, and the Enlightenment, all of which were periods of exponential advancement buoyed by amateurs, as we saw earlier.

British poet, writer and explorer Robert Twigger, just six years my senior and in possession of polymathic insatiety, mused on his own website that what interests him is...

> *"...many things. Too many. From an early age I was entranced by the idea of polymathy. Why can't we be multitudes? I realised that just moving in that direction, rather than its opposite was enough. Almost enough. So polymathy and supporting polymathic activity are things I tend to revolve around, spinning off in various directions to both disrupt*

and instigate. Disrupting by refusing to go along with a jargon riddled, left brain, artificially isolated description of things. Instigating by always looking for the fun in something, the way in, the place where its beating heart may be found…along the way I learnt that the key to learning fast was **micromastery.**"

Twigger tells an important story, in *Aeon Magazine.*[266]

"I travelled with Bedouin in the Western Desert of Egypt. When we got a puncture, they used tape and an old inner tube to suck air from three tyres [sic] to inflate a fourth. It was the cook who suggested the idea; maybe he was used to making food designed for a few go further. Far from expressing shame at having no pump, they told me that carrying too many tools is the sign of a weak man; it makes him lazy. The real master has no tools at all, only a limitless capacity to improvise with what is to hand. The more fields of knowledge you cover, the greater your resources for improvisation."

Twigger goes on, sarcastically, as only the British can:

"The average job now is done by someone who is stationary in front of some kind of screen. Someone who has just one overriding interest is tunnel-visioned, a bore, but also a specialist, an expert. Welcome to the monopathic world, a place where only the single-minded can thrive. Of course, the rest of us are very adept at pretending to be specialists. We doctor our CVs to make it look as if all we ever wanted to do was sell mobile homes or Nespresso machines. It's common sense, isn't it, to try to create the impression that we are entirely focused on the job we want? And wasn't it ever thus?"

It wasn't.

As legend has it, Leonardo da Vinci—one of the greatest creative minds in history—was apparently as proud of his ability to bend iron bars with his hands as he was of the Mona Lisa.

You can't make these things up.

Final Thoughts

None of this is to say that studying is pointless, or that commitment to a given pursuit or line of inquiry is anything less than noble. None of these polymathic amateurs wasn't serious. Quite the opposite: they threw themselves into authentic inquiry because of an inherent passion they held for any given subject.

One cannot make discoveries without intent and focus.

Rather, my point with these musings is that we pay far too much attention to the initials that trail after someone's name, or the number of times we've proven ourselves in any enterprise, and not nearly enough on the quality of the individual and their thinking as we should, because it is almost exclusively the thinking that leads to insight.

Worse still, we have organized education around an Industrial Era model of mastery, and so education is now broken and needs to be fixed to supercharge creative ways of fixing every *other* broken system that the Industrial Era created.

Curiosity isn't the domain of someone with initials; often, it's the opposite. The greatest creative leaps came from the outside in every line of inquiry that matters, including those for which rigor has become the emblem of legitimacy. Aristotle, Newton, Faraday, Mendel, Leavitt, Edison and Tesla—not to mention da Vinci, Alberti, Franklin, Crick and Feynman, the latter of which earned his Nobel Prize in quantum electrodynamics by indulging in his favorite hobby— spinning plates on his finger—sought their inspiration from things outside of the prevailing orthodoxy.

Spinning plates. I told you. You can't make these things up.

To revisit the movie theme for a moment, of my favorite quotes is from a cartoon: Pixar's *The Invincibles.* In it, a caricature of a caricature, Edna Mode—the fashion designer-inventor of hyper-performative super- costumes—revives a century-old quote by Louis Pasteur, the French polymath whose 'pasteurization' has saved countless lives since. Edna says, "Luck favors the prepared, dah-ling…", echoing Pasteur's observation that "In the fields of observation, chance favors only the prepared mind."

"Prepared", in this case, isn't to be confused with "indoctrinated". Rather, it is a broad understanding of the world that emboldens our confidence that the answers to our questions lie outside of that which is known, which is to say, outside of that which is accepted as orthodox truth.

With enough confidence and bravery we can reach beyond what is sanctioned to move humanity forward, one discovery at a time. The amateur is, and always has been, the engine for such leaps.

We would do well to recognize the authenticity *and value* of pure curiosity, indulged.

It travels by the sobriquet "amateur".

In the next two chapters, we will dive into the broken paradigm of our education system, and what some entrepreneurs are doing to revive the polymath.

"The Coding Space" co-founder Eli Kariv works with my daughter, Mia © Anthony Fieldman 2015

21 It's Time to Reinvent Education

Education is broken because it is still largely aimed toward specialization in the name of competition and economic gain. In doing so, it has turned us into blunt weapons ill-prepared for the coming tsunami of change that will see us overcome by things we no longer understand.

Humans evolved to be generalists: to learn everything we could to survive. Over the course of time, those same tools allowed us to make enough connections between things we had learned *ad hoc* to invent systems of increasing sophistication. In short order, we became the dominant species on the planet, ultimately transforming nearly all of it.

Regardless of our inherent capacity for **lateral thinking**, today we largely ignore our own origins in favor of monetizing isolated scraps of it, robbing us of our innate ability to make sense of an increasingly complex world.

It's unfortunate, not the least of which is because we humans are inherently curious creatures. For as long as we've been endowed with the faculties to do so, we've searched for understanding that is both tactical (the "who, what, when, where, and how" of life) and existential (its "why").

Today, our education system decidedly favors the tactical over the existential because, as Waqas Ahmed describes in his excellent book, *The Polymath*:

> *"Somewhere along the line, because of… the predominance of the capitalist paradigm, education came to be seen primarily (and sometimes exclusively) as a means to greater materialistic and social status. Our current institutions and culture have forced us to rely on education as a value-adding process after which we sell ourselves to employers who can be reassured of our ability to contribute to their success. That 'value' is most often judged by how 'specialized' we are. In that sense, education has become a tool to attain stability and status."*

There are two problems with this.

The first is that the dominant Industrial model of education that demands specialization turns jack-of-all-trades into masters of one (if not masters of *one fraction*). This reduces our self-sufficiency as well as our ability to make connections between seemingly unrelated realms the way we did throughout history. The second is that nearly two centuries of specialization have resulted in a spectacularly complex world—far more than would've been possible if the acts of feeding, clothing and sheltering ourselves and our own families still demanded most of our hours. And as a result, while our "progress" is an incredible achievement, more and more decisions are being made by people who *decreasingly* understand the scale and breadth of their decisions' impacts on *other* systems, which paradigm thereby exponentially increases risk for things to go cataclysmically wrong.

See: climate, economics, technology—A.I., specifically—and social systems.

Today, we outsource nearly *all* of life to third parties.

While our problems predate the Industrial Age, it supercharged our transformation into specialists, churning out young adults who were increasingly discouraged from openly exploring their worlds without preconceived outcomes like "correct" answers or targeted application, and who were pushed instead to choose a singular area of focus where, as Ahmed writes, they could distinguish themselves in the name of future economic gain and reputation.

Even 400 years ago, Nicholaus Copernicus, a world-class polymath and the first human to realize the Universe didn't physically revolve around the Earth, maligned the growing trend toward specialization among his peers, as follows:

> *"With them it is as though an artist were to gather the hands, feet, head, and other members for his images from diverse models, each part excellently drawn, but not related to a single body, and since they in no way match each other, the result would be a monster rather than man."*

The human world is now full of economic, environmental, legal, industrial and technological "monsters", as an increasingly specialized workforce tinkers with ever smaller components of an ever more complex set of problems, leaving fewer and fewer people able to broadly navigate our own inventions with the dim hope of synthesizing and distilling broad inputs into holistic insights to help us thrive.

We are now, in many ways, Babel, incarnate.

As E.O. Wilson, a giant in several fields and the "heir" to Darwin, intuited:

"We are drowning in information, while starving for wisdom."

As we discussed in the last chapter, we used to call people whose curiosity fueled open-ended explorations "polymaths". And while every human is capable of polymathy, Ahmed argues, the Western educational paradigm has prevented nearly every student from fulfilling that potential—that is, from turning information into wisdom, or *insight*.

Physical Ease, Intellectual Complexity

We would likely agree that living has become simpler for most than it was in the pre-industrial era. That is, we in the Global West now outsource the creation and delivery of nearly everything we need or want in our lives, most of which we used to have to source or make ourselves: things like food, clothing and shelter, to name just three. Securing resources used to take up most, if not all, of our hours. Today we employ a proxy army for that effort, enabled by our most pernicious creation: money.

The pursuit of money now drives how most of us engage with the world on a daily basis. That includes learning to specialize in something we can charge others for so that we can participate in the cycle of economic exchange.

Life is now mostly *transactional* in that it is framed by exchange between specialists who not only find one another's skills or output useful, but who frankly now *need* these things. That includes the satisfaction of basic needs like food, shelter, water, safety, clothing, and even reproduction for those who engage doctors, nurses and/or midwives during pregnancy, as well as child-rearing for those who hire nannies, babysitters, day care professionals, teachers, and/or activity organizers of every kind. This is a total reversal from pre-industrial times, when most of us farmed, built our homes, dug wells, protected our families, made our clothing, gave birth on the farm, and set our children to work by the age that most in the Global West now begin kindergarten.

The ability to choose to specialize *required* us to outsource things. If we hadn't, we wouldn't have been able to lavish a large amount of energies to just one aspect of needs-meeting. Once we made that trade, two trends emerged: (i) an increase in outsourcing freed up yet more time for individuals to devote to their chosen spheres of specialization; and (ii) this enabled life to reach a level of complexity that would've been difficult otherwise, if at all possible.

The trend toward specialization has only accelerated over time. Today, our systems of governance, finance, production, exchange, communications, and scientific inquiry, not to mention the technological interfaces that increasingly mitigate these things, are all but impossible to navigate without either hyper-specialized and arcane knowledge, a large team of collaborating individuals, or both.

We are now, essentially, unable to navigate the modern world self-sufficiently, without willfully turning our backs on most of it, by choosing to live as though the last century never happened.

We see signs of diminished sense-making everywhere, as polarization and hate crimes increase while tolerance and compromise decrease. This trend makes it imperative that we retool our education system to help us navigate the complexity of human institutions and their physical impacts on people and planet while there's still a hospitable planet to defend.

We desperately need a new education model: one based on *synthesis* that encourages and rewards open-ended inquiry, experimentation, philosophy, discourse, humanism, introspection, collaboration, critical thinking, and creative enterprise. That is, a system that builds on the fact that knowledge is no longer held in ivory towers but on the Internet, and that focuses on teaching us both how to navigate learning and what to do with the things we discover.

Information is now everywhere. As E.O. Wilson said, we are drowning in it. It's formally organized in general e-institutions. At the time of this writing, they include Academic Earth, Khan Academy, W3Schools, Udemy, TeacherTube, EdX, and its subsidiary, MOOC.org, among others. It's hosted at topic-focused learning sites like TED (and TEDx), MasterClass, and SpeakEasy, Inc. It's aggregated in open-source global repositories like *Wikipedia*, YouTube and Vimeo, which have replaced the library for a digital age. It's housed in pragmatic how-to tutorials not only at YouTube and Vimeo, but at sites like eHow, TikTok and Instructables. And it's ubiquitous on digital news and literary sites, including every major media outlet, social media site and on self-publishing platforms, like Medium or Substack.

Not one of these things existed before the turn of the millennium. Most are a mere *decade* old.

In a sense, the entire Internet now exists to connect resources and people, and in a very short time, it has become the driving force of the global economy.

So, what to do with all that data?

Enter the Polymath

I won't repeat the last chapter's thesis. However, it's worth a short discussion of why I believe polymathy is our best hope of saving us from the limiting impacts our own voluntary blinders. And it begins with a retooling of our prevailing systems of education.

As Persian polymath and scholar Seyyed Hossein Nasr warned:

> *"No society can live and survive without the vision of the whole. The polymath renders a service that is absolutely essential for the survival of a civilization in the long term… otherwise everything will become separate from each other like organs of a body with no integrating principle, without which the body will fall apart."*

Nasr sounds a lot like Copernicus.

His contemporary, E.O. Wilson (both men are now in their nineties), had this to say:

"Only fluency across the [disciplinary] boundaries will provide a clear view of the world as it really is, not as seen through the lens of ideologies and religious dogmas or commanded by myopic response to immediate need. A balanced perspective cannot be acquired by studying disciplines in pieces but through pursuit of the consilience among them."

Why is this important? Why isn't it good enough to *only* become the expert in HTML, CDO, 1040's, H1-B, HC-MVEC, 501(c)3, or any other confusing, acronym-heavy human creation? The answer is, it's important because anything isolated and linear is at risk of being automated very, very soon, and because when we hyper-specialize we are blind to the broader impacts of decisions we are making while we remain in our silos.

Opining on the pragmatic application of a polymathic education—how it helps individuals in the near term, in an economic capacity—Anders Sandberg, from Oxford University's Future of Humanity Institute (yup; this exists) has similar advice to E.O. Wilson:

"At least for the next few decades, until machines become smarter than humans, the human polymath will be very important to society. Jobs that can be crisply defined are threatened by automation. Jobs that are hard to define are actually pretty safe. Polymaths are obviously the latter… Not only are they good at doing the jobs that don't have a proper description, but they are, moreover, good at inventing such jobs."

We sorely need an education paradigm that prioritizes the creation of broad thinkers and teaches them how to *apply* the discoveries they make to solving deep problems.

A New Education

Ahmed and I share an optimism about every individual's innate polymathic ability. There will always be outliers, the likes of Aristotle, da Vinci, Newton, Epicurus, Kuo, Tagore, Parks, Franklin, Carver, Alberti and Edison, among countless others. But much as Newton said "If I have seen further, it is by standing on the shoulders of giants," we are all part of the puzzle. Each and every discovery, widget and insight contributes to the collective reach of humanity.

We reviewed this concept in Chapter 5 while discussing Lorenz's Chaos Theory. Everything influences everything else, innovation as much as anything.

The idea, then, *isn't* to stop going about our business as specialists, or to scrap formal education. To the contrary, it is to *enhance* learning by *broadening* it, so that we can in fact "see further" by connecting disparate threads. It is to create *contextual understanding* of any given thing to other things. It is to encourage the exploration of *connections*.

As polymath and scholar Iain McGilchrist said:

"Nothing is what it is except in the context in which it is situated. Take it out and it changes its nature."

Philosopher Edgar Morin refers to this as "blind intelligence."

Edward de Bono, who created the term "lateral thinking", critiqued existing educational institutions for not teaching thinking, and that it was only through deduction, synthesis and application that *information* becomes *knowledge.*

In pursuit of these skillsets, we must also cultivate skepticism: the humble understanding that there is far more that we *don't know* than we know; and that anything known is no more than an imperfect means toward greater *future* understanding, because it, too, is incomplete... if not dead wrong.

Leonardo da Vinci himself said:

"The greatest deception men suffer from is their own opinions."

Mihaly Csikszentmihalyi, who named the concept of "flow" or "flow state", referred to creative people like polymaths as being multitudes rather than individuals.

One of the most illuminating parts of Ahmed's book is his review of what neuroscientists are discovering about the distinct roles of each brain hemisphere—divisions that McGilchrist dubs *The Master and his Emissary*, in his book of the same name.

"During a creative moment, the left hemisphere barely reacts but the right becomes more active, showing a striking increase in gamma waves. Brain cells on the left hemisphere have short dendrites, useful for pulling in information from nearby, but the cells on the right branch out much further and pull together distant unrelated ideas."

Via our dendrites, it appears, our right-brained creative hemisphere makes biologically shallow and broad connections across distinct areas of the brain, while our analytical left-brained hemisphere is limited in its reach, drawing instead on nearby—and related—data.

If nothing else, this speaks to the need for our educational institutions to amplify right-brain creativity, to develop the "ideas, analogies, patterns and perspectives from outside the domain [of inquiry]" that cognitive psychologist Rand Spiro cites as foundational to the development of future polymaths.

Putting Humpty Dumpty Back Together

If the Machine Age was about shattering the spherical holism of human understanding and activity into thousands of fragments in service of targeted advancements and their *monetization*, the post-industrial Information Age should be about putting Humpty Dumpty together again.

Our misguided subdivision of everything we touch and do, however incredible human systems may be, has led us to make products and decisions that are ultimately harmful to ourselves.

We parse what and how we eat into component nutrients rather than consume whole foods that interact nutritionally. We "treat diseases, not people," as my late brother—a Harvard-trained doctor—once chastised his colleagues during his valedictory speech there, which leads to sub-standard outcomes in human health. We grow and harvest fragments of the world's resources (think bluefin tuna or mahogany trees), ignoring how doing so destroys entire ecosystems as "collateral damage". We we treat one another transactionally rather than as complex human beings, reducing the richness of connection into transacted loneliness. And we rob ourselves of the sense-making apparatus to thrive, both as individuals and as a species, by teaching fragments in lieu of synthesis.

It is high time for us to retake the mantle of polymathy through a retooling of our educational system, because the fact is that there is only one planet, and it acts invariably like the ecosystem that it is. It can't do otherwise.

Every part of the planet and its constituent parts exerts an influence on every other part.

The 2022 invasion of Ukraine proved that there is only one economy, and it's global. It triggered record energy and food price inflation, disrupted global supply chains, and increased poverty.[267] A market in Wuhan proved that there is only one macrobiome, and it's global. A rotating garbage patch three times the size of France[268] (among many, many others) proves that there is only one waste stream, and it is global. Runaway cyclones, rainstorms, hurricanes, heat waves, wildfires, desertification, ocean acidification, colony collapse and melting ice caps the world over all prove that there is only one climate, and it is global. And a world-wide web where all of human knowledge and commerce now lives and interacts—one which despots in isolated places will do anything to limit—proves that there is only one meta-source of exchange, and it is global.

And so, to solve global problems today we need a global understanding of the world, and not *only* how to harness the individual components of an increasingly complex set of problems, but critically how those constituent pieces interact and impact potential outcomes, so that we might stand a chance of directing human effort toward favorable outcomes for *all*.

Final Thoughts

According to the late education expert Sir Ken Robinson, whose video "Do Schools Kill Creativity?" is the most watched TED talk of all time, believes the current model of education...

"...is grossly outdated; it is still based on a model that Victorian Britain installed, which fostered a culture of 'linearity, conformity and standardization,' whereas today we are faced with a different world, one that is 'organic, adaptable and diverse.' This incongruence affects the students' intellectual and professional prospects. So treating children like robots doesn't even suit the twenty-first-century job market."

Mathematician and philosopher Alfred North Whitehead called these "inert ideas". Ahmed calls them "compartmentalized, fragmented information thrown at students at school without any unifying framework."

As a result, students are not only less able to make sense of how these fragments of knowledge transmitted to them in various classes are relevant to *each other*, but even how they are relevant *to their own lives*. There is simply no context, and therefore little internalization.

So, what to do?

To reprise what I wrote earlier, we need an education model of synthesis, for children and adult learners, alike, that encourages and rewards something like the following learning sets, as a sort of meta-curriculum, or "Ten Principles for a Polymathic Education":

1. Open-ended inquiry and Cognitive Science
2. Exploration and Experimentation
3. Philosophy and History
4. Discourse and Debate
5. Empathy and Humanism
6. Introspection and Reflection
7. Collaboration and Social Organization
8. Critical thinking and Deduction
9. Sense-Making and Meaning
10. Creative enterprise and The Arts

I'm sure there are many others.

There are rich sources of all of these things online. Visiting any of the few dozen portals I listed earlier in this chapter could send any one of us down rabbit holes into which we could easily disappear, at length. The trick, of course, is in teaching children and adults alike how to navigate an infinite information stream in service of productive sense-making, and to find and enfranchise collaborators in the process.

Polymaths like Aristotle did exactly this, millennia ago.

All of us—not just the professionals we currently pay pittance to outsource our children's education—are responsible for maximizing human potential in every person, at every age.

Educators, families, employers, service providers and lawmakers each have a role in aiming individual and collective energy toward sense-making and synthesis. Respectively, these groups are responsible for teaching and connecting toolsets (educators), establishing moral and ethical frameworks (families), advancing direct contributions to the living world (employers), distributing resources (service providers), and ensuring that equitable access and protections are encoded in law (lawmakers), to ensure that everyone has a chance to maximize their contribution to their and others' thriving.

It's time for us to reinvent education, learning from our own long-term history to guide a new generation of polymaths, and our short-term past to avoid repeating the negative impacts of fragmented human activity.

All the answers are there. We simply need to synthesize them.

22 Learning Reboot

The Industrial model of education that fueled the modern era and its dizzying reach did its job incredibly well. Its prime accomplishment was the expansion of our ability to *abstract the world.* Until then pragmatism reigned, limiting most people's thoughts and interactions primarily because we lacked the time and tools to extrapolate information and wield it for things that lay beyond obvious applications.

That is, most humans couldn't see patterns behind inputs, because doing so required us to be able to entertain abstract concepts. And our education was what led us there.

If the idea that we were largely unable to see patterns sounds implausible to you, it did to me, too, until I read David Epstein's fascinating book, *Range: Why Generalists Triumph in a Specialized World.* Early on, he introduces us to **Raven's Progressive Matrices**: essentially the gold standard for general human intelligence tests, because it transcends education and culture.

Using Raven's Matrices, a New Zealand psychologist named James Flynn was the first person to amalgamate existing studies from around the world to test how results from Raven's Matrices changed over time. His discoveries in 1981, dubbed the Flynn Effect, proved across generations and nations that whether or not general scholastic intelligence climbed or fell, Raven's scores *always* went up.

In the Machine Age, for the very first time, the general workforces needed knowledge of STEM subjects in order to take advantage of new machines and work processes. This allowed us to extrapolate information from abstract concepts like math or scientific inquiry which we used to make sense of increased complexity.

Modern education introduced the public at large to things that had hitherto existed only in rare imaginations or in ivory towers. Most of these things had remained hidden from us because they required an abstract level of thinking that was never taught at large, but was now suddenly within the grasp of the masses. With modern educational pedagogy, it wasn't long until novel inventions began to blossom prodigiously.

That's not to say that invention or innovation began with the Industrial Revolution. It didn't. The Ancient Babylonians, Egyptians, Persians, Greeks, Romans, Ottomans and Anglo-Saxons were all wildly inventive. The difference was that in pre-modern times, education wasn't formalized, standardized, and democratized. The Machine Age, however, demanded it.

With some exceptions, the new education system was aimed at one end and one end only: specialization, necessitated by new complexity.

We remain there today.

Missing the Forest for the Trees

The learning systems that made societies like the Ancient Greeks so prolific as inventors of nearly every conceptual system that still underpins society today—medicine, ethics, philosophy, logic and democracy among them—bore no resemblance to our current educational paradigm. While Aristotle and Co. also excelled in abstraction, they used it to opposite ends from ours.

They *generalized* knowledge.

"Flynn's greatest disappointment," Epstein writes, *"is the degree to which society, and particularly higher education, has responded to the broadening of the mind* [under abstraction] *by pushing specialization, rather than focusing early training on conceptual, transferable knowledge."*

In other words, the abstraction that led to progress in the Modern Era also painted itself into a corner by removing the very quality that would allow us to escape the limits of our own inventions. This is because specialization is about the selective *removal* of variables in order to enable the deepening of a *singular* skill or expertise possible. The trade-off with this kind of training is that we become less able to engage in discussions about, or participate in, things that lie outside of our chosen area(s) of focus.

Not infrequently, specialists miss the forest for the trees. The expression, "To a hammer, everything is a nail," comes to mind.

In his writing, Flynn illustrates study after study, spanning nations and decades, in which the modern educational gift of abstraction—a transcendent sign of intelligence, as we saw in Raven's Matrices—has been squandered because we have aimed that broad potential to narrow ends. The reason we've done so is because modern society values predictable and monetizable outcomes above all (the kind that specialists excel in) over open-ended inquiry that may *someday* lead us *somewhere*.

Unfortunately, most schoolchildren are taught that the world is predictable. We teach *rules:* in language, biology, physics, history, chemistry and mathematics. Then we test for *fact retention*, or rote regurgitation. Thus our education system equips us well for things we have experienced before and expect to stay that way, while leaving us extremely ill-equipped for everything else. The modern world has demanded this of us.

Says Epstein:

> *"A rapidly changing 'wicked' world demands conceptual reasoning skills that can connect new ideas and work across contexts."*

Ready for Change

Today, we refer to the solution to our problems by many names: lateral, horizontal, divergent, or critical thinking. These differ from what is taught in most classroom settings—*convergent* thinking—insofar as the latter is *deductive* and focuses on driving toward a single, well-established answer, while the others are *generative* or *expansive* in that they resist conclusions in favor of exploration.

Most educational systems and the societies in which we are raised and taught downplay the importance of expansiveness, focusing instead on preparing students to differentiate themselves from future competitors by *out-mastering* them.

Post-school-age learning follows a similar trajectory, in which adults pay to specialize even further, for competitive advantage.

But, to paraphrase Jack Cecchini—one of the world's great multi-genre musicians—there is a huge difference between creation and *re-creation*.

Alas, specialization, it turns out, is the enemy of lateral thinking; and worse, it turns out that once our minds are hard-wired to specialize, it can be an uphill—even insurmountable—battle to grasp things that challenge our well-formed and deeply grooved beliefs. Said another way, rules thwart creativity.

Throughout his book Epstein introduces us to world-renowned musicians, scientists, and athletes, among others, taking us through their life journeys. With few exceptions, their trajectories follow a similar arc: those who *dabbled* the most early in life—who resisted depth in favor of open-ended and self-directed play, then chose to train their focus on one thing only later, and even then, never *exclusively*—invariably reached greater levels of virtuosity than those who didn't. Moreover, the self-directed group stayed at those heights even as the world changed around them. The early specialists didn't.

Importantly, that same group of creative dabblers were more often than not *innovators* within their chosen fields, as well—not just masters of a prevailing paradigm, the way their expert peers were.

Epstein believes we need to be taught is how to be ready for change in a quickly changing world—not how to dominate a field that may disappear overnight.

We'll do a deeper dive into this subject in the next chapter.

Intra-Disciplinary

The word "interdisciplinary" is a modern one. I've never liked it. Most of my colleagues use it daily as a badge of honor to describe how well we work together. But if we look beneath the obvious benefit of sharing skillsets in a genial and collaborative manner, the fact is that "interdisciplinary" was an idea borne out of the fact that we are no longer able to easily skate between knowledge sets, and thus require a *team* to solve the same problems we might have solved on our own before we turned our backs on general learning in favor of specialization.

Interdisciplinary teams, in the way that I see them, are a reminder of everything we've given up on the route to specialization. In my view, we'd be better served by a different goal. In lieu of seeking *inter*-disciplinary partnerships, we could instead aspire to reach **intra-disciplinary fluency**— that is, turning inward to cultivate our innate polymathic ability.

We could retool the primary and secondary educational paradigm to be intentionally broad and equally resistant to convergent thinking, leaving specialization to undergraduate or post-graduate education, as we do now. If we did, then every child would benefit from years of divergent thinking at the age of maximum neuroplasticity like the exemplars in Epstein's book, and *still* have the same choices they have today for those who elect a specific path.

If we developed an intra-disciplinary fluency, we would be better primed to solve "wicked" problems per se without regard for prevailing orthodoxies or rule sets of any kind. That's because knowledge sets are resources to draw upon, and the intersection *between* broad ones is where insight and innovation can be found.

Whether we do this solo or collaborate with others isn't the point. What is the point is that every person contributing to a creative problem would bring better contextual tools to the undertaking, allowing us to individually and collectively reach farther than we could by subdividing tasks and applying discrete lenses to the bits.

In the Industrial era, we have excelled in the creation of new *objects*. Ancient Greece, by contrast, excelled in the creation new *systems of thought*, as we saw in the last chapter.

My field of business is a complex one. Some buildings whose design I've led have required teams of 100 or more, sustained over a 5-plus year period, simply to *draw* works *on paper* that guide construction activities during which *hundreds more* might turn them into things we occupy and use. What makes me an effective leader is not any singular expertise. Rather, it is the ability to know *enough* about *enough* things, including each team member's *own* spheres of expertise, to best guide them and their teammates toward harmonic, and on occasion innovative, works of architecture.

In a way, my job to **design the system that leads to great outcomes**.

The ability to tackle problems from a variety of angles through broad learning and the playful trial and error that they precipitate seems to show up consistently among the most creative people in *any* field. And our education has not fully prepared us for this.

In the modern era, we have fallen out of love with polymathy—so much so that we frequently use its analogues as insults. "Amateur" and "jack of all trades (master of none)" are wielded largely to disparage or impugn people for lacking sufficient expertise to warrant our attention, or speak with *authority*.

When was the last time sportscasters brought in an engineer to comment on plays, or conference organizers invited a mathematician to opine on the latest political scandal, or the CDC brought in a philosopher to share her thoughts about COVID-19?

And yet: from Aristotle to Da Vinci to Newton to Darwin to Edison and beyond, these polymaths' outsize contributions to humanity (engineering, math and philosophy included) emerged from lives spent resisting depth in favor or indulging their curiosity wherever it took them, then building insights from the *outside*. In the process, they invented things in fields in which they had no standing, but which fields they transformed or *created*, nonetheless.

Self-Directed and Test-Free

Self-directed learning is another subject frequently touched upon in Epstein's book. Most of the stories he tells about various fields' brightest luminaries start in the very same place: with children who resisted being boxed in or told what to do, actively rejecting things that didn't interest them in favor of indulging their casual curiosity.

There's even a term for that: **interleaving**.

Interleaving "involves mixing together different topics or forms of practice in order to facilitate learning". Interleaving has been shown to improve *inductive* reasoning. While *deduction* is inference based on widely accepted facts, *induction* is inference based on observation alone—often just a sample. Said another way, deduction draws truths from facts. Induction questions the facts themselves.

While we may not want to build a rocket ship on induction alone, this type of "ballpark learning" allows broad threads to be pulled together into a gestalt whose end goal is contextual understanding.

Interleaving is how Darwin, an amateur naturalist, induced the principles of evolution. It's how Newton, an amateur scientist, induced the laws of thermodynamics, gravity among them. It's how Da Vinci invented scuba diving, the airplane and war machinery, while sneaking into graveyards to disinter bodies so that he could dissect them and understand how mechanics functioned.

Imagine if, instead of teaching Suzie and Jamal that 2+2=4, we told them to go home, gather groups of objects together, and work with their classmates to invent games with the goal of exchanging them. I think they'd learn math pretty quickly.

Whether or not that's a good illustration, I'm proposing a focus on investigation rather than conclusion. To teach question-seeking rather than answer-finding. To encourage children to explore their worlds *without regard for being "wrong"*, and to share the questions and thoughts that emerge from their activities; then to gather the collected reflections of the entire class as a pretext to structured learning.

The Japanese do just that. It's called **bansho**.

Bansho celebrates "the class's collective intellectual voyage, dead ends and all."

The prevailing Western educational paradigm, by contrast, and the parents who raise their children within it, teach and test for "right and wrong", rather than gray. In doing so, we lead children (and adults) toward efficient answers rather than effective questions; toward monetizing adulthood instead exploring childhood; toward guiding mastery over something that will differentiate them, in lieu of encouraging something that may have no clear application but could seed long-term resilience.

As Epstein's book cautions, the tide of rapid change is rising, and the one thing A.I. cannot yet do—and may never do—is draw *illogical* connections between seemingly unrelated (non-linear) things in ways that lead to novel strategies and solutions.

Learning, it turns out, benefits more from self-directed mistakes than it does from correct answers.

How? Cognitive psychologist Nate Kornell and psychologist Jane Metcalfe separately tested sixth-graders and ivy-league university students on vocabulary. They alternated between giving the students a definition and word together, or giving only the definition and asking the student to come up with the word themselves.

What they found was that "being forced to generate answers [on one's own] improves subsequent learning even if the generated answer is wrong." This is due to a *hypercorrection* effect. The more wrong the answer, the bigger the correction and the bigger the impact when the right answer is learned. They concluded that tolerating big mistakes can create the best learning opportunities.

To reprise the quote I shared in Chapter 9, when Edison was questioned about his missteps in creating the electric light, he said, "I have not failed 10,000 times. I've successfully found 10,000 ways that will not work."

I think we know how that one ended.

Final Thoughts

The prevailing pedagogy does us a disservice by being too fixated on the short-term conclusions we draw from what we're taught or otherwise learn, because our socio-economic value system demands it from us. It demands answers and certainty as the defining measures of human value.

If I'm not an expert, then what good am I to an employer, or the world for that matter?

What is my *purpose*?

Abstraction has led us to fantastic things: the creation of machines and systems our ancestors could only imagine. At the same time, our drive to specialize, as children and adults, has cheated us out of our full potential.

In a 21st century world, where A.I. and machines will increasingly outperform people on rote tasks, lateral thinking will add value and longevity to our productive lives. Like the Ancient Greeks before us and the polymaths who engaged their worlds with broadly applied curiosity rooted in ideation free of preconceptions, we would be well-served by guiding children and adults through a life of open-ended co-exploration.

Summing up his thoughts on the matter, Epstein cites Shinichi Suzuki, a grittily self-taught musician who nonetheless became a renowned music educator:

> *"Children do not practice exercises to learn to talk… children learn to read after their ability to talk has been well established."*

He's saying that humans are hard-wired to *act* first *then* learn from what we've already done. And yet: in schools, we do the opposite. The exercises come first in the hopes that they result in learning.

"In totality," Epstein writes, "breadth of training predicts breadth of transfer. That is, the more contexts in which something is learned, the more the learner creates abstract models, and the less they rely on any particular example. Learners become better at applying their knowledge to a situation they've never seen before, which is the essence of creativity."

It's time for learning to prepare us for the unknown. It's time for an education reboot.

Now let's discuss how we aim all that learning, as adults.

WORK:

Meaning and Cities

DEST Charleston. © Anthony Fieldman 2021

23 The Future of Work:
Self-Directed and Digital

Work is broken, in several ways. First, the places many of us spend most of our waking hours are frankly terrible. Second, the competition they fuel makes as many enemies as friends. And third, our relationships at work are invariably tainted by hierarchies and competing interests. The combination of these things—and seismic advances in remote access to key resources that put the power of a team in our phones or laptops—is why more people are fleeing the paradigm than ever before.

For more than a decade, I have consistently said that the future of work will be self-powered, ever-changing and decentralized, comprising a network of entrepreneurs who *collaborate dynamically*, rather than an assembly line of specialists who *produce linearly*.

I think centralized employment will likely go the way of the record: never quite gone, but relegated to specialized applications.

I came to those conclusions within days of launching my own company in 2012 at a NYC-based co-working innovation hub called NeueHouse. There, I was introduced to an ecosystem of fellow entrepreneurs I'd never have met if I'd simply leased space in a building and siloed my employees in our own little bubble, like nearly everyone other professional service company did, at the time.

Often, the lines blur between companies when you're in a multi-business environment that cultivates fluid connection and collaboration over rigid corporate orthodoxy. At NeueHouse, most days, what started as a social moment often evolved into a business opportunity *or vice versa*, as clients became friends, friends became collaborators, and some became all three.

The primary reason this happened is that none of us had any obligations to one another. There was no ladder to climb, no hierarchy to navigate, no conflicts of interest to solve, and no favors to curry. Everyone was on equal footing. Each of us had paid our dues to be there, and none of our successes depended on what the others did, *directly*. All that remained were people to meet, discoveries to be made, and relationships to be forged, by *choice*.

It was the best workplace I never knew was missing, until I had it.

Pretty much *everyone* loved it, from new graduates to titans of industry who had conventional offices elsewhere, but who nonetheless preferred NeueHouse's rich connectivity to their own siloed kingdoms.

I realized that the "office" was not only uninviting; it was a leftover from another era—one in desperate need of reinvention. It dawned on me that the concept of employment itself emerged in that same era—the Industrial Revolution—and that industrial methodologies, too, required a significant rethink.

Many people I speak with scoff at the idea that employment (by others) is dying. They point out that business is booming, that not everyone is cut out to be an entrepreneur, that there will always be leaders and followers, that job security matters to most, and that for many people, "work isn't everything", and they "just want a job".

Yes, yes, yes, yes and yes. But it's not that simple.

There are several forces that conspire to rewrite what work is, and we're already in the "initial thrust" phase of that particular rocket trip.

Why Work is Changing

Corporations face pressures that demand ever-increasing levels of efficiency, market share capture, and profitability. In this paradigm, employees are *resources first* and *people second*.

These metrics are an ever-tightening belt that demands continual "weight loss". As such, corporations can't help but streamline or automate the jobs they can, cut costs everywhere possible, and even reconsider full-time employment altogether, with its expensive benefits programs, comp time, and absenteeism.

Even before the pandemic super-charged the phenomenon, there was a huge increase over the preceding decade in people working part-time because they wanted to. The allure of working for a single company full-time is eroding. A key reason for this is that there's been a wholesale change in incentive—the "why" of work. For many, employment is becoming more closely aligned to—and driven by—their values. That is, work is decreasingly "work" and increasingly "the means by which they practice what fulfills them".

For white-collar workers, especially, human flourishing has increasingly replaced productivity as the modus operandi of work. That is, work is being influenced by *values*, and values are sticky. When given the opportunity, we now live our values at play, at work and with family. We increasingly live in one bucket.

Consider the following statistics:

- Before tariff wars and global gyrations led to "job hugging", 85% of U.S. employees planned to quit within six months, in 2023[269]
- As a result of uncertainty, 65% of employees in 2024 felt "stuck"—as in, unable change jobs, even if they wanted to[270]
- "Productivity anxiety" now affects 80% of the workforce[271]
- This has led to "quiet cracking" i.e.: worker disengagement, costing the world $438 billion in lost productivity, in 2024[272]
- 81% of U.S. adults were worried about losing their job, in 2025[273]

Since the onset of COVID-19, the data has consistently trended toward increased dissatisfaction, disengagement, and/or job stresses within the workforce. What the statistics suggest is that the existing paradigm of work is no longer working for sizable subset of people.

What one does for work is increasingly a reflection of self. And self is non-transferable. Values can be shared between people, but how we apply them varies greatly and evolves alongside us. Work has nearly always consisted of some form of give and take—of negotiation and teamwork. However, because the definition of work has grown to more strongly reflect our values, and because we now have powerful toolsets, technologies, and collaborators at our disposal, I believe that the future of work will look like a dynamic network in which we assemble for a discrete period of time to achieve a specific outcome, whether that's out of pure convenience, or better, the alignment of values.

How we aim our energies toward productivity will, I believe, become increasingly dynamic. Simply put, feeling fulfilled will likely play an increasing role in our choices, as the available toolsets continue to empower us.

The Future of Work, by the Numbers

The data suggests that self-directed work is here to stay. Consider the following statistics shared by April Rinne in her mind-expanding and empowering book, *Flux*:

- Since 2008, 94% of net new job creation in the United States has been part-time work or self-employment
- Independent workers and freelancers are growing at three times the rate of the rest of the labor force
- By 2019, 35% of the entire American workforce were freelancers
- By 2027, it is expected that freelancers will outnumber employees
- 77% of full-time freelancers report having better work-life balance
- 90% of all freelancers say the best days are ahead of them

Rinne provides other statistics that are accelerating this trend:

- 43% of recent college grads hold jobs that don't require a college degree
- Nearly 67% of recent college grads remain *underemployed* after five years

All of these stats *preceded* the pandemic. Consider the possibility that work, by which we define where, to what and when we contribute our energies to earn money, has changed drastically since COVID-19 unmoored so many of us. Consider as well that a large contingent of the work force doesn't go into a workplace at all, goes far less often, or only does when they're *willing to.*

Overnight, because of COVID-19, for many of us, our workplaces became our computers and phones, at least during the acute phase of the pandemic. Six years later, the genie is *still* out of the bottle, and dancing. Work, for a large contingent of the 58% of Americans who qualify as "professionals,"[274] is now increasingly something we can take with us, *anywhere.*

On the flip side, and compounding the issue, the professional sector is shrinking for the first time. In 2024, 1 in 4 jobs lost were in that sector, many to A.I.; and a large number of knowledge workers in the most affected fields are having a hard time finding work.[275] In Chapter 25, we will revisit this subject in detail.

Cue the digital nomad.

Temporary? Likely not. Some of us—myself included—believe a majority of people will never return to work full time, and that a large chunk of those may never return at all. In my own 600-person design studio, my partners and I initially presented our employees with 3 choices following COVID-19's lockdowns: **remote** (<1 day/week in the studio), **hybrid** (2–3 days), or **full-time** (4–5 days). We decided we would give everyone agency in their own lives. The feedback blew us away. Fewer than 8% of our staff—one in twelve—opted to return "full time". Moreover, most of those were my partners—a decidedly empowered demographic. 70% chose "hybrid", while the remaining 22%—one in five—chose never to return.

Several years later, it is still largely their choice; and though we *expect* people to work in person at least three days a week now [on which, it must be said, we don't *all* agree], we have allowed many to decamp to other states or even countries and continue their employ with us, from wherever they feel most fulfilled.

It's entirely conceivable that full-time mandated work will become the exception to the rule in the near term, and that everyone (read: big business) just hasn't gotten the memo.

The biggest exceptions to this trend are in healthcare, education, construction and retail, for now. And even those fields are in jeopardy of going increasingly virtual, and separately, increasingly technological. We'll discuss this last point in the final chapter.

Final Thoughts

From robots that operate, and A.I. that diagnoses illnesses, to storied educational institutions that deliver content online at a sliding scale of costs [these are called "Zombie colleges" for their physical closure and online rebirth—a growing trend[276]], to factory and in-situ robots that construct our buildings safely, to retail kiosks that make our coffee, and fulfillment bots that send our Amazon wares to our homes, the transformation is just beginning, and will likely only accelerate.

The shifts from employee to independent contractor, from office to home (or beach), and from human to A.I. workforce would *each* be seismic impact. Together, they spell out a potential rewrite of work as we know it and open the door to transformational creativity for those brave enough to take matters into their own hands and create their future.

Already, a near-majority of the workforce is doing just that. With 94% of all job growth being part-time and freelance growing at 3x the rate of conventional employment, that particular debate is now moot.

All of it points toward two things: a future in which individuals are increasingly the captains of our own ships; and an expanding amount of work moving online to avail itself of global resources, including collaboration and customer networks.

We are in the infancy of these things, yet the pace of change is astonishing. Companies that have doubled down on bricks and mortar workplaces without adequate investment in decentralized online platforms will plausibly experience increased pressures to compete for people and market share. If that happens, power will continue to shift downward and outward, whether through shared ownership of companies with full-time employees or the continued "freelancification" of the workforce.

The real question is: what will our downtowns look like, once the workplaces are (mostly) gone?

24 Where We Will Work: City 3.0 – A Vision

If the office is broken and dying (I think it is), what will replace it? And what will we do with all that empty space?

This chapter outlines a personal vision of what cities *could* look like in the context of municipal governance that leads with optimism as a driving force of decision-making, based on the premise that "abundance" is no longer a *speculative* ideal but a technically feasible condition; and that it is primarily blocked by outdated incentives, political capture, and unexamined human fear. As such, I sometimes use declarative words like "will" instead of "could" to bolster the vision, which I believe is eminently achievable with the right framework.

We may finally be on the doorstop of just such a revolution.

The Central Business District (or CBD) was an outcome of the Industrial Era's focus on financial productivity. All CBDs are recognizable by their skylines: towers thrust upward—punctuations in largely horizontal landscapes—huddled together to maximize the density of nestled and stacked human beings toiling away to achieve peak output for economic gains.

Inside they are often dystopian, comprised of repetitive work pods made of industrial materials, and glistening under the hum of fluorescent lighting. No one would choose to spend time in them if they had a choice (they do now; thank you, COVID). Foosball tables notwithstanding, most offices were never designed with people in mind, but for our capacity and willingness to function like machinery in environments that fuel it, performing repetitive on-demand acts—ad infinitum—to stoke the global economy.

The "office" is just a clean factory.

The lingua franca of the planet's humans today is economics. Its lexicon consists of words everyone understands because they largely drive human behavior, and most non-social interaction. There are literally hundreds of terms that comprise the de facto language of human energy. And simply put, buildings that see humans as engines of economic capital are primarily designed to optimize for that.

I came to this conclusion as an architect who authored several of these monuments and whose colleagues designed countless more during the large portion of my career that I spent employed by three of the planet's largest design firms.

CBDs were designed as paeans to human industriousness. Towers of Babel, they reached to the sky as proof positive that captains of industry were gods, and that their command over a portion of the human world was worth memorializing, and announcing to the world.

Enter COVID-19

It took no more than a few weeks to send everyone home, apart from those who had sworn to uphold public safety and essential wellbeing. What happened next surprised all of us. The economic universe didn't collapse. What *did* happen is that for the first time since the Industrial Revolution cratered the once-dominant "cottage industry", most humans began working again amid plush furnishings made of natural materials, and under soft- or day-lighting, surrounded by things (and often people) that duly reflected the lives they had *chosen for themselves* when they weren't at work.

It's called "home".

And they liked it.

Our homes are a reflection of what buttresses our emotional and social wellbeing. For sure, they are limited (or enabled) by our access to capital and to the ages, demands and decibel levels of the "other occupants": our dependent-age children, and/or partners. But the choices we make at home, within our means, are made for one reason only: to support our thriving.

So, why don't workplaces look or feel like home? For one category of the workplace, the better ones increasingly do. These are called co-working spaces, and they represent the most recent major leap in workplace design—now just a decade-and-a-half old. At Soho Works, NeueHouse, Industrious, the Battery, or scores of others, we would be hard-pressed to tell the difference between them and well-appointed living space; or at least, a cozy boutique hotel.

They feel *great*.

Beyond aesthetics, the allure of co-working is fed by three forces. The first of these is our digital autonomy, which allows a now-majority of the labor force to work from anywhere. This phenomenon is increasing with the continued growth of the service economy, which in its entirety now comprises 79% of all U.S. workers.[277] The second force is our core social need to build community. More on this below. And the third force spurring change is the stratospheric rise of self-employment. As we saw in the last chapter, this accounts for 94% of all new jobs, at three times the growth rate of conventional employment. Accordingly, the demand for places where people can work *without costly or inflexible overhead* is increasing.

Consider the following:

- The co-working 'footprint' has doubled in three years at a pace that keeps accelerating,[278] and now comprises 8,400-plus U.S. locations totaling 150 million sq. ft.[279]
- While office demand shrinks, co-working is growing robustly[279]
- As of late 2025, 41% of employees would not *consider* jobs that don't offer remote work[280]

The writing is on the wall for full-time employees, as well:

- Despite the COVID-19 pandemic, JLL predicts 30% of all office space will be consumed flexibly by 2030[281]
- 58% of CBRE respondents are either exploring or executing more flexible expansion/contraction options for their office needs[282]
- 35% of 2025 World Economic Forum survey respondents (comprising employers, organizations, and employees) support changes to labor laws related to remote work[283]
- In 2025, Pew Research found that 34.5% of all workers would quit their

jobs if told to return to office full time[284]

The Fifteen-Minute City

As convenient as home is, what it doesn't do is build community. The better co-working spaces offer great tech, great food, work-and-social events, and people to meet: new friends, collaborators, and/or clients. At NeueHouse, which I've discussed, and whose own global expansion I also helped its founders explore, I met all three. Frankly, it was so good and filled so many needs, I was loathe to leave it, but for the fact that my team outgrew it.

At NeueHouse, I had found my "third place".

The downside to co-working facilities today is that they are still mostly centralized rather than spread out to better meet local needs, within walking distance of home. That is, there are still too few of them to serve a truly distributed workforce. Nearly six years after so many of us sequestered in our homes for varying amounts of time, a large share of the workforce *just isn't willing* to submit to pre-pandemic office life, at least partly because the "office" always sucked.

With too-few people willing to re-commit to long commutes to expensive CBDs just to spend their days in sterile work environments, and unable to move flexibly between home and nearby work to attend to a variety of personal needs that support their wellbeing, I would submit that the future of work—the future of communities, really—will quite likely evolve into "**fifteen-minute cities**".

Also called "complete communities", the fifteen-minute city, first envisioned by French-Colombian scientist Carlos Moreno, has been described as a "return to a local way of life", where home, work, and play all converge within walking distance.

We used to call these things villages. In them, relationships ran deep because they played host to home, work, and play; because the quality of the neighborhood impacted all of its members; and because we saw the same people day in and day out, drawing us closer together, if for no reason other than increased social overlap (i.e.: fewer degrees of separation).

An increasing number of commercial developers are looking to capitalize on the fifteen-minute city phenomenon, as priorities shift from job-seeking to life-balancing. Millions of people are leaving careers—and money on the table—for a greater life-work balance. Many are prioritizing fulfillment over structures that maximize income.

This is a *massive* shift from the Industrial Model, and a welcome one.

As I noted in the last chapter, prior to the current "job hugging" panic set in, 85% of U.S. employees planned to quit within six months due in part to an increase in values-driven choices. There is no reason to believe that at least *some* won't do just that, as soon as fears subside.

The chief cost to retooling cities will likely be in "de-infrastructuring" the CBD, to borrow a term from the Urban Land Institute (ULI). And so, to mitigate the abandonment of large chunks of infrastructure, CBDs may be forced into post-business makeovers, while bedroom communities simultaneously undergo "post-home" ones, too. If this happens, the largely 20th century phenomenon of single-function districts will likely be remade into complete communities, catering to a full life at the scale of the pedestrian, with each neighborhood reflecting the cultural micro-climates of their residents.

In this new paradigm, the "CBD" will lose its "C" and its "B".

The No-Longer-Central, No-Longer Business-Fueled District

The future of neighborhood-centric workplaces will likely look a lot like the co-working spaces of today, but will be sized for neighborhoods and cater to local needs and interests with culturally inflected social programs, food and beverage, and other services that support the community. At the same time, the future of giant office towers in former CBDs will need to look very, very different if they are to draw a reluctant workforce to their distant doors.

More on this shortly.

Before we head downtown, let's review how co-working spaces will operate in the neighborhoods. For this to work at scale, with choice in each neighborhood, third-party companies specializing in hospitality will increasingly build and operate a network of work-and-play spaces to cater to the needs of a distributed workforce, not unlike several "third place" food and beverage operators do today. These will presumably offer tiers of membership, from local to regional access, and plausibly also provide special (and more costly) resources in discrete locations, of which members can avail themselves if they are willing to travel to use them. We all do this regularly when we seek food, entertainment, or special services, today.

This idea—special offerings—is likely to be the impetus behind the future of CBD-centric "headquarters" for the still-employed. Rather than providing places to work, employment motherships would do well to become places where employers focus on building community and culture, because these are the primary qualities within companies that are truly "sticky": meaning, things that keep people inspired and aligned.

Angela Ahrendts, then SVP of Retail at Apple, was the first to realize that with the demise of brick-and-mortar's primacy, the future of retail was no longer necessarily driven by direct sales, but rather as places to provide brand-enhancing education and culture. Apple doesn't care where you buy its gizmos. It mostly cares that you feel supported in your needs, which it does by minimizing frustration with its Genius Bars, and by allowing Apple to provide a foundational (and self-serving) education that *empowers you in your purpose*, both online and in in-store Discovery Centers.

So, too, must the office evolve, really, from a place where work gets done (many of us can increasingly work *anywhere*, just as we can buy Apple products *anywhere*) to one where culture and community are built around things that engender and galvanize both.

In my vision of it, the "office" will be rebranded as "experience center". It will be mostly opt-in, food-centered (free lunch!) and a programming-rich environment with too-good-to-ignore tech, where participants willing to commute to them can share an experience that reinforces the values of the business, and that they can't duplicate at or near home. No doubt these will be aimed at building skillsets, inspiring the workforce, and creating opportunities for unscripted interactions—water cooler talk—to coalesce.

Because headquarters will be smaller, in my conception of them, many would be well served moving downstairs, in whole or in part, into all of those empty retail shops that Amazon and other online businesses have been decimating.

High-touch, high-food, and high-tech, these new experience centers could be Apple store-like, whether or not they sell products. Hands-on workshops, inspirational guest speakers, and committed mentors could help employees improve business acumen, bond, and grow.

As I see it, those who do these things first will retain their employees *better*, while those who don't will be saddled by expensive and empty infrastructure, a dwindling workforce, and an inability to compete.

While the sweeping vision I'm laying out for the future of work may take decades to replace what we have, the transformation is underway nonetheless because eventually, the *majority* and *laggards* will catch up to wherever the *innovators* and early *adopters* are taking us, as Everett Rogers' use of the bell curve has proven time and again.

I believe employees' visits to HQ will bring co-employed people together episodically, while their local co-working community will bring them into contact with people in *other often complementary or collaborative businesses* far more frequently—perhaps daily, or several times a week, for an hour or all day. The richness of flexibility and interactions there will provide members with natural and elastic networks, which should be of interest to *any* company.

Businesses hoping to retain their employees could buy "hours" or "seats" from these third-party providers, to support a workforce where it chooses to be. Many already are. According to *Fortune Business Insights'* 2025 analysis[285]:

"Globally, major companies have moved many of their employees to co-working office spaces, including Bank of America, Ernst & Young, Facebook, HSBC, IBM, Jaguar Land Rover, Microsoft, Salesforce, Shell Global, Starbucks, and UBS."

Moreover, market share for co-working—or "the global flexible office market", as some officially call it—"is projected to grow from USD 45.24 billion in 2025 to USD 136.46 billion by 2032, exhibiting a CAGR of 17.08% over the forecast period," according to that same report.

The "office" as such, whether it's in CBDs, in neighborhoods, or in homes, will plausibly coalesce into a constellation of spaces from which we can dynamically contribute our professional energies.

With an increasing number of empty office towers flooding the market, some will convert to residential to house increasingly mixed communities, and prices will likely reflect the glut. They already are. As we discussed in Chapter 19, the primary idea being floated in cities across the U.S. and Canada, in the context of a cratering asset class, is to convert end-of-life, mostly Class B and C office towers into residential high-rises.

As these are far denser than horizontal neighborhoods, residents of to-be-former CBDs could benefit from more robust entertainment offerings—restaurants, bars, stores, and other cultural assets—that cater to people who value and prioritize these things, as so many urbanites do. New York City is the obvious existing exemplar, when it comes to high-rise residences.

But not all office towers will lend themselves to conversion, as we've discussed, nor will the market demand support it. Here, other uses will have to be imagined. These could include vertical entertainment centers (like Hong Kong's Times Square Building in Causeway Bay—the world's first "vertical mall" covering *nine floors*, and a favorite venue of mine when I lived there); farming skyscrapers (they're coming! see Chapter 19) and even "parks with a view", as the public realm moves truly vertically for the first time, comprising **self-contained "five-minute cities" at the speed of an elevator**, the likes of which were illustrated a century ago, then again in the '70s, in architectural luminary Rem Koolhaas's seminal book *Delirious New York*.

Today, four such "parks" that I know of (two very high, and two low, but still elevated) are drawing legions of visitors, for no other reason than they're *delightful* spaces to stroll, sit, or enjoy a drink or swim. One is the Marina Bay Towers, in Singapore. I'll admit to skepticism upon seeing it published. Nonetheless, it was one of the most memorable afternoons I can recall spending "in" a building, sitting poolside, drink in hand, people-watching some 55 stories above the fray. Likewise with San Francisco's Salesforce Park's

5.4 acres of amphitheaters, trails, playgrounds and a gondola in the sky. NYC's High Line—one of the city's top ten tourist attractions—and Hudson Yards' Edge—the highest observation deck in the Western Hemisphere and home to pop-up yoga sessions and DJ concerts—round out my perfunctory list.

There are doubtless many others. The point is, the right kind of innovation transforms communities *and* draws people for no other reason than they're *fun*.

The Big Crunch

The reason CBDs will transform isn't *only* because we can create a better model of living, or even because people are no longer commuting regularly to work. In most cases, it certainly doesn't *feel* as though people aren't commuting anymore. In the cities I frequent—New York, Toronto, and San Francisco, primarily—traffic is frankly getting worse. But the numbers don't lie, and the statistics are jarring.

The primary catalyst of CBD change will flow from the fact that a fifth of all office space in the United States is already empty. While everyone's crystal balls differs in the details, a recent report by Bloomberg forecasts office vacancy to rise to one quarter of *all* supply by 2026, wiping out $250 billion in commercial property value.[287]

Today, large office buildings are being shed by owners whose debt now exceeds the value of their assets. In fact, 44% of all loans on commercial office buildings are now in "negative equity", according to a 2024 paper by the National Bureau of Economic Research[288] I've seen reports of *many* buildings selling for as little as 10¢ on the dollar from their valuation less than a decade earlier.

And so, it's not just because enough people are choosing *not* to commute for enough days of the week that downtowns are cratering. In my view, it's a wholesale reappraisal of what daily life is meant to look like—or at least, *could* look like—if our communities better reflected our ideals. While the pandemic may have been the catalyst (it was), the gyrations are now working their way through the system, and the opportunities to remake cities (curbside dining instead of parked cars, anyone?)[289] are here, and in severe need of triage.

An increasing number of humans are regaining the upper hand in how we aim our energies and days toward finding and expressing shared values domestically, commercially, and communally.

The office is dead. Long live the human.

Defining City 3.0

To understand where we're going, we need to revisit where we've been, and why. It's worth an abbreviated history lesson to set the context.

City 1.0

The city's origins were humble. It was all about food. Until 12,000 years ago, for all of human existence, we lived in Dunbar-sized groups of 100–150 stable members comprised of people we knew and trusted; and we foraged and hunted for food, like every other animal.

The early rise of agriculture in the fertile river valleys of Mesopotamia, India, China and Egypt thousands of years ago changed that, allowing us to produce, gather, and store prodigious amounts of surplus food for the first time. Suddenly, the small tribes of trusted members we lived among were supplanted by large swarms of transacting strangers to manage the bounty. Mistrust ensued, which precipitated the invention of systems for cooperation and governance. Divisions of labor, infrastructure, laws, and narrative identities were all created to aim and align human activity among strangers.

As so-called "city-states" stabilized, some blossomed into empires, empowering them to prey on the bounty of weaker sovereign states. The Sumerian and Egyptian Empires were the first. In time, they gave rise to the empires of Persia, Greece, Rome, China, the Indus, and much later, the Khmer, Mongols, Aztecs, Incas, and a few hundred others.

Two hundred years ago, it all changed.

City 2.0

City 2.0 was incubated over the course of two Industrial Revolutions. New and complex tools required specialized workers, who in turn could earn more by participating than they could as farmers and cottage workers. As we saw in Chapters 20 thru 22, economics were the de facto engine of City 2.0.

For the first time in human history, productivity was no longer limited by the human body. Fueled by powerful machines and the people who operated them, cities boomed.

The invention of capitalism—an ideology born in the fertile imagination of Scottish economist Adam Smith—coincided with this period. In fact, these two things depended on one another to succeed. As the history books show, Smith envisioned an underclass of "laborers" that could be held down by low wages to boost productivity and profit, and to give rise to a wealthy "master class" of industrialists. Class divisions increased dramatically under capitalism, and it remains that way today.

The "invisible hand" of competition and demand in Smith's "free market" was, in reality, a steady stream of workers who were forced to accept tiny wages, immensely bad working conditions, and long work hours to afford basic food and shelter necessities.

City 2.0 is largely the product of Smith's vision. Until then, urbanization was *flat* throughout history. For centuries, less than 10% of the world lived in cities.[290] In a single generation, Smith's *The Wealth of Nations* was published, the Spinning Jenny, the Iron Smelter and the Steam Locomotive were all invented, and cities exploded with growth.

To say it again, more than half of the world now lives in one, while in the US, that number is 79%. The United Nations projects that by 2050, two third of humans worldwide will likely be urbanized.[291]

City 3.0 – A Long-Term Vision

That projection may not become reality. And if it does, it will likely look very different from how the UN and everyone else might have imagined it, just a few years back.

City 3.0 was born exactly six years ago, when the world shut down, sending workers home. Until then, the engine of City 2.0 had been jobs, even though many workers hated city life.

The post-war birth of the suburb was American workers' attempt to have their cake and eat it, too. By living "in nature" and commuting (though in reality, suburbs are anything but natural), people could spend weekdays where the jobs demanded and weekends and evenings wherever they wished, within commuting limits.

In 2013, a staggering 86% of Americans commuted to work by car, according to the US Census Bureau. That's a cumulative 29.6 billion hours, per year, in America alone.[292]

In New York, until March 2020, one million of these day workers coursed in and out of the city, every day. All of a sudden, it stopped. As we all know now, suburbanites stayed home as cities went on lockdown, worldwide. Traffic dried up, trains sat empty, and work goods—printers, chairs, desks and high-def cameras—became as rare as hand sanitizer, as work went remote.

In just days, only "essential workers" whose job it was to treat, feed people, or deliver things were moving around. Without the dynamism of city life, swaths of the "bricks and mortar" economy cratered.

Well, as I've proposed at length here, I think it's never going back to how it was.

That's because COVID-19 didn't *create* this situation. It just *accelerated* a trend that was already gathering steam.

The Internet, with limitless resources and global connectivity, has long made it possible to decouple work and the office. The Digital Age has fed a massive expansion of self-employment, as we've seen. And yet, before capitalism took over, self-employment was the *default.*

To repeat a statistic, today over one-third of the U.S. workforce is already self-employed and has grown by 50% in the last decade alone. In the U.K., it grew by 88% in fifteen years.[293] Everywhere, it seems, self-employment is increasing, dramatically.

The gig economy was already bound to be the future of work, in my view, for two likely reasons: the wild growth in self-employment strongly suggests it; and many whose work requires a physical presence—such as hospitality, healthcare, and education—are increasingly leaving those jobs for more remote-friendly options.

The Great Resignation was highest in these sectors;[294] and retaining and attracting workers has become more acute in industries and locations that cannot offer as much remote work due to job constraints.[295]

So, what will happen to all that real estate, and to streets that are suddenly free of traffic, blaring horns and pollution? Why move to—or even stay in—a city at all, if its primary draw—economics—is now increasingly moot?

Many people will leave cities for good, and overall, I believe, they will shrink. I have friends who have already decamped to the Adirondacks, Charleston, Costa Rica, Mexico, Connecticut and Bali, effectively choosing to live where they want, and adjusting their work circumstances to suit the environment.

This directly contravenes a two-hundred-year trend.

Most white collar workers will likely remaining in cities, but in my view, it will be for a desired *lifestyle* instead of *employment*.

We will revisit this idea in the next and final chapter.

Regardless, if the city isn't a jobs engine, then what exactly is it?

There are many answers, but I believe the city will remain strong. And to everyone's benefit, it will *have* to evolve it in order for it to succeed in its new role(s).

Creative Density

A rich exchange of ideas is the de facto source of innovation. Creative hubs like Industry City, Newlab, the Starrett-Lehigh Building, the Brooklyn Navy Yards and the Made In New York Campus, among many others, are as much what makes New York City what it is, as anything, these days. The rising creative class, powered by tech and one another, intuitively coalesce into clusters because that's what fuels their creative reach.

Cities, therefore, will continue to attract people because of *other people* with whom they can build relationships, share resources, and incubate ideas in an era of rapid innovation and unbound creativity.

We are social creatures, to our cores. For as difficult as the trade-offs of city living have been in the modern era, they are a wellspring of rich social, creative exchange. There is no force on Earth that will change that.

Culture Vultures

It's not just for work that cities will continue to thrive. As I mentioned earlier, the biggest ones have long been centers of culture—places where the arts flourish, like live music (Austin), theatre (London), fine arts (New York), museums (Mexico City), the spoken word (San Francisco), culinary arts (Kyoto), fashion (Milan), nightlife (Berlin), and so on. Cities will remain magnets for those seeking to learn, collaborate, be inspired, or simply enjoy the fruits of others' creative labors, as part of an audience. The cultural landscapes in cities will likely deepen and become a larger part of cities' identities, as economy workers flee.

To expand on this idea, let's look at the "mean streets" era of New York. The City's most financially downtrodden decades, fueling countless cautionary tales and plummeting population, was also arguably *the most socially and creatively dense time in the city's history*, giving birth to many of the legacies we all still talk about, when we conjure thoughts of the Big Apple in our minds.

A brief appraisal tells the story:

There was **CBGB's**, founded in 1973, birthing the careers of Patty Smith, Blondie, and the Ramones; **Max's Kansas City**, which hit its fever pitch in the 70's as home to art powerhouses Andy Warhol, John Chamberlain, Robert Rauschenberg, Larry Rivers, Robert Smithson, Donald Judd, Richard Serra, Dan Flavin and Donald Judd; literary icons William S. Burroughs and Allen Ginsburg; and musical legends Lou Reed and the Velvet Underground. Then, there was **Studio 54**, birthed in 1977: the single most legendary nightclub in history. The list is too long to include here, but everybody who was anybody was there, sometimes naked on horseback, at the greatest party on Earth. Owner Ian Schrager said it was like "standing on stardust", and it left glitter that could be found months later in attendees' clothing and homes. Finally, there was **the Bronx**. Journalist Will Hermes described the era thus: "Kool Herc, Afrika Bambaataaa, and Grandmaster Flash hot-wired street parties with collaged shards of vinyl LPs."[296] There, they invented the first real, ultimately global, new music genre, in ages: **Rap**. Its influence on the world of fashion, music, language, and culture is perhaps the biggest cross-cultural phenomenon to come out of New York to date.

And this was during New York's undisputed economic *nadir;* all to say, more often than not and perhaps, invariably, culture thrives in the context of upended norms, as extreme forces give birth to the new.

Which is precisely what's happening around the world, *right now*.

Car-free

Morgan Stanley found that cars are used on average just 4% of the time and cost owners $9,000 a year.[297] The age of car ownership is, I'd wager, nearly over. Ride share options like Uber and Lyft, and on-demand rentals like Zipcar and CitiBike, among others, will combine with "clean tech" like zero-emission and driverless vehicles (hello, Waymo!) to make self-driving, pollution, and gridlock all a thing of the past, just as soon as we can get humans out of the driver seat.

It's not just companies like Tesla and Rivian, or conventional automakers' increasingly electric fleets, whose near- or fully self-driving cars are moving the industry toward autonomy. Alphabet (Waymo), Avride (with Uber), Amazon (Zoox), Aptiv (Motional, in partnership with Hyundai), Baidu (Apollo Go), Intel (Mobileye), and other tech players are also investing heavily in this space.

In 2015, a Columbia University study showed that "with a fleet of just 9,000 autonomous cars, Uber could replace every taxicab in New York City, and that passengers would wait an average of 36 seconds for a ride that costs about \$0.50 per mile.[297] The convenience and low cost will plausibly make car ownership less attractive, while a "transportation cloud" could quickly become the dominant form of movement."

Price Waterhouse Coopers has predicted that a staggering 99% of cars could come off the road in this scenario.[297] If so, or if even *half* of that were to happen, traffic would crater in cities. With enough of a reduction, the presence of parking, traffic signals, greenhouse gases, delays and parking lanes could all be reduced drastically, if not effectively disappear. In that scenario, emergency vehicle responsiveness would improve drastically, and the majority of motor vehicle deaths and injuries would plummet.

Urban Farming

Food production, as we saw in Chapters 18 and 19, would become hyper-local, in my vision of City 3.0. It would take over underutilized rooftops and also go vertical, in garages and former office buildings everywhere. Our all-season, soil-free, and indoor food supply, at scale, would catalyze the reduction of our carbon footprint dramatically, while freshness, nutrient quality and shelf life would all increase. In the presence of these forces, the cost to market would continue to plummet as techniques and scale evolved, and like Ford, we would ideally pass on the savings to those who eat it, limiting our greed in service of our collective thriving.

Courageous politicians and lawmakers could enable, subsidize, or enforce it.

Delivery Network

With the low cost and high convenience of on-demand, at-grade travel, the entire underbelly of the city—the subway system—could be adapted into a network for commercial and retail deliveries, finally taking trucks off a largely pedestrianized streetscape. These subterranean fleets could feed a distributed network of holding facilities for local pick up, or use human and robotic couriers to bridge depot and doorstep, mostly underground.

In 2017, Amazon filed a patent for this exact thing.[298] In spite of it, though, they weren't first to market. In 2023, a startup called Pipedreams launched the world's first underground autonomous robot delivery system, in Atlanta, proving that pipe dreams can in fact be realized.[299] I would be shocked if others don't follow.

So what would we do with all that newly available public space?

The public realm—streets, sidewalks, etc.—comprise roughly 50% of any city's footprint. With 99% fewer cars on the roads—or half that reduction—the city's most drastic makeover could take place there.

The street could belong, once again, to the pedestrian. New York's High Line points to one version of what streets could begin to look like. Asphalt would no longer be king. Every road could become a plaza, a park, or a playground of sorts; and like 12,500 restaurants in New York City during the pandemic, sidewalk dining could supercharge the public realm *and* the economy, given that the city's "COVID experiment" generated $370 million of new wages and 12,000 new jobs.[300]

The street could look a lot like old Europe.

Right-Sizing

In the long term, cities will shrink, I believe, since people who otherwise don't like city living won't need to stay. This is a cataclysmic change for the "Smithian Faithful"—the capitalists—who see cities as engines of economic growth rather than places for people.

Regardless, for those who remain, the draw will increasingly become one of *choice* rather than one of forced drudgery.

That means that cities will no longer be the only—or even prime— economic engines anymore. A global fragmentation of the workforce will allow people to choose the beach or the forest over the concrete jungle. Like a snowshoe, the workforce will be distributed, everywhere.

Smaller, globally wired communities heretofore mostly seen in hyper- wealthy enclaves could arise broadly for the first time since before City 1.0, as like-minded, Dunbar- or even Mondragón-sized groups pool resources to live with the land, rather than against it. They would transact with the rest of the world digitally, as Hall's Civium Project and Kosters' Edge City, both discussed in Chapter 13, have proposed. Other so-called Game-B communities,[301] the likes of which are being pioneered in online fora, could incubate new models of living, enabled by digital ubiquity.

All to say, cities would do well to become more livable in their bid for post-CBD relevance, as the commercial tax base dries up. The public realm, the cultural landscape, the institutions that support quality living, and ultimately, the cost of living itself—equity and affordability—are all ripe for improvement and may well have to evolve, *if* the city is to survive these changes.

Once the CBD is no longer king, cities will have to adapt, or die.

To be clear, I am not saying the city will no longer be an economic engine, or that people will not live there to work for a company that insists their employees show up, in person, five days a week. I *am* saying that this is a dying model. That eventually, the late majority and laggards will be forced to accept that a five-day office job is a vestige of another era. That CBDs everywhere will take a major hit, and are already being re-distributed, courtesy of the Great Resignation, which saw 98.3 million Americans—one third of the total workforce—quit for a better fit, and redistribute themselves in what we could easily call a "Great Migration", too. That we will have choices to make. And that the primary value proposition of cities will move from purely economic to something more overtly social and cultural.

Community

Larger residential (multi-family) buildings could finally become true micro-communities, inside of which intentionally social amenities deepen bonds between residents while tempering anonymity in the process. Spaces for intrinsically participatory activities like gardening, cooking, maker spaces, and co-working, among existing luxe offerings like on-site playrooms, barbecue pits, and dog runs, could emerge to finally engender successful vertical living communities, rather than boxes in the sky full of strangers. Through these new connections, riding the elevator could *finally* feel less awkward, and because enough of our neighbors would no longer be strangers, we would spend less time staring at the floor indicators or our phones to avoid too-common feelings of discomfort. Buildings could also share access to resources with one another to bridges *between* micro-communities.

Net-Positivity

Finally, the truly sustainable city is nigh, and it's super-green. The Paris Agreement was just one high-profile initiative. While legally binding, it operates nationally. Solutions will need to be more granular, and more responsive.

The C40 Cities Climate Leadership Group is a collection of 97 cities worldwide representing one ninth of the world's population. C40 is more than a commitment by sovereign cities to clean up their own houses. It is first and foremost a network, and as such, it's been set up to *pool* research, knowledge management, peer-to-peer exchange, and communications, ensuring that cities move farther, faster, toward curbing carbon emissions.

New York, Washington, D.C., Vancouver, Stockholm, and London have already enacted strict EUI (energy use intensity) caps on new construction, which include timelines and penalties. Other signatories, like Paris, Toronto, San Francisco, Seattle, and Portland, are in the planning stages of similar policies.

We'll get there.

Final Thoughts

In my vision, when cities are no longer smog engines or polluters; when their streets are green, healthy, and richly programmed; when their cultural investments blossom; when food is produced everywhere, near you; when the chief reasons to leave home are to collaborate, socialize, and/or play; when the physical environment of the city supports us as we always wished, supplying copious amounts of choice, dynamism, energy, friendship, and creativity; and when most building's doors lead to on-demand spaces and services; then City 3.0 will flourish.

It will surely be the very best version of cities yet. And when it's here, people will flock to municipalities everywhere, delivering—for a very different set of reasons—on the UN's now-obsolete, employment-based projection of increased urbanization. However, it will be because cities are the most dynamic, richly textured, creative, diverse, social, tolerance-incubating, inclusive, and exciting places to be.

And there's nothing that could ever replace that.

There's just one more thing lurking in the shadows, and that's the nagging question about whether (and how) the emergence of A.I. will transform not just *where* and *how* we work, but *if we will continue to work at all*, in City 3.0.

In the next and final chapter, we will discuss the possibility that work—the very force that has monopolized our energies for millennia—may finally give way to a new model of being.

25 The Rise of the "Useless Class"

Artificial intelligence is here. McKinsey believes that "current-gen A.I. and other technologies have the potential to automate work activities that absorb up to 70 percent of employees' time today", and will force millions of Europeans and Americans to change jobs.[302] Whether or not these are replaced remains the realm of crystal ball-gazing.

We just don't know.

Today, there is no shortage of crises to fret over. To reprise some ideas shared elsewhere in the book, global politics are fanning the flames of rising extremism and terrorism, both domestic and foreign. A climate crisis not only risks displacing 1.2 billion humans, but is also fueling the planet's sixth mass extinction. We've already destroyed half the life on Earth, including 83% of wild animals[303], and over one million additional species are at risk, today.[304] And recently, a virus menaced our entire planet, resulting in more than seven million deaths.[305]

Our health, safety and welfare are all being attacked. Psychologically, we have become increasingly addicted to toxic digital platforms, fueling record cases of depression and suicide, as we saw earlier in this book. Corporeally, Class II ("severe") obesity now afflicts 1 in 8 humans and is rising quickly,[306] fed by a broken food system that is consolidating control, and is increasingly effective in profiting from our illness. And brinkmanship and autocratic rule are both on the rise in an astonishing recalibration of the world order, unfolding in real time in courts, congresses, streets and seas.

To be alive today is to live in a treacherous world few would design, as such, but that we must now all navigate to survive regardless—no one more than the young.

There's more.

If McKinsey and others are right, we could potentially be facing the demise of our own livelihood. In the study cited at this chapter's outset, McKinsey estimates that up to 800 million jobs could be lost to automation, <u>this decade</u>. Of a three billion-strong global labor force, that's more than a quarter of all jobs, worldwide. In a twist of irony, rich countries would suffer *more* than poor ones because we can better afford to automate. In the wealthy world, between 30% and 60% of jobs risk disruption due to A.I., according to the IMF.[307]

Stephen Hawking famously said two things:

"Success in creating A.I. would be the biggest event in human history. Unfortunately, it might also be the last."

He later said:

"The development of full artificial intelligence could spell the end of the human race."

Let's assume that A.I. doesn't kill us. Nor the aforementioned extremists, bad political actors, the coronavirus, climate collapse, or our diets. What it will do—and groups like McKinsey are pointing out—is force us to *consider* what it is to live without life-defining labor, as it's understood today.

Along with love and belonging, finding **purpose** is one of our foundational needs. If love helps us feel alive and belonging makes us feel connected, then purpose is what gives our lives *meaning* and *direction*, while simultaneously helping us to feel that we are contributing to the collective wellbeing of our communities.

Purpose is a wholly collectivist concept. Frankly, all three of these are. That's because to be human is to be, first and foremost, a social creature. There's no love or belonging without other people.

For many, right or wrong, our job is our **default purpose**. We feel that by focusing our energies from adulthood to retirement on *something*, we are somehow of value, at least to someone. For a large portion of us, that job is creating and raising a family. For others, it's proselytizing about a deep belief, like religion, civil rights, or "truth", to guide or influence others. But for a majority of us, it takes the form of employment, in the hopes that we feel accomplished in whatever it is that we've chosen to practice, professionally. The flip side of this is to feel like a failure—in our efforts, or lack thereof—or that we "wasted" our lives by doing something other than what we feel we *should have.*

These are the exact things most of us apparently rue, on our deathbeds. Author and palliative care nurse Bronnie Ware spent eight years developing a list of her patients' **top five end-of-life regrets**, then collected them into a book she titled, *The Top Five Regrets of the Dying.* How these all connect to one another is germane to the subject of this chapter, in which work itself may cease to be a central means by which we establish and *apply* meaning. Her interviewees' biggest regrets were:

- not living a life *true to themselves*, rather than other's wishes
- not staying more connected to their friends
- not expressing their [true] feelings
- not letting themselves be *happier*
- not having worked *less hard*

"Living a true life" and "working less hard" are only at odds with one another when one's daily activities *don't* contribute to one's feelings of living authentically. "Staying more connected to friends" and "expressing true feelings" are both social paradigms, and are the chief means by which we feel we bond and find belonging. And "being happier" is an *outcome* of the other four activities [they are all *actions*], which brings us back to the seismic importance of what we *do* in our daily lives in the hopes of satisfying the things that we all—by extrapolation of Ware's interviewees—cherish most in life.

Simply put, if we were to fill our daily lives with *personally meaningful* activities, we might not feel such regret in our final hours, when we finally pause long enough to assess what it is we did with the gift of living.

So, what happens if a quarter to a third (or more) of us are out of a job, and would that help or hinder us in connecting with meaning?

Three Potential Scenarios

There are many potential directions human purpose could take in the wake of mass job loss. Let's look at three of them. First is the possible need to re-educate and retrain large swaths of the workforce with increasing frequency: not just once, but with every advancement of automation into territory we now occupy. Second is the concept of retirement from work altogether, wherein our resources for financing necessities is recast in post-capitalist terms. And third is the reinvention of work itself, from a means of value creation to *an expression of passion*, in which machines and algorithms provide for our needs, so that our pursuit of authentic purpose may more closely align with what drives us internally, absent the pressures of survival.

Retraining (With Increased Frequency)

Sixty-two percent of executives surveyed believe they will need to retrain or replace more than a quarter of their workforce due to advancing automation and digitization. So says McKinsey.[308] Whether their timetable trails by a half-decade or more, if it comes true, it portends the single largest, fastest, and most consequential retraining of a population in history.

The last time anything of this scale happened was in the transition from agriculture to industry, 150-ish years ago. The material difference between then and now is that during the Industrial Revolution we had over 100 years for change to fully upend norms. The span between 1850 and 1970 saw agricultural employment plummet from 60% of US employment to just 5%.[309] China's was faster. Between 1990 and 2015 —just a quarter century—33% of their workforce were forced to retrain.

The good news is that as drastic a change as this was, overall employment continued to grow, in both places. Meaning, there were not only enough jobs for those in transition; there were enough for the growing population, and then some.

As capital-fueled production skyrocketed, employment turned on its head because while agriculture jobs plummeted, an entire industry around trade, brokerage, manufacture, repair, and professional services emerged to profit from it. Moreover, jobs in education aimed at retraining the majority of the workforce expanded dramatically, as well. Eventually, tertiary businesses emerged, like financial services to manage new wealth, and entertainment & leisure activities to service a new idle class that was no longer tied to the farm.

Simply put, jobs weren't lost. They just changed.

This time, however, we may not have the luxury of a century—or even, possibly, a generation—to retrain people.

Which is where the worry starts.

One of the biggest impediments to retraining at scale is that many of the low-skill, low-wage jobs now being lost to robots and A.I. are being replaced by higher-skill openings that require longer training and transition times. In a 2019 study, IBM found that "workers need[ed] 36 days of training to close a skills gap (it took just 3 days in 2014.)[310] That represents a twelvefold increase in training needs, in a half-dozen years.

Still, thirty-six days isn't much in the context of work. But that investment doesn't generate the *expertise* workers had before they lost their jobs, any more than three days in 2014 did. The loss to productivity and likely reductions in salary or status will be enormously disruptive to those seeking new jobs. And it will likely begin to happen *more frequently*.

Anyone with an aged parent knows that they are continually confounded by "new-fangled" technologies. My own mother calls herself a technological "troglodyte," and it usually takes me a half-hour to guide her toward a 30-second fix that is second nature to those of us who have grown up alongside these things, or whose younger brains are more neuroplastic. My father used to call once a month to check in on me. It grew tenfold in recent years, and invariably consists of him yelling at me about his "broken machines", and no matter how patiently I try to troubleshoot over the phone, he nearly always yells at me for going too fast for him to follow.

While neither of them is seeking jobs retraining, the point is that generational familiarity and neuroplasticity both play a huge role in whether or not we can, and how long it will take, to retrain a subset, if not the majority, of the workforce.

Forbes reported that "while the [studies claim] that employees can learn new skills, its logic is suspect to the realities." The seismic shift in work goes beyond what Tom Friedman calls "thick-fingered" jobs.

Forbes continues, "There's no hiding from the robots. Well-trained and experienced doctors will be pushed aside by sophisticated robots that can perform delicate surgeries better and read x-rays more efficiently and accurately to detect cancerous cells that can't be readily seen by the human eye."[311]

Five years ago, *Nature* wrote an article about how this phenomenon was already upending norms. It described British, German, and American medical researchers, doctors, and programmers collaborating to build A.I. engines that read pathologies and cancer tissue, then delivered diagnoses. Two such engines found that 12–14% of brain tumors had been misdiagnosed by trained pathologists. The machines got them *right*. Another engine outperformed seasoned radiologists, reducing the number of false positives by 11% and negatives by 5%, in assessments of lung cancer.[312]

Apart from those whose A.I.-fueled diagnoses improve their chances of survival, the winners of this shift from human-based diagnosis to a computational one will be the coders and computer engineers... at least until, as *Forbes* puts it ominously, "A.I. can learn to code as well as—or better than—the humans."

That's already happening. Demand for junior developers is flagging. The unemployment rate for new graduate engineers in 2025 was double the U.S. average, and employment shrunk by 26% for "computer programmers" between 2022 and 2024, alone.[313]

"Even those developing [technologies] don't fully understand how it works or what direction it's taking," *Forbes* continues. "Recent advances in machine learning have shown that a computer—given certain directives—can learn tasks much faster than humans thought possible even a year ago."

All of this points to a potential catastrophic loss of *existing* jobs, at a pace and direction that are bafflingly out of our hands. And while on balance a workforce could be retrained, the speed of change, the power of science, machine learning, and biological limits will all conspire to make this unlike anything humans have faced, and thus may well drive us toward what some—like Elon Musk and Stephen Hawking—have famously insisted is the inescapable outcome of a human world integrated with A.I.

It is the rise of what I'm calling a "**Useless Class**", and if it comes to pass, human governments will be forced to deal with a population no longer able to find meaningful employment, or at least earn enough to be able to afford food, shelter, and a modicum of pleasure—as we should all be able to do—given a reasonable investment of time and energy.

Enter retirement.

Retirement (with a Universal *Human* Income)

A friend and I were chatting recently about how stunning a shift there was in people's patterns the moment we all went into hiding from a novel coronavirus, just a half dozen years ago. In particular, we were talking about inertia—again, the tendency of a body at rest to stay that way. In this case, the bodies are humans, and productivity is the thing that would typically get us moving.

She said, "The less we need to do, the less we seem to be doing." She added that she doesn't see us reverting to our past patterns; that we will settle into a "new normal" in which we simply do less. To make her point, she brought me past a lingerie store as we walked down the street. "Look," she said. "What do you see?" Stunned by the contents of the window, I said, "Well, what I *don't* see is lingerie." "Precisely," she said, smiling. "What they're selling now is what people are buying, which isn't lingerie but some form of what you always call *street pajamas*," invoking my preferred taunt of the decreasing effort people make to dress up, and an increase in what is frankly is *indistinguishable* from what they wear to bed, minus the sneakers.

I digress.

We are all, somewhat alarmingly, becoming more and more like the morbidly obese, mechanically conveyed blobs in Pixar's WALL-E: unable to walk, even, doing nothing but leisure activities daily, and outsourcing every erg of work energy to a legion of robots and algorithms.

In response to my friend's provocation, I said that while I might agree wholeheartedly with her observations of *some humans'* inherent laziness (we need look no further than the trillions of dollars humans spend on things that help us all to do *less*), we won't have that luxury until our governments encode our ability to *stop working* in law, *and* bridge our impending loss of income.

Which is where people's opinions start to go crazy.

As we covered in Chapter 12, the idea of a Universal Basic Income (or UBI) has been floated and tested for years now. Its origins are even older. English statesman and philosopher Thomas More first proposed it in his book, *Utopia*, written in 1516, over five hundred years ago.[314] More, whose ideas inspired the American Revolution, proposed a tax plan that would *provide a stream of government-provided income to every person*, rich or poor.

In *Utopia*, he wrote the following:

> *"No penalty on earth will stop people from stealing, if it's their only way of getting food. Instead of inflicting... horrible punishments, it would be far more to the point to provide everyone with some means of livelihood, so that nobody's under the frightful necessity of becoming first a thief, and then a corpse."*

Martin Luther King, Jr., the African-American civil rights leader, proposed a similarly "guaranteed income" in his book *Where Do We Go From Here: Chaos or Community?*, back in 1967.

Even Nobel Prize winning economist Milton Friedman—the small government and free market godfather whose views helped reshape capitalism in the last half-century—wrote, in *Capitalism and Freedom*, that a "negative income tax" (or UBI) would help overcome a mindset where citizens aren't inclined to make sacrifices if they don't believe others will follow suit.

A UBI may become a necessary reality, if McKinsey, IBM, and others' prophecies come to pass, leading to unemployment on a scale never before seen.

As we also reviewed in Chapter 12, scores of countries are experimenting with UBI today on various scales, touching every populated continent. Not to repeat those stories, I'll add a few more examples here. Spain tested a UBI with 850,000 of the nation's poorest households, providing each with monthly payments of €1,015. Within 4 hours of launching, their website had already logged 50,000 applicants.[315] In Finland, 2,000 unemployed Finns were each paid €560/month over a two-year period, from 2017–2018 to bridge loss of income until they *rejoined* the labor force; but the anticipated 'boost' did not materialize the hoped for reductions in overall unemployment.[316]

This supports my friend's central thesis: perhaps some people simply don't *want* to work, if given the chance not to. Perhaps, if a viable alternative to doing so existed, we would welcome it and ride into the sunset, permanently retired. If the Finns took the money and simply used it—not to fuel their return to work, but to cushion their leisure—then maybe we are involuntarily hinting at our inherent inner sloth, and the end state of employment altogether, à la WALL-E.

Certainly, that's what people mean when they decry the potential creation of a "welfare state".

Well, we may not have the choice. 25% is a huge percentage of the workforce. If even a small portion of that group leaves the labor pool permanently, countries will have no choice but to fill the gap or crater, both economically and societally. Whether directly (through loss of revenues) or indirectly (as a large out-of-work population aims its energies destructively), an unemployed population can, and often does, ruin a nation's fortunes.

Paul Collier, the British economist, is famous for modeling the causes of civil wars, arguing that unemployed people—especially young men— are those most likely to be recruited voluntarily to armed groups; and that unemployment is a strong probable cause or motivating factor behind violence and violent conflict."[317]

Even with Spain's leadership in beta-testing UBI, the idea that families can thrive long-term and fully meet even their most basic needs with just a few thousand dollars per month, is woefully off the mark.

A *true* replacement for work in the form of a government-subsidized existence would require a seismic shift—one we have never fully tested—from the prevailing life focus of adults, worldwide.

Perhaps, instead of thinking of it as a universal *basic* income, we'd do well to re-conceive of it as a **universal *human* income**, or UHI. That is, not a handout, but a basic human right. "Universal Basic Income" is a policy instrument. "Universal Human Income" is a claim about what being human *entitles* you to.

In a post-A.I. labor world, the concept of a UHI is *existential*.

Reinvention (From Need to Choice)

Let's say we figure this out, and that with adequate social scaffolding, *enough* people would be able to redirect their energies toward meaning-driven contribution. What would life look like in a world where an ever-diminishing percentage of human beings earn money through effort? While robots and A.I. aren't projected to *fully* supplant human labor as much as to supplement it, even a modest—but permanent—reduction in employment will likely force governments to do *something* to support those humans. The alternative is a bifurcation of a population, with healthy, well-cared for, and wealthy citizens on one hand, and those who descend into some hellish form of terrestrial mayhem, on the other.

It's hard to imagine any even pseudo-democratic government allowing that to happen to a double-digit percent of its population.

So let's imagine for a minute that our non-human labor pool made of bots and A.I. is *benign*, and doing exactly what we designed it to do, to great success. This could spur nations to reap huge rewards from the output of this 24/7, predictable, tireless army, capable of Herculean feats of strength and Einsteinian intellectual prowess.

If the bots are doing the work and generating not just income, but also paying taxes (in the *Forbes* article, none other than Bill Gates has called for a tax on robots due to the disruption they will cause and a corollary reduction in human tax—*deflation, anyone?*), then what's coming down the road is a potential boon to humanity, *isn't it?*

Wouldn't it mean that we could potentially, fully, support a new Useless Class (we will rename this, obviously, into something evocative like "Leisure Class") with our creations? Said another way, wouldn't it mean that we could move from a population that *needs* to work into one that *chooses* to? That we would all, finally, be free to pursue our passion projects—the ones that so many of Ware's dying interviewees lamented *not* doing that it constituted one of the *greatest forms of regret that they had*, over an entire lifetime?

Here, my friend's prophecy is troubling. "The less we need to do, the less we seem to be doing." To make her point, she listed a number of friends who have dreamed of having time to do things that—guess what?—they suddenly had time for at home during COVID-19's forced quarantine (this was in Canada). They ranged from spring cleaning to incubating new businesses. The upshot? Not one of these people did any of it. What most of them did instead was to sit on their sofas, binge-watching Netflix, and doom scrolling.

In the same way that many (most?) of us are most productive under constraints like deadlines, or threats to our job security, when those pressures to produce lessen, many of us give in to our inner sloth.

And there's another price to pay. A 2019 *The Atlantic* article about happiness and leisure time cited research pointing to the fact that the happiest people were the ones who were busiest, *not* the most idle.[318] Their research confirms my own belief about humans *needing purpose to feel good about life*.

So, let's just say that we do put down our phones and remotes, keep the weight off and continue to resemble our sinewy ancestors, rather than WALL-E's blobs. What would that even look like?

In my own mind, work Nirvana might look more than a little like the non-profit world. Not-for-profit organizations exist to generate collective public or social benefit, in contrast with entities that exist solely or primarily to generate business profit for their owners and shareholders. In other words, NPOs, as they're called, exist *to do good*, reflecting or supporting the moral and ethical values of a society.

That's a world I'd like to live in.

So, while many of us might binge-watch ourselves into a popcorn-tinged stupor, others would undoubtedly use the opportunity to connect with their inner passions and invest in them, aiming their continued contributions to the human world: if not for financial gain, then because they find it *meaningful*, and it makes them *content*.

If—and it may be a long shot—our basic needs were underwritten by a non-human workforce, and this same army of bots and A.I. engines generated *adequate* revenues and paid *adequate* taxes to support the Useless Class, then it's entirely conceivable that humans would focus on helping other humans, agnostic to the economic dimensions of their energies, as **shareholders in the corporation of their home nation**.

This would be fantastic indeed. A human race aimed at communal wellbeing is Utopian, to its core. It is the Platonic idea of collectivism—that the good of the many supersedes the good of the few—writ large.

Collectivism's greatest impediments have been twofold: the fact that until recently, were have never been able to supply all of our needs without human labors; and more troublingly, that a bevy of ever-present baser human qualities—greed, resentment, and fear, among them—have perverted early attempts at collectivist initiatives like socialism, communism, and anarchy, by perverting these structures to surreptitiously feed the *few*. Those early experiments turned collectivism on its head, into some form or another of capitalism.

Capitalism and communism, as practiced by nations who identify with either one, *really* aren't much different from one another. In both, an already-elite individual or group seeks then attains power, doing everything possible to amass increasing amounts of it, while the human labor force underpinning it unwittingly contributes to their scheme—whatever we end up calling it— because the choice they have in front of them is stark: "participate or suffer." Capitalist and communist nations alike comprise a super-rich and/or legacy elite who have close ties to the ruling party—however they got there—and who are more often than not *also* super-rich, if not initially, then certainly by the time they consolidated their power base by cozying up to the rulers. This elite enjoys access to things, people, and services that few of their fellow citizens do, while the majority of the work force plods along, plying wares to varying degrees of success, sending a portion of their earnings to a government which in turn doles out varying levels of social services and makes infrastructure investments, in order to keep the engine that feeds them humming. And as long as any member of the establishment/aristocracy doesn't make waves that gainsay those in (political) power, they are left alone. When they *do* criticize the ruling class, on the other hand, they are punished, censored, stripped of their power, and sometimes disappear.

In the foregoing paragraph, I could just as easily be describing Russia, China, Canada, Turkey, the United States, or most other nations.

And so, in a new collectivist future fueled by A.I., robotics, and the resultant Useless Class, the large swath of humans who are driven by the greed motive and given to undermining one another in competition will likely need to be robbed of their chief weapons—those of unchecked power and economic subterfuge—in order for this scheme to work. If they aren't, then the drive for dominance or self-preservation could bifurcate humanity into two imbalanced camps *again*: a tiny class of super-wealthy aggressors with power, and a majority underclass of subsistence earners without any choice but to be thankful for what the bots produce, and their rich overlords mete out.

Brave New World warned us of just such a construct.

The only way a collectivist future of mutual wellbeing works is if *everyone is in it*, as Kaakinen plainly put it. If not, competition will conspire to have all of humanity scrambling to be on the upside of an upended boat.

If we can somehow see our way to regulating and taxing bots (and their owners!) the way Gates advises us, and doling out a truly livable UHI (or UBI 2.0), perhaps starting with those who increasingly need it, and for whom King, Jr. advocated with his "Poor People's Campaign", then we may yet get to a place of equilibrium with our metal-and-silicon Frankensteins.

Then, and only then, we could spur the next wave of growth: an era of peace and wellbeing in which the primary (or even sole) focus of our energies is improving our collective lot in whatever way inspires us as individuals; because if we did, *our passions and our energies would no longer be at potential odds*, the way they are today all too often.

Our future could ruled by the *heart*, while today it is mostly ruled by the *pocketbook*. For those who opt out altogether in favor of street pajamas, bonbons, and doom-scrolling?

Well, to each his/her/their own.

The Post-Work World

It's a long shot. We haven't shown ourselves to be altruists, as civilized humans. We are consummate competitors, whether we aim those energies at the Earth itself or at one another. We have done a good job of destroying our planet and our health in the name of the almighty dollar (or yuan, or pound, or dinar). Still, there is a path there. At the 2017 World Economic Forum (WEF), British professor and co-founder of the Basic Income Earth Network (BIEN) Guy Standing pointed to something under our very noses: that in the U.S., if the Federal Reserve's four-year $475 billion in QE plan would've been paid out as a basic income instead, it would've netted every non-millionaire household *$56,000 each,* over that period.[319]

Because economics are a major force in unrest, Standing believes a UBI could liberate countries from the instability that has led to, among other things, the election of increasingly autocratic leaders. Fear of lost jobs is a huge part of that, and many would-be autocrats' biggest base is the working poor. "Basic economic security is behind this drift to populism," Standing warned. "The emancipatory value of basic income is greater than the monetary value."

The world is taking note. India, now the world's most populous country, is looking seriously at the feasibility of adopting a national UBI. They're not alone. Dozens of countries, including half of Europe's, are experimenting with this.

Even in the U.S., there's a long-standing UBI hiding in plain sight. As I briefly mentioned in Chapter 12, Alaska's Permanent Dividend Fund has been pumping out checks to every Alaskan for nearly *fifty years,* effectively turning every resident into an automatic shareholder in the revenue generation of the state itself. By law there, a minimum of 25% of certain mineral revenues are deposited into a public savings account, and paid out, annually.[321]

That idea—that every citizen should be deemed, through their residency alone, a "shareholder in the corporation of the state or nation"—is one of the *least* crazy ideas I've ever heard, and what I mean when I advocate for a UHI.

As to whether the world will fall apart if we aren't working? To reprise and expand the list that I shared in Chapter 1, in which *Forbes* referenced "three types of people who prove that you don't need a job to have meaning", here are <u>five</u> reference populations endemic to *every country* that provide a glimpse at what a post-work life could look like:

- **children**
- **the retired**
- **stay-at-home parents**
- **the idle rich**
- **the unemployed**

In the United States, as of late 2025, there are 75 million minors supported by their parents or extended families; 50 million retirees living off social security and savings; 11.3 million stay-at-home parents; an unspecified number of idle rich (it's far from zero; let's just agree on that); and 31.8 million unemployed workers, a large majority of whom are not *also* retirees.

In all, that's ~165 million Americans—effectively <u>half</u> of us—who *already* don't work, as such, regardless of who pays for the privilege.

The bots are coming, whether or not we like it. And if analysts are right, it will quite likely hit this decade, in full force. Even if that horizon extends, it's a matter of *when*, not *if*. Whether or not we regulate and tax them remains to be seen. Whether or not UHI is understood for what it could be—a boon to humanity and a means of sunsetting Earth-killing economics—is within view and being seriously studied.

Deflation—also called "degrowth" by some, such as Dr. Jason Hickel— could get us most the way there, if we were to let the natural course of things play out. Bots and A.I. could easily do the rest, with the right legislative framework. Only politics and a slavish adherence to the existing world order, armed by those who have the most to lose in the transition, could stand realistically in its way.

Those voices, as most of us know, are loudest.

And so, what remains to be seen is what appetite those in charge of making these decisions—our elected or self-appointed leaders—have for this looming transition while they can still avert the disaster of a global Useless Class without the means to survive, let alone thrive.

The payoff for playing ball? At the 2017 World Economic Forum, Harvard professor Michael Sandel suggested—to thundering applause—that a UBI ought to come coupled with some kind of requirement of all citizens who receive it. He called it "A sense of mutual indebtedness wedded to a sense that everyone has a duty to contribute to the common good."

Final Thoughts

To my ears, Sandel's musing sounds a lot like collectivism, the way Plato described it in his Socratic dialogue, *Republic*. In *Republic*, Plato illustrated our innate draw to societal and political justice, giving it precedence over individualism.

To describe his ideas, Plato used his brother in real life, Glaucon, who travels with Socrates to visit city-states filled with "purely just" and "purely unjust" souls. In the purely just places they discover gender equality (this is over 2,000 years ago!), universal education, and societally empowering institutions. After spending enough time in one, Glaucon declares that he wishes to remain, and loses any interest he once had in going home.

The story is far more complex than this, but it stands nonetheless as a philosophical guidepost for the human potential to overcome its own baser instincts. It was penned by a member of the very same population—the Ancient Greeks—who *also* invented philosophy and myriad other schools of thought and governance, direct democracy among them.

We are at a crossroads. For now, we still have the power to direct outcomes. If we do so to everyone's benefit—without undue bias toward our own selfish interests, and by encoding virtuous behaviors and equitable governing structures in the process—then the next wave of human development could well be the best one yet.

No matter whether or not we do this, Hawking was right. A.I. might well be the last invention we make. Which means, we may get just one shot at aiming it.

It is my deep hope that we are able to overcome our baser instincts for the benefit of those—like my own daughter, Mia, her generational peers, and the next wave of children—who are still young enough that their futures will be defined by the outcome of our choices. And because if we choose the "purely unjust" route, then while we may win in the short term, we will no longer be able to outthink or outrun our own creation. In that case, Hawking's final fear—the destruction of mankind—may be the future we create.

On the other hand, if we choose the "purely just" path and focus our emerging armies of physical robots and silicon brains on the labors that mankind has undertaken manually for millennia, *and also* reap the rewards together as shareholders in the corporations of our independent states or nations—or even as citizens of the planet itself, post-nationalism—then we may just enfranchise a global population suddenly left to explore their passions, in the name of building what the machines cannot:

Meaning.

EPILOGUE
The (Potential) Path to Abundance

I began this book with a personal story about my own brokenness and how that led me on a multi-year search for meaning, in order to reclaim an innate optimism that a half-century of living had bled out of me.

As I wrote in the Preface, in the process of trying to heal myself, I found beauty and creativity in places I didn't realize existed, which have influenced my own creative path, and which did no less than restore my faith in *people's inherent goodness.*

I wanted to share that message using the tools at my disposal: design systems thinking fed by voracious reading, a mind for understanding the "why" beyond the "what", a career spent crafting spaces for living, learning, working, transacting, and bonding, a ripe imagination primed for projecting a future in which the "better angels of our nature" guide our current acts, and the ability to identify and connect initiatives that could lead us to these outcomes, in real life.

Certainly, the world feels like it needs that right now.

To reiterate an idea, I believe our most destructive behaviors—toward planet and one another—stem from internal pain. And that pain has precipitated the "meaning crisis", leading us to record levels of anxiety, depression and suicide.

At the same time, in spite of it all, there are people incubating *profoundly restorative alternatives* to the problems we have largely wrought.

And so, this book is about the people who are toiling away furiously on ideas for improving our many broken systems, for no reason other than so that we can flourish together, as a human community.

In many ways, this is a book about grounded hope.

Project Human

There have been two macro-phases of human presence on Earth. During the first of these, we lived *with* Nature, like every other animal. During this second phase, we are still at war with it, squandering our inheritance and driving us to the brink. It's time for a Phase III for Project Human—one borne of Epoch B, post-inflection point. Luckily, our transformation is already underway.

Like so many others, I am aghast at some universally ruinous aspects of human behavior that seem to transcend time and culture and drive us to inflict damage on one another and on nature in spite of possessing all of the tools we need to do otherwise. I'm speaking of our too-common penchant for competing, warring, killing, dominating, and desecrating people and planet in the name of nationhood, culture, race, sex, religion, and the most powerful god of all, economics.

It needn't be this way.

We have the means of thriving, as individuals and as a collective, without any of the deleterious impacts we've had on all of it. We are so industrious and creative as a species that we alone are able to manifest what has yet to exist, in addition to fully harnessing what already does, to near-infinite ends.

We can grow food on a postage stamp, in the middle of a city. We can create protein literally from the air itself; earlier, I mentioned my friend who has tried it, and couldn't distinguish it from chicken (insert joke here). We can power all industry from the only infinite resource we have—the sun—not to mention the myriad other finite sources within our terrestrial marble. And we can 3D-print houses for the cost of two-and-a-half to three months of average U.S. rent *today*, or finance a $50,000 prefabricated one for less than $900/month, owning it outright in just 5 years.

Those are just the basics. We can reverse desertification, as the Israelis have done; end homelessness, as the Finns have done; clean the oceans of plastic, as private industry is now doing; eradicate infectious diseases, as the Gates Foundation is doing; and even—*even*—overcome the crippling effects of late stage capitalism on human and natural populations everywhere, as

Mondragón—the 84,000-strong conglomerate thriving in Spain since the time of Franco, bolstering its GDP and avoiding every economic downturn that has dogged its home country—has been showing us again and again and again is not only possible, it is an incredibly effective means to get out of our destructive path and onto a new one that leads toward global thriving.

While none of these innovations has become dominant yet beyond its current borders, every one of them has proven that we have the means of doing all of it, <u>today</u>. And because as-yet-undreamt wizardry seems to emerge daily from the minds of *homo sapiens sapiens*, I can only imagine the wonders we will create in the coming years—wonders we will most certainly take for granted, within our lifetimes, once they become commonplace, as Everett Rogers showed us.

The Potential Path to Abundance

And so, on occasion, I indulge my mind and visit the future I wish to see—that by all measures, can *easily* exist in a world where these constraints have been deliberately addressed. In those moments, I dream of a world in which…

… fresh food is grown in our neighborhoods and homes, ending hunger and food-fueled illnesses.

… houses are produced in factories for the price of a car today, while social programs bring everyone into the fold of independent living, collectively ending homelessness.

… science mitigates illnesses as they evolve, thereby removing impediments to harnessing the full potential of human energy, such as physiological and mental illnesses.

… the seventh-generation principle[322] once again guides our behaviors, and short-term gains take a back seat to long-term thriving.

…the common good outweighs the good of the individual in all thinking and acts.

… natural ecosystems thrive once again in a new form of planetary homeostasis that includes Project Human.

… nature powers all of human activity, the way it powers every other thing on Earth, without depleting it.

… nations finally acknowledge the inescapability of the Butterfly Effect and evolve beyond nationalism, racism, sexism, and other fictitious systems into a planetary family, reflecting our digital, taxonomic, pathological, environmental and economic oneness.

… we can once again care for one another as friends and collaborators, not nemeses and competitors, as toxic narratives and systems have fooled us into believing are necessary.

… we recognize the inherently *deflationary* nature of human progress: that the true cost to produce food, clothing, medicine, homes, and products of every single kind lowers consistently with time; that the true cost of sharing what we know with one another by means of education, advisory services and training is already negligible; and that in the *near* future, A.I., robotics, and other production innovations will continue to reduce the true cost of living (to manufacturers and service providers, if not customers) to <u>zero</u>, precluding—if the savings are passed on, rather than hoarded—the need for competitive systems, and guaranteeing everyone's universal human needs are met, marginally for *free*.

The recognition of these things, and the corollary change in human behaviors will, if pursued broadly, unlock our inner reserves to pursue our life's purpose *as we each define it*, because doing so is in our fundamental nature.

To dive into this last point a bit more, the truth is that every human on Earth, bar none, seeks purpose. Our three universal life drivers are, as I've posited before, love, belonging and purpose. In past writings, I have called this **The Light Triad**.

Regarding purpose:

"Why am I (and why are we) here?"

"What should I do with my life?"

"What do I love and wish I had more time to try/do/develop/pursue?"

"What really matters to me, deeply?"

As Bronnie Ware's dying patients showed us, each one of us asks a version of at least one of these questions, at some point in our lives. The trick is to do so while we still have the resources to act on the answers we find. Pundits will warn that if we give people anything for free, it will disincentivize us and we will become lazy; that our inherent sloth will emerge, and humans will descend into sin.

Well, the opposite is true. That's because without purpose—aimed—we feel inherently discontented or incomplete, even in the face of being loved, and feeling we belong. People *also* need to identify and feel engaged in accomplishment and achievement, not because we need to pay the bills, but because in that way we feel there is purpose to our being alive.

Final Final Thoughts

If we acknowledge that we are already in possession of the answer key to most or all of the puzzles that dog humankind—our poverty, hunger, illness, war, homelessness, stress, inequality, and planetary imbalance—and that all we lack is the will to systemically support the development and/or deployment of these things on a planetary scale, then we should all feel at least some comfort in knowing that our future can not only be bright, it can be radiant; and that the intractable problems facing us are in fact no more than failures to act, because our current systems are at odds with *the solutions we have in hand to fix all of it.*

These are largely, if not entirely, no more than design problems. If we can dream up solutions that fix them all—and we *have*, as I have endeavored to highlight throughout this book—then success is only a matter of implementation, not possibility.

To fix things, I would propose, we need to lead with an "abundance mindset."

The Path to Abundance is at hand. If only we could get over our fear of walking through that door together, we could get there.

The Japanese concept of kintsugi speaks to this.

Kintsugi posits that things that are broken, once mended, can make the formerly broken object *even more beautiful.* It effectively reframes damage as a catalyst for transformation. To the Japanese, kintsugi is not about pottery, per se, though the "art" focuses on the repair of vessels. Rather, it is reflective of a larger philosophy about healing, resilience, design, identity, and aging.

In that regard, kintsugi shares much with the song I referenced in the book's opening chapter. To paraphrase it again here, **the "crack in everything" is how the light gets in**.

Thank you, Mr. Cohen.

Indeed it is.

Notes

Chapter 1 (Notes 1-12)

1.   National Museum of the American Indian, 'Do All Indians Live in Tipis?,' (Washington, DC: Smithsonian Books, 2018), 78–79

2.   Hooijer, A., Vernimmen, R. 'Global LiDAR land elevation data reveal greatest sea-level rise vulnerability in the tropics,' Nat Commun 12, 3592 (2021). https://doi.org/10.1038/s41467-021-23810-9 (accessed January 27, 2026)

3.   Lane Beckes, James A. Coan, Karen Hasselmo, Familiarity promotes the blurring of self and other in the neural representation of threat, Social Cognitive and Affective Neuroscience, Volume 8, Issue 6, August 2013, Pages 670–677, https://doi.org/10.1093/scan/nss046 (accessed January 27, 2026)

4.   Liz Moyer, 'When Heirs Collide,' https://www.wsj.com/articles/when-heirs-collide-1411749577 (accessed January 27, 2026)

5.   Special Report, 'How Housing Became the World's Biggest Asset Class,' https://www.economist.com/special-report/2020/01/16/how-housing-became-the-worlds-biggest-asset-class (accessed January 27, 2026)

6.   'Health effects of dietary risks in 195 countries, 1990–2017: a systematic analysis for the Global Burden of Disease Study 2017,' Afshin, Ashkan et al. The Lancet, Volume 393, Issue 10184, 1958 - 1972

7.   'Industrial Animal Agriculture's Large Footprint on Global Land,' https://pbfinstitute.org/blog/industrial-animal-agricultures-large-footprint-on-global-land# (accessed January 27, 2026)

8.   'Wardenclyffe Tower,' https://en.wikipedia.org/wiki/Wardenclyffe_Tower (accessed January 27, 2026)

9.   Wallace Edward Brand, 'Rereading the Supreme Court: Tesla's Invention of Radio,' https://mercurians.org/antenna-newsletter/rereading-the-supreme-court-teslas-invention-of-radio/ (accessed January 27, 2026)

10. The global poverty gap is falling. Billionaires could help close it. Laurence Chandy, Lorenz Noe, and Christine Zhang, Brookings Institute, January 20, 2016

11. Janna Anderson, Lee Rainie, 'Artificial Intelligence and the Future of Humans,' https://www.pewresearch.org/internet/2018/12/10/artificial-intelligence-and-the-future-of-humans/ (accessed January 27, 2026)

12. Calum Chace, '"The Price Of Tomorrow" by Jeff Booth - Book Review,' https://www.forbes.com/sites/calumchace/2020/08/18/the-price-of-tomorrow-by-jeff-boothbook-review/ (accessed January 27, 2026)

Chapter 2 (Notes 13-20)

13. Dryden, Howard, and Diane Duncan. 2022. "Climate Disruption Caused by a Decline in Marine Biodiversity and Pollution". International Journal of Environment and Climate Change 12 (11):3413-35. https://doi.org/10.9734/ijecc/2022/v12i1111392. (accessed January 27, 2026)

14. https://goesfoundation.com/ (accessed January 27, 2026)

15. NOAA, 'How much oxygen comes from the ocean?,' https://oceanservice.noaa.gov/facts/ocean-oxygen.html (accessed January 27, 2026)

16. Cai Z, Li M, Zhu Z, et al. Biological Degradation of Plastics and Microplastics: A Recent Perspective on Associated Mechanisms and Influencing Factors. Microorganisms. 2023;11(7):1661. Published 2023 Jun 26. doi:10.3390/microorganisms11071661

17. 'U.S. total food expenditure,' https://humanprogress.org/dataset/u-s-total-food-expenditure/ (accessed January 27, 2026)

18. 'Agricultural Productivity in the United States - Summary of Recent Findings,' https://www.ers.usda.gov/data-products/agricultural-productivity-in-the-united-states/summary-of-recent-findings (accessed January 27, 2026)

19. S. Asseng, J.R. Guarin, M. Raman, O. Monje, G. Kiss, D.D. Despommier, F.M. Meggers, & P.P.G. Gauthier, 'Wheat yield potential in controlled-environment vertical farms,' Proc. Natl. Acad. Sci. U.S.A. 117 (32) 19131-19135, https://doi.org/10.1073/pnas.2002655117 (2020).

20. 'The Global Findex Database 2021 survey headline findings on financial wellbeing,' https://www.worldbank.org/en/publication/globalfindex/brief/the-global-findex-database-2021-chapter-3-financial-resilience/ (accessed January 27, 2026)

Chapter 4 (Notes 21-26)

21. Bernard Marr, 'How Much Data Do We Create Every Day? The Mind-Blowing Stats Everyone Should Read,' https://www.forbes.com/sites/bernardmarr/2018/05/21/how-much-data-do-we-create-every-day-the-mind-blowing-stats-everyone-should-read/ (accessed January 27, 2026)

22. 'Time Flies: U.S. Adults Now Spend Nearly Half a Day Interacting with Media,' https://www.nielsen.com/insights/2018/time-flies-us-adults-now-spend-nearly-half-a-day-interacting-with-media/ (accessed January 27, 2026)

23. R.I.M. Dunbar, Neocortex size as a constraint on group size in primates, Journal of Human Evolution, Volume 22, Issue 6, 1992, Pages 469-493, ISSN 0047-2484, https://doi.org/10.1016/0047-2484(92)90081-J. (https://www.sciencedirect.com/science/article/pii/004724849290081J)

24. Madeleine North, '7 ways AI is transforming healthcare,' https://www.weforum.org/stories/2025/08/ai-transforming-global-health/ (accessed January 27, 2026)

25. "Pengcheng Li, Yanbing Chen, Xiaochuan Guo, Digital transformation and supply chain resilience, International Review of Economics & Finance, Volume 99, 2025, 104033, ISSN 1059-0560, https://doi.org/10.1016/j.iref.2025.104033. (https://www.sciencedirect.com/science/article/pii/S1059056025001960)"

26. https://theoceancleanup.com/ (accessed January 27, 2026)

Chapter 6 (Notes 27-61)

27. Victoria Masterson, 'What has caused the global housing crisis - and how can we fix it?,' https://www.weforum.org/stories/2022/06/how-to-fix-global-housing-crisis/ (accessed January 27, 2026)

28. Rebecca Baird-Remba, Alex Horowitz, 'How States and Cities Decimated Americans' Lowest-Cost Housing Option,' https://www.pew.org/en/research-and-analysis/issue-briefs/2025/07/how-states-and-cities-decimated-americans-lowest-cost-housing-option/ (accessed January 27, 2026)

29. Adam, Klaus & Kuang, Pei & Marcet, Albert. (2012). 'House Price Booms and the Current Account,' NBER Macroeconomics Annual. 26. 77-122. 10.1086/663990. https://www.researchgate.net/publication/259710502_House_Price_Booms_and_the_Current_Account#pf9

30. Alan Durning, 'Yes, Other Countries Do Housing Better, Case 2: Germany,' https://www.sightline.org/2021/05/27/yes-other-countries-do-housing-better-case-2-germany/ (accessed January 27, 2026)

31. Jenny Schuetz, 'Rethinking homeownership incentives to improve household financial security and shrink the racial wealth gap,' https://www.brookings.edu/articles/rethinking-homeownership-incentives-to-improve-household-financial-security-and-shrink-the-racial-wealth-gap/ (accessed January 27, 2026)

32. Briana Sullivan, Shomik Ghosh, 'Wealth of Households: 2022,' https://www2.census.gov/library/publications/2024/demo/p70br-202.pdf (accessed January 27, 2026)

33. 'US rental market: What is the average rent in US?,' https://www.zillow.com/rental-manager/market-trends/united-states/ (accessed January 27, 2026)

34. Katharina Buchholz, 'U.S. Home Prices Continue To Climb,' https://www.statista.com/chart/32922/median-home-sales-price-in-the-us-per-month/ (accessed January 27, 2026)

35. Na Zhao, 'Top Posts – Inadequate Shelter: Millions of U.S. Homes Fail to Meet Standards.' https://eyeonhousing.org/2025/12/top-post-inadequate-shelter-millions-of-u-s-homes-fail-to-meet-standards/ (accessed January 27, 2026)

36. National Center for Healthy Housing, 'Executive Summary,' https://nchh.org/tools-and-data/data/state-of-healthy-housing/executive-summary/ (accessed January 27, 2026)

37. Homestead Act (1862), https://www.archives.gov/milestone-documents/homestead-act/ (accessed January 27, 2026)

38. Gregory P. Asnwer, Ph.D, 'Measuring Carbon Emissions from Tropical Deforestation: An Overview,' https://www.edf.org/sites/default/files/10333_Measuring_Carbon_Emissions_from_Tropical_Deforestation--An_Overview.pdf (accessed January 27, 2026)

39. Global Burden of Disease, https://www.thelancet.com/gbd (accessed January 27, 2026)

40. 'Vertical Farming Market Size (2024-2030),' https://virtuemarketresearch.com/report/vertical-farming-market (accessed January 27, 2026)

41. Kate Taylor, 'These 10 Companies Control Everything You Buy,' https://www.businessinsider.com/10-companies-control-food-industry-2017-3/ (accessed January 27, 2026)

42. 'History of agriculture in the United States,' https://en.wikipedia.org/wiki/History_of_agriculture_in_the_United_States/ (accessed January 27, 2026)

43. Jake Edmiston, 'Safety Net: A flock of chickens, held for ransom — Growing cyberattacks on Canada's food system threaten disaster,' https://financialpost.com/cybersecurity/growing-cyberattacks-canada-food-system-threaten-disaster/ (accessed January 27, 2026)

44. Air Protein, https://www.airprotein.com/ (accessed January 27, 2026)

45. 'Why Are Americans Paying More for Healthcare?,' https://www.pgpf.org/article/

46. Beth McGroarty, 'US Leads Overall Spend in $828 Billion Physical Activity Market, But Ranks 20th in Participation, Indicating a Sharp Divide in Wellness "Haves and Have-Nots",' https://globalwellnessinstitute.org/press-room/press-releases/us-leads-overall-spend-in-828-billion-physical-activity-market/ (accessed January 27, 2026)

47. Beth McGroarty, 'US Physical Activity Market: Ranks #1 in Spend, but Lags in Participation,' https://globalwellnessinstitute.org/global-wellness-institute-blog/2020/01/28/us-physical-activity-market-ranks-1-in-spend-but-lags-in-participation/ (accessed January 27, 2026)

48. 'Agrochemicals Market: Global Forecast to 2028,' https://www.marketsandmarkets.com/Market-Reports/global-agro-chemicals-market-report-132.html (accessed January 27, 2026)

49. Beth Mole, 'Big Pharma shells out $20B each year to schmooze docs, $6B on drug ads,' https://arstechnica.com/science/2019/01/healthcare-industry-spends-30b-on-marketing-most-of-it-goes-to-doctors/ (accessed January 27, 2026)

50. Meagan C. Fitzpatrick, Seyed M. Moghadas, Abhishek Pandey, Alison P. Galvani, 'Two Years of U.S. COVID-19 Vaccines Have Prevented Millions of Hospitalizations and Deaths,' https://www.commonwealthfund.org/blog/2022/two-years-covid-vaccines-prevented-millions-deaths-hospitalizations (accessed January 27, 2026)

51. Janet Burns, 'Artificial Intelligence Is Helping Doctors Find Breast Cancer Risk 30 Times Faster,' https://www.forbes.com/sites/janetwburns/2016/08/29/artificial-intelligence-can-help-doctors-assess-breast-cancer-risk-thirty-times-faster/

(accessed January 27, 2026)

52. 'U.S. Healthcare Generative AI Market Trends,' https://www.grandviewresearch.com/industry-analysis/us-healthcare-generative-ai-market-report (accessed January 27, 2026)

53. Camilo Maldonado, 'Price Of College Increasing Almost 8 Times Faster Than Wages,' https://www.forbes.com/sites/camilomaldonado/2018/07/24/price-of-college-increasing-almost-8-times-faster-than-wages/ (accessed January 27, 2026)

54. Maureen Milliken, 'The Demographics of Household Debt In America,' https://www.debt.org/faqs/americans-in-debt/demographics/ (accessed January 27, 2026)

55. Statista Research Department, 'Number of internet and social media users worldwide as of October 2025,' https://www.statista.com/statistics/617136/digital-population-worldwide/ (accessed January 27, 2026)

56. Lexie Pelchen, 'Internet Usage Statistics,' https://www.forbes.com/home-improvement/internet/internet-statistics/ (accessed January 27, 2026)

57. Sarah Perez, 'AI art apps are cluttering the App Store's Top Charts following Lensa AI's success,' https://techcrunch.com/2022/12/12/ai-art-apps-are-cluttering-the-app-stores-top-charts-following-lensa-ais-success/ (accessed January 27, 2026)

58. Ariana Baio, 'Celeb surgeons say people are asking to look like their Lensa AI avatars,' https://www.indy100.com/science-tech/lensa-ai-plastic-surgery-celebrity-surgeons/ (accessed January 27, 2026)

59. Morgan Smith, '64% of workers would consider quitting if asked to return to the office full-time,' https://www.cnbc.com/2022/04/28/64percent-of-workers-would-consider-quitting-if-asked-to-return-to-office-full-time.html (accessed January 27, 2026)

60. Berenika Teter, 'RTO: Return-to-Office Statistics,, Rsearch & Trends [2026],' https://archieapp.co/blog/return-to-office-statistics/ (accessed January 27, 2026)

61. Graig Paglieri, 'Why The Future Of Work Could Take Place In The Metaverse,' https://www.forbes.com/councils/forbestechcouncil/2022/09/08/why-the-future-of-work-could-take-place-in-the-metaverse/ (accessed January 27, 2026)

Chapter 7 (Note 62)

62. Thomas B. Edsall, 'The Moral Chasm That Has Opened Up Between Left and Right Is Widening,' https://www.nytimes.com/2021/10/27/opinion/left-right-moral-chasm.html (accessed January 27, 2026)

Chapter 8 (Notes 63-64)

63. 'Starvation Response,' https://en.wikipedia.org/wiki/Starvation_response/ (accessed January 27, 2026)

64. Balasubramanian V. 'Brain power,' Proc Natl Acad Sci U S A. 2021;118(32):e2107022118. doi:10.1073/pnas.2107022118, (accessed Jan. 27, 2026)

Chapter 10 (Notes 65-70)

65. 'Survey from Fidelity Investments®, Business Group on Health: Employers View
    Well-Being as Key Part of Workforce Strategy, Despite Economic Pressures,'
    https://www.businessgrouphealth.org/newsroom/news-and-press-releases/press-
    releases/2023-fidelity-survey/ (accessed January 27, 2026)
66. Soeren Mattke, Harry H. Liu, John P. Caloyeras, Christina Y. Huang, Kristin R.
    Van Busum, Dmitry Khodyakov, Victoria Shier, Ellen Exum, Megan Broderick,
    'Do Workplace Wellness Programs Save Employers Money?,' https://www.rand.
    org/pubs/research_briefs/RB9744.html (accessed January 27, 2026)
67. Stephan Meier, Lea Cassar, 'Stop Talking About How CSR Helps Your Bottom
    Line,' https://hbr.org/2018/01/stop-talking-about-how-csr-helps-your-bottom-
    line/ (accessed January 27, 2026)
68. Elizabeth Pollman, 'Startup Failure,' https://corpgov.law.harvard.edu/2023/09/29/
    startup-failure/ (accessed January 27, 2026)
69. 'Statistics on U.S. Generosity,' https://www.philanthropyroundtable.org/almanac/
    statistics-on-u-s-generosity/ (accessed January 27, 2026)
70. David Morris, 'The Mondragón System: Cooperation at Work,' https://www.ilsr.
    org/wp-content/uploads/files/images/mondragon.pdf (accessed January 27, 2026)

Chapter 11 (Notes 71-79)

71. 'Cooperative,' https://en.wikipedia.org/wiki/Cooperative/ (accessed January 27,
    2026)
72. College Raptor Staff, 'Timeless Knowledge: The 15 Oldest Universities in the
    World,' https://www.collegeraptor.com/find-colleges/articles/college-search/
    oldest-universities-in-the-world/ (accessed February 16, 2026)
73. Supriya Kumar, 'Membership in Co-operative Businesses Reaches 1 Billion,'
    https://cdi.coop/new-report-highlights-role-of-cooperatives-worldwide/ (accessed
    January 27, 2026)
74. Courtney Berner, 'Where Are New Co-ops Emerging? The Changing Map of
    Co-op Development,' https://nonprofitquarterly.org/where-are-new-co-ops-
    emerging-the-changing-map-of-co-op-development/ (accessed January 27, 2026)
75. 'Friedman Doctrine,' https://en.wikipedia.org/wiki/Friedman_doctrine/ (accessed
    January 27, 2026)
76. Elise Gould, Josh Bivens, Jori Kandra, 'CEO pay increased in 2024 and is now 281
    times that of the typical worker,' https://www.epi.org/blog/ceo-pay-increased-in-
    2024-and-is-now-281-times-that-of-the-typical-worker-new-epi-landing-page-
    has-all-the-details/ (accessed January 27, 2026)
77. International Cooperative Alliance, 'Key Figures,' https://coops4dev.coop/
    en/4devasia/india/ (accessed January 27, 2026)
78. Milton Friedman, 'Henry George,' https://cooperative-individualism.org/

friedman-milton_henry-george-1970.htm (accessed January 27, 2026)

79. 'Cooperative,' https://en.wikipedia.org/wiki/Cooperative/ (accessed January 27, 2026)

Chapter 12 (Notes 80-86)

80. Lawrence Mishel, Elise Gould, Josh Bivens, 'Wage Stagnation in Nine Charts,' https://www.epi.org/publication/charting-wage-stagnation/ (accessed January 27, 2026)

81. James Manyika, Susan Lund, Michael Chui, Jacques Bughin, Lola Woetzel, Parul Batra, Ryan Ko, Saurabh Sanghvi, 'Jobs lost, jobs gained: What the future of work will mean for jobs, skills, and wages,' https://www.mckinsey.com/featured-insights/future-of-work/jobs-lost-jobs-gained-what-the-future-of-work-will-mean-for-jobs-skills-and-wages/ (accessed January 28, 2026)

82. Sarah Li-Cain, 'Silicon Valley has the nation's largest wealth gap — just 9 households control more than the bottom half,' https://finance.yahoo.com/news/silicon-valley-nations-largest-wealth-110200665.html (accessed January 28, 2026)

83. State of Alaska: Department of Revenue, Permanent Fund Dividend, https://pfd.alaska.gov/ (accessed January 28, 2026)

84. Singh P, Brown R, Copeland WE, Costello EJ, Bruckner TA. Income dividends and subjective survival in a Cherokee Indian cohort: a quasi-experiment. Biodemography Soc Biol. 2020;65(2):172-187. doi:10.1080/19485565.2020.1730155, (accessed January 28, 2026)

85. 'Minors Trust Fund,' https://www.ebci.gov/minors-trust-fund/ (accessed January 28, 2026)

86. Sigal Samuel, 'Everywhere basic income has been tried, in one map,' https://www.vox.com/future-perfect/2020/2/19/21112570/universal-basic-income-ubi-map/ (accessed January 28, 2026)

Chapter 13 (Notes 87-106)

87. School Authors, Milton Leitenberg, 'Deaths in Wars and Conflicts in the 20th Century,' https://cissm.umd.edu/research-impact/publications/deaths-wars-and-conflicts-20th-century/ (accessed January 28, 2026)

88. 'Global Burden of Disease,' https://www.thelancet.com/gbd (accessed January 28, 2026)

89. Stephen Devereux, 'Famine in the Twentieth Century,' https://www.socialscienceinaction.org/resources/famine-in-the-twentieth-century/ (accessed January 28, 2026)

90. David Wallace-Wells, 'Just How Many People Will Die From Climate Change,' https://www.nytimes.com/2024/02/22/opinion/environment/climate-change-death-toll.html (accessed January 28, 2026)

91. R.J. Rummel, 'Death By Government,' https://www.hawaii.edu/powerkills/NOTE1.HTM/ (accessed January 28, 2026)

92. 'Around 8% of The Supply Exists In Cash, The Rest, Faith-based Currency,' https://www.newsbtc.com/news/around-8-money-supply-exists-cash-rest-just-faith-based-currency/ (accessed January 28, 2026)

93. Eliana Zeballos, Wilson Sinclair, 'Total food spending reached $2.58 trillion in 2024,' https://www.ers.usda.gov/data-products/chart-gallery/chart-detail?chartId=58364/ (accessed January 28, 2026)

94. Dr. Robert Pearl, MD, 'U.S. Healthcare's Biggest Problem: Overcoming the $5 Trillion Gorilla,' https://www.forbes.com/sites/robertpearl/2025/11/17/us-healthcares-biggest-problem-overlooking-the-5t-gorilla/ (accessed January 28, 2026)

95. Mark Abadi, 'Modern technology is slowly killing the mood in the 'happiest country in the world'' https://www.businessinsider.com/bhutan-happiness-technology-2018-8/ (accessed January 28, 2026)

96. Zach Patton, 'What Cities Can Learn From Burning Man,' https://www.governing.com/archive/gov-burning-man.html (accessed January 28, 2026)

97. Emily Badger, 'A Nobel-Winning Economist Goes to Burning Man,' https://www.nytimes.com/2019/09/05/upshot/paul-romer-burning-man-nobel-economist.html (accessed January 28, 2026)

98. Paul M. Romer, 'Endogenous Technological Change,' The Journal of Political Economy, Vol. 98, No. 5, Part 2: The Problem of Development: A Conference of the Institute for the Study of Free Enterprise Systems. (Oct., 1990), pp. S71-S102., https://web.stanford.edu/~klenow/Romer_1990.pdf (accessed January 28, 2026)

99. Lauren Tierney, Shelly Tan, 'The Rise of Burning Man,' https://www.washingtonpost.com/graphics/2018/lifestyle/burning-man/ (accessed January 28, 2026)

100. Statista Research Department, 'Share of households in the United States in 2024, by income group,' https://www.statista.com/statistics/203183/percentage-distribution-of-household-income-in-the-us/ (accessed January 28, 2026)

101. Giles Tremlett, 'Mondragón: Spain's giant co-operative where times are hard but few go bust,' https://www.theguardian.com/world/2013/mar/07/mondragon-spains-giant-cooperative/ (accessed January 28, 2026)

102. 'Edge City,' https://www.edgecity.live/ (accessed January 28, 2026)

103. Jordan Hall, 'The Civium Project 01: Civium vs City,' https://www.youtube.com/watch?v=3CH4mlDX-fc/ (accessed January 28, 2026)

104. 'The Voicecraft Network,' https://www.voicecraft.network/ (accessed January 28, 2026)

105. Twenge JM. 'Increases in Depression, Self-Harm, and Suicide Among U.S. Adolescents After 2012 and Links to Technology Use: Possible Mechanisms.' Psychiatr Res Clin Pract. 2020;2(1):19-25. Published 2020 Sep 9. doi:10.1176/appi.prcp.20190015 (accessed January 28, 2026)

106. Dan Witters, 'U.S. Depression Rates Reach New Highs,' https://news.gallup.com/poll/505745/depression-rates-reach-new-highs.aspx (accessed January 28, 2026)

Chapter 14 (Notes 107-134)

107. Daniil Filipenco, 'Homelessness statistics in the world: causes and facts,' https://www.developmentaid.org/news-stream/post/157797/homelessness-statistics-in-the-world/ (accessed January 28, 2026)

108. United Nations, 'Around 300 Million People Are Homeless Worldwide, and Nearly 2.8 Billion Lack Adequate Housing,' https://social.desa.un.org/world-summit-2025/blog/300million-people-homeless-worldwide/ (accessed January 28, 2026)

109. 'How Finland's Housing First model makes real progress against homelessness,' https://finland.fi/life-society/how-finlands-housing-first-model-makes-real-progress-against-homelessness/ (accessed January 28, 2026)

110. About Us, https://ysaatio.fi/en/about-us/ (accessed January 28, 2026)

111. Republic of Finland, 'Housing First policy in Finland provides long-term housing & stability to homeless populations,' https://the-atlas.com/projects/finland-housing-first-homelessness/ (accessed January 28, 2026)

112. 'Nordic Model,' https://en.wikipedia.org/wiki/Nordic_model/ (accessed January 28, 2026)

113. 'Ranking of Countries by Quality of Democracy,' https://www.democracymatrix.com/ranking/ (accessed January 28, 2026)

114. 'Quality of Life,' https://www.usnews.com/news/best-countries/rankings/quality-of-life/ (accessed January 28, 2026)

115. 'GDP per Capita (2025) - IMF,' https://www.worldometers.info/gdp/gdp-per-capita/ (accessed January 28, 2026)

116. 'Christian Socialism,' https://en.wikipedia.org/wiki/Christian_socialism/ (accessed January 28, 2026)

117. 'Socialism,' https://en.wikipedia.org/wiki/Socialism/ (accessed January 28, 2026)

118. 'List of countries by total private wealth,' https://en.wikipedia.org/wiki/List_of_countries_by_total_private_wealth/ (accessed January 28, 2026)

119. Apryl A. Alexander, 'Laws banning sleeping outdoors criminalize homelessness,' https://www.apa.org/monitor/2024/10/camping-bans-homeless/ (accessed January 28, 2026)

120. Kushel MB, Evans JL, Perry S, Robertson MJ, Moss AR. 'No Door to Lock: Victimization Among Homeless and Marginally Housed Persons.' Arch Intern Med. 2003;163(20):2492–2499. doi:10.1001/archinte.163.20.2492, (accessed January 28, 2026)

121. Jennifer Ferreira, 'The toll COVID-19 is taking on Canada's homeless,' https://www.ctvnews.ca/lifestyle/article/the-toll-covid-19-is-taking-on-canadas-homeless/ (accessed January 28, 2026)

122. Olivia Little, 'People living in Toronto's banned tiny shelters share how they've changed their lives,' https://www.blogto.com/city/2021/01/people-living-in-toronto-tiny-shelters-what-its-like/ (accessed January 28, 2026)

123. Toronto Tiny Shelters, 'Tiny Shelters Testimonials,' https://www.youtube.com/watch?v=AdbmLKaGleg/ (accessed January 28, 2026)

124. Olivia Niland, Megan Specia, 'Los Angeles declares war on tiny houses donated to the homeless,' https://mashable.com/2016/02/26/la-clears-tiny-homes-for-homeless/ (accessed January 28, 2026)

125. Gale Holland, 'L.A. is seizing tiny homes from the homeless,' https://www.latimes.com/local/lanow/la-me-ln-tiny-houses-seized-20160224-story.html (accessed January 28, 2026)

126. 'Public social expenditure as a share of GDP,' https://ourworldindata.org/grapher/social-spending-oecd-longrun?tab=discrete-bar&time=latest&country=GRC~CAN~AUS~JPN~USA~SWE~ITA~DEU~NLD~FRA~GBR~FIN~AUT~BEL~DNK~ESP~NZL~PRT~NOR~LUX/ (accessed January 28, 2026)

127. Mitchell Thompson, 'Canada's Social Spending is Still Among the Lowest in the Industrialized World,' https://pressprogress.ca/canadas-social-spending-is-still-among-the-lowest-in-the-industrialized-world/ (accessed January 28, 2026)

128. Statista Research Department, 'Value added to the gross domestic product of the United States in 2024, by industry,' https://www.statista.com/statistics/247991/value-added-to-the-us-gdp-by-industry/ (accessed January 28, 2026)

129. Statista Research Department, 'Gross Domestic Product (GDP) of Canada in June 2025, by industry,' https://www.statista.com/statistics/594293/gross-domestic-product-of-canada-by-industry-monthly/ (accessed January 28, 2026)

130. Shauna MacKinnon, 'Successfully housing the homeless: A Finnish perspective,' https://www.policyalternatives.ca/news-research/successfully-housing-the-homeless-a-finnish-perspective/ (accessed January 28, 2026)

131. 'Housing assistance in Australia,' https://www.aihw.gov.au/reports/housing-assistance/housing-assistance-in-australia/contents/summary/ (accessed January 28, 2026)

132. 'Housing Mobility and Conditions,' https://www.abs.gov.au/statistics/people/housing/housing-mobility-and-conditions/2019-20/ (accessed January 28, 2026)

133. 'How many people live in subsidized housing in the United States?,' https://usafacts.org/answers/how-many-people-live-in-subsidized-housing/country/united-states/ (accessed January 28, 2026)

134. Sophia Weeden, 'Greater Assistance Needed to Combat the Persistence of Substandard Housing,' https://www.jchs.harvard.edu/blog/greater-assistance-needed-combat-persistence-substandard-housing/ (accessed January 28, 2026)

Chapter 15 (Notes 135-182)

135. Alex Gailey, Chris Kahn, 'Priced out of 75% of the market, Americans' dream of

homeownership has become a luxury,' https://www.bankrate.com/mortgages/american-dream-of-homeownership-turning-into-luxury/ (accessed January 28, 2026)

136. Nijskens, Rob & Lohuis, Melanie & Hilbers, Paul & Heeringa, Willem. (2019). 'Hot Property The Housing Market in Major Cities: The Housing Market in Major Cities.' 10.1007/978-3-030-11674-3. https://www.researchgate.net/publication/333782084/ (accessed January 28, 2026)

137. Višnjički, Siniša, Bosna, Jurica. (2015). 'Causes and measures for preventing future crises in E.U.,' Review of Innovation and Competitiveness. 63. 63-80. https://www.researchgate.net/figure/US-housing-price-index-since-1900_fig1_320243821/ (accessed January 28, 2026)

138. 'A History of the Rise of Homeownership in the United States,' https://www.huduser.gov/portal/pdredge/pdr-edge-housingat250-article-071025.html (accessed January 28, 2026)

139. 'Residential mortgage-backed security,' https://en.wikipedia.org/wiki/Residential_mortgage-backed_security/ (accessed January 28, 2026)

140. United States Government, Financial Crisis Inquiry Commission, 'Chapter 8: The CDO Machine,' https://fcic-static.law.stanford.edu/cdn_media/fcic-reports/fcic_final_report_chapter8.pdf/ (accessed January 28, 2026)

141. Diana Olick, 'Investors are making up the highest share of homebuyers in 5 years,' https://www.cnbc.com/2025/10/07/home-sales-investors-make-up-highest-share-of-buyers-in-5-years.html (accessed January 28, 2026)

142. Miles, David & Monro, Victoria. (2019). UK House Prices and Three Decades of Decline in the Risk-Free Real Interest Rate. SSRN Electronic Journal. 10.2139/ssrn.3508653. 'Figure 1: Real house price growth in G7 countries (1980-2018), OECD housing prices database,' https://www.researchgate.net/figure/Real-house-price-growth-in-G7-countries-1980-2018-a-a-OECD-housing-prices-database_fig1_338168248/ (accessed January 28, 2026)

143. Yasuhiro Kitagawa, 'Japan's Housing Surplus Began in 1968—Despite Only 5% of Land Being Livable,' https://dovetail.co.jp/en/japans-housing-surplus-began-in-1968-despite-only-5-of-land-being-livable/ (accessed January 28, 2026)

144. Sami Sparber, 'America's housing shortage explained in one chart,' https://www.axios.com/2023/12/16/housing-market-why-homes-expensive-chart-inventory/ (accessed January 28, 2026)

145. 'The Problem,' https://nlihc.org/explore-issues/why-we-care/problem/ (accessed January 28, 2026)

146. 'The National Zoning Atlas is a collaborative project digitizing, demystifying, & democratizing ~30,000 U.S. zoning codes.' https://www.arcgis.com/home/item.html?id=13d78ab5ad5b4651a1c21524daab7fd1/ (accessed January 28, 2026)

147. 'Creating the National Zoning Atlas,' https://www.huduser.gov/archives/portal/pdredge/pdr-edge-featd-article-071123.html (accessed January 28, 2026)

148. Qiaoyu Pan, Kuniaki Sasaki, 'Verifying the effectiveness of area division for

land and population: The case of the Kofu urban area, Japan,' Asian Transport Studies, Volume 10, 2024, 100124, ISSN 2185-5560, https://doi.org/10.1016/j.eastsj.2024.100124. (https://www.sciencedirect.com/science/article/pii/S2185556024000026)/ (accessed January 28, 2026)

149. 'Household net worth,' https://www.oecd.org/en/data/indicators/household-net-worth.html (accessed January 28, 2026)

150. OECD, 'Society at a Glance 2024: OECD Social Indicators,' https://doi.org/10.1787/918d8db3-en (https://www.oecd.org/en/publications/society-at-a-glance-2024_918d8db3-en/full-report/income-and-wealth-inequalities_7ac4178f.html/) (accessed January 28, 2026)

151. Eddy Duan, Akemi Terukina, 'Japanese Savers Have a Quadrillion Yen Stashed Away. Here's How Much That Is,' https://www.bloomberg.com/news/articles/2024-03-21/japanese-savers-have-a-quadrillion-yen-stashed-away-here-s-how-much-that-is/ (accessed January 28, 2026)

152. Dorothy Neufeld, 'The State of U.S. Household Finances in 2025,' https://www.visualcapitalist.com/state-of-u-s-household-finances-in-2025/ (accessed January 28, 2026)

153. Lisa Camner McKay, Kenneth Cowles, 'Who is homeless in the United States? A 2025 update,' https://www.minneapolisfed.org/article/2025/who-is-homeless-in-the-united-states-a-2025-update/ (accessed January 28, 2026)

154. Cristian Martini Grimaldi, 'The invisible homeless in Japan,' https://www.examiner.org.hk/2025/01/17/the-invisible-homeless-in-japan/features/ (accessed January 28, 2026)

155. Allison Hanley, 'Rethinking Zoning to Increase Affordable Housing,' https://www.nahro.org/journal_article/rethinking-zoning-to-increase-affordable-housing/ (accessed January 28, 2026)

156. Daniel Hernandez, Matthew Lister, and Celine Suarez, Jonathan Rose Companies, 'Location Efficiency and Housing Type,' https://www.epa.gov/sites/default/files/2014-03/documents/location_efficiency_btu.pdf/ (accessed January 28, 2026)

157. Cummings Realty, 'Why Multifamily Properties Are Outperforming Single-Family Homes in 2025,' https://www.cummingsrealty.properties/blog-content/why-multifamily-properties-are-outperforming-single-family-homes-in-2025/ (accessed January 28, 2026)

158. Noah Kazis, 'New York's ideas for zoning reform offer many paths to tackling the housing crisis,' https://www.brookings.edu/articles/new-yorks-ideas-for-zoning-reform-offer-many-paths-to-tackling-the-housing-crisis/ (accessed January 28, 2026)

159. 'Ford Model T-1911,' https://www.heritagesociety.org/ford-model-t/ (accessed January 28, 2026)

160. 'The Ford Model T,' https://www.blueoceanstrategy.com/blue-ocean-strategy-examples/the-ford-model-t/ (accessed January 28, 2026)

161. '1927 Ford Model T Touring Car, The Fifteen-Millionth Ford,' https://www.thehenryford.org/collections-and-research/digital-collections/artifact/212759/ (accessed January 28, 2026)

162. 'Model T,' https://www.detroithistorical.org/learn/online-research/encyclopedia-of-detroit/model-t (accessed January 28, 2026)

163. 'Henry Ford,' https://www.philanthropyroundtable.org/hall-of-fame/henry-ford/ (accessed January 28, 2026)

164. 'Sears Modern Homes,' https://en.wikipedia.org/wiki/Sears_Modern_Homes/ (accessed January 28, 2026)

165. Daniel Leussink, 'Toyota remains world's top-selling automaker; chairman apologises over scandals,' https://www.reuters.com/business/autos-transportation/toyota-keeps-crown-worlds-top-selling-automaker-2023-2024-01-30/ (accessed January 28, 2026)

166. Management, 'The Benefits of Not Focusing on the Figures--How Akio Toyoda Transformed Toyota's Profit Structure,' https://toyotatimes.jp/en/spotlights/14_year_trajectory/002_1.html (accessed January 28, 2026)

167. 'Housing,' https://unhabitat.org/topic/housing/ (accessed January 28, 2026)

168. 'Strategies to Lower Cost and Speed Housing Production,' https://ternercenter.berkeley.edu/blog/833-bryant-street-sf-case-study/ (accessed January 28, 2026)

169. Realtor.com, 'San Francisco - Median Home Listing Price: Historical Chart,' https://www.macrotrends.net/4850/san-francisco-median-home-listing-price/ (accessed January 28, 2026)

170. Ezra Klein, 'The Problem With Everything-Bagel Liberalism,' https://www.nytimes.com/2023/04/02/opinion/democrats-liberalism.html (accessed January 28, 2026)

171. Malea Martin, 'Google gives an update on its $1B commitment to combat Bay Area housing crisis,' https://www.almanacnews.com/news/2022/07/29/google-gives-an-update-on-its-1b-commitment-to-combat-bay-area-housing-crisis-2/ (accessed January 28, 2026)

172. 'Apple commits $2.5 billion to combat housing crisis in California,' Press Release, https://www.apple.com/newsroom/2019/11/apple-commits-two-point-five-billion-to-combat-housing-crisis-in-california/ (accessed January 28, 2026)

173. Conor Dougherty, 'Facebook Pledges $1 Billion to Ease Housing Crisis Inflamed by Big Tech,' https://www.nytimes.com/2019/10/22/technology/facebook-1-billion-california-housing.html (accessed January 28, 2026)

174. Karen Weise, 'Microsoft Pledges $500 Million for Affordable Housing in Seattle Area,' https://www.nytimes.com/2019/01/16/technology/microsoft-affordable-housing-seattle.html (accessed January 28, 2026)

175. Flixxy, '30-Story Building Built In 15 Days (Time Lapse),' https://www.youtube.com/watch?v=rwvmru5JmXk (accessed January 28, 2026)

176. The Wall Street Journal, 'Watch a 57-Story Building Go Up in 19 Days | WSJ,' https://www.youtube.com/watch?v=N6f_sayw0mM (accessed January 28, 2026)

177. @SolarPaths, 'This 10-Story Building Was Built in Just 28 Hours!', https://www.youtube.com/shorts/ktQ-kDKA2AU (accessed January 28, 2026)

178. '26 Stories in 5 Days - How BROAD Sustainable Building is Redefining the Speed of Modular,' https://www.modular.org/2024/01/24/26-stories-in-5-days-broad-group-jindu-tower/ (accessed January 28, 2026)

179. Lauren Hilgers, 'Meet the Man Who Built a 30-Story Building in 15 Days,' https://www.wired.com/2012/09/broad-sustainable-building-instant-skyscraper/ (accessed January 28, 2026)

180. Report, 'Building Materials And The Climate: Constructing A New Future,' https://www.unep.org/resources/report/building-materials-and-climate-constructing-new-future/ (accessed January 28, 2026)

181. 'Volumetric Building Companies and Polcom Group Complete Merger,' https://www.modular.org/2022/01/12/vbc-polcom-compete-merger/ (accessed January 28, 2026)

182. Nate Hendley, 'The Modular Construction Industry Makes Monumental Strides,' https://constructioninfocus.com/2024/11/the-modular-construction-industry-makes-monumental-strides/ (accessed January 28, 2026)

Chapter 16 (Notes 183-205)

183. Elizabeth Pennisi, 'Earth home to 3 trillion trees, half as many as when human civilization arose,' https://www.science.org/content/article/earth-home-3-trillion-trees-half-many-when-human-civilization-arose/ (accessed January 28, 2026)

184. World Economic Forum in collaboration with Visual Capitalist, 'Here's how the Earth's forests have changed since the last ice age,' https://www.weforum.org/stories/2022/04/forests-ice-age/ (accessed January 28, 2026)

185. Aleena, 'The Return of Flora and Fauna in the Atlantic Forest,' https://about.restor.eco/blog/the-return-of-flora-and-fauna-in-the-atlantic-forest/

186. National Statistic Services, Urban Audit, 'Suburban, Core & Urban Densities by Area: Western Europe, Japan, United States, Canada, Australia & New Zealand,' http://demographia.com/db-intlsub.htm/ (accessed January 28, 2026)

187. 'Rewilding,' https://en.wikipedia.org/wiki/Rewilding/ (accessed January 28, 2026)

188. Sid Perkins, 'Is Agriculture Sucking Fresh Water Dry?' https://www.science.org/content/article/agriculture-sucking-fresh-water-dry/ (accessed January 28, 2026)

189. Jens Heinke, Mats Lannerstad, Dieter Gerten, Petr Havlík, Mario Herrero, An Maria Omer Notenbaert, Holger Hoff, Christoph Müller, 'Water Use in Global Livestock Production—Opportunities and Constraints for Increasing Water Productivity,' First published: 20 November 2020, https://doi.org/10.1029/2019WR026995, (https://agupubs.onlinelibrary.wiley.com/doi/full/10.1029/2019WR026995) (accessed January 28, 2026)

190. UNM Sustainable Studies Program, 'Why are Cattle in the Desert?' https://abqstew.com/2019/04/04/why-are-cattle-in-the-desert/ (accessed January 28,

2026)

191. 'Food's Big Water Footprint,' https://watercalculator.org/footprint/foods-big-water-footprint/ (accessed January 28, 2026)

192. 'COP26: Agricultural expansion drives almost 90 percent of global deforestation,' https://www.fao.org/newsroom/detail/cop26-agricultural-expansion-drives-almost-90-percent-of-global-deforestation/en (accessed January 28, 2026)

193. Charlene Watson, ODI and Liane Schalatek, HBS, 'Climate Finance Thematic Briefing: REDD+ Finance,' https://climatefundsupdate.org/wp-content/uploads/2020/03/CFF5-2019-ENG-DIGITAL.pdf (accessed January 28, 2026)

194. 'Major reductions of greenhouse gas emissions from livestock within reach – UN agency,' Report, https://news.un.org/en/story/2013/09/450752/ (accessed January 28, 2026)

195. 'Vertical Farming,' https://en.wikipedia.org/wiki/Vertical_farming/ (accessed January 28, 2026)

196. Plenty, https://www.plenty.ag/ (accessed January 28, 2026)

197. 'Statistical Review of World Energy,' https://www.energyinst.org/statistical-review/ (accessed January 28, 2026)

198. Michael Taylor, Sonia Al-Zoghoul and Pablo Ralon (IRENA), Olga Sorokina (European Energy Link Group), 'IRENA (2023), Renewable power generation costs in 2022, International Renewable Energy Agency, Abu Dhabi.' ISBN 978-92-9260-544-5, https://www.irena.org/-/media/Files/IRENA/Agency/Publication/2023/Aug/IRENA_Renewable_power_generation_costs_in_2022_SUMMARY.pdf (accessed January 28, 2026)

199. Lazard, Teneo, Roland Berger, 'Levelized Cost of Energy +,' https://www.lazard.com/media/uounhon4/lazards-lcoeplus-june-2025.pdf/ (accessed January 28, 2026)

200. Saied Dardour, Deborah Ayres and Lourdes Zamora (IRENA), 'IRENA (2025), Renewable power generation costs in 2024, International Renewable Energy Agency, Abu Dhabi.,' ISBN: 978-92-9260-669-5, https://www.irena.org/-/media/Files/IRENA/Agency/Publication/2025/Jul/IRENA_TEC_RPGC_in_2024_2025.pdf/ (accessed January 28, 2026)

201. 'Buildings,' https://www.iea.org/energy-system/buildings/ (accessed January 28, 2026)

202. 'Energy subsidies in the United States,' https://en.wikipedia.org/wiki/Energy_subsidies_in_the_United_States/ (accessed January 28, 2026)

203. 'List of countries by renewable electricity production,' https://en.wikipedia.org/wiki/List_of_countries_by_renewable_electricity_production/ (accessed January 28, 2026)

204. 'CO2 Emissions by Country,' https://www.worldometers.info/co2-emissions/co2-emissions-by-country/#google_vignette/ (accessed January 28, 2026)

205. Paige Bennett, 'Climate change is costing the world $16 million per hour: study,' https://www.weforum.org/stories/2023/10/climate-loss-and-damage-cost-16-

million-per-hour/ (accessed January 28, 2026)

Chapter 17 (Notes 206-227)

206. Stephen Adams, 'Obesity killing three times as many as malnutrition,' https://
www.telegraph.co.uk/news/health/news/9742960/Obesity-killing-three-times-as-
many-as-malnutrition.html (accessed January 28, 2026)
207. Colin Barras, 'Ancient leftovers show the real Paleo diet was a veggie feast,' https://
www.newscientist.com/article/2115127-ancient-leftovers-show-the-real-paleo-
diet-was-a-veggie-feast/ (accessed January 28, 2026)
208. Rob Dunn, 'Human Ancestors Were Nearly All Vegetarians,' https://www.
scientificamerican.com/blog/guest-blog/human-ancestors-were-nearly-all-
vegetarians/ (accessed January 28, 2026)
209. Wilson J. Warren, 'Meat Makes People Powerful: A Global History of the Modern
Era,' https://uipress.uiowa.edu/books/meat-makes-people-powerful/ (accessed
January 28, 2026)
210. 'Biodiversity,' https://populationmatters.org/biodiversity/ (accessed January 28,
2026)
211. A. Mood, P. Brooke, 'Estimating The Number of Fish Caught in Global Fishing
Each Year,' https://fishcount.org.uk/published/std/fishcountstudy.pdf/ (accessed
January 28, 2026)
212. Anthony Fieldman, 'Death and Diet — Chart: Leading Causes of Death in
the United States,' https://anthonyfieldman.medium.com/death-and-diet-
69d46c917767/ (accessed January 28, 2026)
213. 'Dietary Fiber,' https://en.wikipedia.org/wiki/Dietary_fiber/ (accessed January 28,
2026)
214. Kostovcikova K, Coufal S, Galanova N, et al. 'Diet Rich in Animal Protein
Promotes Pro-inflammatory Macrophage Response and Exacerbates Colitis
in Mice.' Front Immunol. 2019;10:919. Published 2019 Apr 26. doi:10.3389/
fimmu.2019.00919/, (accessed January 28, 2026)
215. Kristeen Cherney, Alana Biggers, 'Why Scar Tissue Pain Occurs and What You
Can Do About It,' https://www.healthline.com/health/scar-tissue-pain/ (accessed
January 28, 2026)
216. Lasse Bruun, Christina O'Sullivan, 'COP out no more: It is time to address
livestock production waste,' https://www.aljazeera.com/opinions/2021/12/16/cop-
out-no-more-we-can-no-longer-ignore-the-wast/ (accessed January 28, 2026)
217. Hannah Ritchie, Pablo Rosado, Max Roser, 'Meat and Dairy Production,' https://
ourworldindata.org/meat-production/ (accessed January 28, 2026)
218. Hannah Ritchie, 'If the world adopted a plant-based diet, we would reduce global
agricultural land use from 4 to 1 billion hectares,' https://ourworldindata.org/land-
use-diets/ (accessed January 28, 2026)
219. 'Time left to the end of commercial seafood,' https://www.theworldcounts.com/

challenges/planet-earth/oceans/overfishing-statistics/ (accessed January 28, 2026)

220. 'Water Scarcity,' https://www.unicef.org/wash/water-scarcity/ (accessed January 28, 2026)

221. Kenny Torrella, 'This is how much meat and dairy hurt the climate,' https://www.vox.com/future-perfect/22905381/meat-dairy-eggs-climate-change-emissions-rewilding/ (accessed January 28, 2026)

222. Seth Millstein, 'How Many Animals Are Killed for Food Every Day?,' https://sentientmedia.org/how-many-animals-are-killed-for-food-every-day/ (accessed January 28, 2026)

223. 'Holocene extinction,' https://en.wikipedia.org/wiki/Holocene_extinction/ (accessed January 28, 2026)

224. Damian Carrington, 'Humanity has wiped out 60% of animal populations since 1970, report finds,' https://www.theguardian.com/environment/2018/oct/30/humanity-wiped-out-animals-since-1970-major-report-finds/ (accessed January 28, 2026)

225. Rachael Garrett, Joice Ferreira, 'For cattle farmers in the Brazilian Amazon, money can't buy happiness,' https://theconversation.com/for-cattle-farmers-in-the-brazilian-amazon-money-cant-buy-happiness-85349/ (accessed January 28, 2026)

226. Sarah Wells Kocsis, Alisha Sud, Anita Totten, 'Modernizing Care for Obesity as a Chronic Disease: A How-To Guide for Employers,' https://milkeninstitute.org/content-hub/research-and-reports/reports/modernizing-care-obesity-chronic-disease-how-guide-employers/ (accessed January 28, 2026)

227. Michael Pollan, "In Defense of Food' Author Offers Advice For Health,' Morning Edition, https://www.npr.org/2008/01/01/17725932/in-defense-of-food-author-offers-advice-for-health/ (accessed January 28, 2026)

Chapter 18 (Notes 228-249)

228. Hiroko Tabuchi, Brad Plumer, 'How Green Are Electric Vehicles?,' https://www.nytimes.com/2021/03/02/climate/electric-vehicles-environment.html/ (accessed January 28, 2026)

229. 'How much carbon dioxide does the United States and the World emit each year from energy sources?,' https://www.usgs.gov/faqs/how-much-carbon-dioxide-does-united-states-and-world-emit-each-year-energy-sources/ (accessed January 28, 2026)

230. 'Map of Worldwide Croplands,' https://www.usgs.gov/media/images/map-worldwide-croplands/ (accessed January 28, 2026)

231. Hannah Ritchie and Max Roser (2019) - "Half of the world's habitable land is used for agriculture" Published online at OurWorldinData.org. Retrieved from: 'https://archive.ourworldindata.org/20251125-173858/global-land-for-agriculture.html' [Online Resource] (archived on November 25, 2025)/ (accessed January 28, 2026)

232. Alabama Forestry Commission, 'Guidelines to measure carbon sequestration in Alabama forests,' https://www.forestry.alabama.gov/Pages/Management/Forms/Carbon_Baseline_Inventory_Procedures.pdf/ (accessed January 28, 2026)

233. Alabama Forestry Commission, 'Guidelines to measure carbon sequestration in Alabama forests,' https://www.forestry.alabama.gov/Pages/Management/Forms/Carbon_Baseline_Inventory_Procedures.pdf/ (accessed January 28, 2026)

234. Jocelyn Durkay, Jennifer Schultz, 'The Role of Forests in Carbon Sequestration and Storage,' https://www.ncsl.org/environment-and-natural-resources/the-role-of-forests-in-carbon-sequestration-and-storage/ (accessed January 28, 2026)

235. Oliver Milman, 'Earth has lost a third of arable land in past 40 years, scientists say,' https://www.theguardian.com/environment/2015/dec/02/arable-land-soil-food-security-shortage/ (accessed January 28, 2026)

236. 'Vertical Farming,' https://en.wikipedia.org/wiki/Vertical_farming/ (accessed January 28, 2026)

237. Richard Gray, 'Why soil is disappearing from farms,' https://www.bbc.com/future/bespoke/follow-the-food/why-soil-is-disappearing-from-farms/ (accessed January 28, 2026)

238. Chelsea Harvey, 'Alarming research finds humans are using up far more of Earth's water than previously thought,' https://www.washingtonpost.com/news/energy-environment/wp/2015/12/03/alarming-research-says-humans-are-using-up-far-more-water-than-previously-thought/ (accessed January 28, 2026)

239. Chris Arsenault, 'Only 60 Years of Farming Left If Soil Degradation Continues,' https://www.scientificamerican.com/article/only-60-years-of-farming-left-if-soil-degradation-continues/ (accessed January 28, 2026)

240. 'Vertical Farming,' https://en.wikipedia.org/wiki/Vertical_farming/ (accessed January 28, 2026)

241. Saloni Walimbe, '3 emerging trends in vertical farming that will cultivate the future of agriculture,' https://www.intelligentliving.co/3-emerging-trends-in-vertical-farming/ (accessed January 28, 2026)

242. Sasha Moonilal, 'Vertical Farming: The Future of Agriculture?,' https://www.cengn.ca/information-centre/innovation/vertical-farming-the-future-of-agriculture/ (accessed January 28, 2026)

243. 'Food Availability (Per Capita) Data System - Food Loss,' https://www.ers.usda.gov/data-products/food-availability-per-capita-data-system/food-loss/ (accessed January 28, 2026)

244. Dr. Kai-Shu Ling, Dr. James Altland, 'Vertical Farming – No Longer A Futuristic Concept,' Interview, https://www.ars.usda.gov/oc/utm/vertical-farming-no-longer-a-futuristic-concept/ (accessed January 28, 2026)

245. Jack Rogers, 'Vertical Farming Industry to Grow 25% Annually Through 2030,' https://www.globest.com/2024/02/01/vertical-farming-industry-to-grow-25-annually-through-2030/ (accessed January 28, 2026)

246. 'Controlled Environment Agriculture,' https://en.wikipedia.org/wiki/Controlled-

environment_agriculture/ (accessed January 28, 2026)

247. Sophie Egan, 'Are Hydroponic Vegetables as Nutritious as Those Grown in Soil?,' https://archive.nytimes.com/well.blogs.nytimes.com/2016/12/23/are-hydroponic-vegetables-as-nutritious-as-those-grown-in-soil/ (accessed January 28, 2026)

248. Gosia Wozniacka, 'Can regenerative agriculture reverse climate change? Big Food is banking on it.,' https://www.nbcnews.com/news/us-news/can-regenerative-agriculture-reverse-climate-change-big-food-banking-it-n1072941/ (accessed January 28, 2026)

249. A. Arcasi, A.W. Mauro, G. Napoli, F. Tariello, G.P. Vanoli,, 'Energy and cost analysis for a crop production in a vertical farm, Applied Thermal Engineering, Volume 239, 2024, 122129, ISSN 1359-4311, https://doi.org/10.1016/j.applthermaleng.2023.122129. (https://www.sciencedirect.com/science/article/pii/S1359431123021580)/ (accessed January 28, 2026)

Chapter 19 (Notes 250-264)

250. Ermengarde Jabir, PhD, Ricardo Rosas, Isabella Grande, Julianne Wiley, 'A new working order: Reimagining offices in a hybrid world,' https://www.moodys.com/web/en/us/insights/data-stories/us-commercial-real-estate-vacancies-downtown-vs-suburbs.html (accessed January 28, 2026)

251. Kathryn Brenzel, 'Office-to-resi conversions are financially feasible, but just barely: report,' https://therealdeal.com/new-york/2023/08/08/report-identifies-nyc-offices-ripe-for-resi-conversion/ (accessed January 28, 2026)

252. Abby Corbett, Kevin Thorpe, David Smith, 'Obsolescence Equals Opportunity,' Report, https://www.cushmanwakefield.com/en/united-states/insights/obsolescence-equals-opportunity/ (accessed January 28, 2026)

253. Martin Z. Braun, 'NYC Property Tax System Cushions Near-Term Blow to Revenue,' https://www.bloomberg.com/news/articles/2023-06-29/nyc-property-tax-system-cushions-near-term-blow-to-revenue/ (accessed January 28, 2026)

254. Alex Armlovich, 'People Are Worrying About the Wrong Downtowns,' https://www.theatlantic.com/ideas/archive/2023/11/downtown-building-maintenance-costs/675848/ (accessed January 28, 2026)

255. Kate Taylor, 'These 10 companies control everything you buy,' https://www.businessinsider.com/10-companies-control-food-industry-2017-3/ (accessed January 28, 2026)

256. Charli Shield, 'Who controls the world's food supply?,' https://www.dw.com/en/agriculture-seeds-seed-laws-agribusinesses-climate-change-food-security-seed-sovereignty-bayer/a-57118595/ (accessed January 28, 2026)

257. James Rundle, 'Food Producers Band Together in Face of Cyber Threats,' Wall Street Journal, https://www.wsj.com/articles/food-producers-band-together-in-face-of-cyber-threats-8aa2e3ca/ (accessed January 28, 2026)

258. Sarah Rehkamp, 'A Look at Calorie Sources in the American Diet,' 12/5/2016,

https://www.ers.usda.gov/amber-waves/2016/december/a-look-at-calorie-sources-in-the-american-diet/ (accessed January 28, 2026)

259. Miranda Lipton, 'Grain Farming Goes Indoors,' https://modernfarmer.com/2023/01/grain-farming-goes-indoors/ (accessed January 28, 2026)

260. Rice Today, 'Singapore harvests its first batch of rice grown in a vertical farm,' https://ricetoday.irri.org/singapore-harvests-its-first-batch-of-rice-from-vertical-farm/ (accessed January 28, 2026)

261. Air Protein, https://www.airprotein.com/ (accessed January 28, 2026)

262. Onego, https://www.onego.bio/ (accessed January 28, 2026)

263. Quorn, https://www.quorn.us/mycoprotein/ (accessed January 28, 2026)

264. TRD Staff, 'Banks' exposure to CRE triggers "doom-loop" fears,' https://therealdeal.com/national/2023/09/06/bank-exposure-to-commercial-real-estate-estimated-at-3-6-trillion/ (accessed January 28, 2026)

Chapter 20 (Notes 265-266)

265. 'Aristotle,' https://en.wikipedia.org/wiki/Aristotle/ (accessed January 28, 2026)

266. Robert Twigger, Ed Lake, 'Master of many trades,' https://aeon.co/essays/we-live-in-a-one-track-world-but-anyone-can-become-a-polymath/ (accessed January 28, 2026)

Chapter 21 (Notes 267-268)

267. Caitlin Welsh, 'Russia, Ukraine, and Global Food Security: A Two-Year Assessment,' https://www.csis.org/analysis/russia-ukraine-and-global-food-security-two-year-assessment/ (accessed January 28, 2026)

268. 'The Great Pacific Garbage Patch,' https://theoceancleanup.com/great-pacific-garbage-patch/ (accessed January 28, 2026)

Chapter 23 (Notes 269-276)

269. '85% of US employees plan to quit in next six months,' https://www.staffingindustry.com/news/global-daily-news/85-us-employees-plan-quit-next-six-months/ (accessed January 28, 2026)

270. Sasha Rogerlberg, 'Workers are 'job hugging' in a stagnant labor market, but growing resentment means they could bail as soon as the next Great Resignation comes,' https://fortune.com/2025/08/18/what-is-job-hugging-next-great-resignation/ (accessed January 28, 2026)

271. Bryan Robinson, Ph.D, '80% Of Employees Report 'Productivity Anxiety' And Lower Well-Being In New Study,' https://www.forbes.com/sites/bryanrobinson/2024/06/15/80-of-employees-report-productivity-anxiety-and-lower--well-being-in-new-study/ (accessed January 28, 2026)

272. Emma Burleigh, Orianna Rosa Royle, "Quiet cracking' is spreading in offices: Half of workers are at breaking point, and it's costing companies \$438 billion in productivity loss,' https://fortune.com/2025/08/18/quiet-cracking-workplace-culture-employees-burnout-disengagement-mental-health-billions-business-loss-managers-ai-promotions/ (accessed January 28, 2026)

273. Amrita Ahuja, '81% of US workers worried about job loss in 2025,' https://www.staffingindustry.com/news/global-daily-news/81-of-us-workers-worried-about-job-loss-in-2025/ (accessed January 28, 2026)

274. 'The Professional and Technical Workforce: By the Numbers,' https://www.dpeaflcio.org/factsheets/the-professional-and-technical-workforce-by-the-numbers/ (accessed January 28, 2026)

275. Giulia Carbonaro, 'White-Collar Jobs Are Disappearing,' https://www.newsweek.com/white-collar-jobs-disappearing-2031221/ (accessed January 28, 2026)

276. Chris Quintana, 'Zombie colleges? These universities are living another life online, and no one can say why,' https://www.usatoday.com/story/news/investigations/2024/05/09/zombie-colleges-taking-applications/73546247007/ (accessed January 28, 2026)

Chapter 24 (Notes 277-301)

277. Aaron O'Neill, 'Distribution of the workforce across economic sectors in the United States from 2011 to 2021,' Statista (Feb. 2, 2024), (accessed January 28, 2026)

278. Abby McCain, 'Co-working statistics: Facts and trends,' Zippia (Feb. 2, 2023), (accessed January 28, 2026)

279. Andreea Neculae, 'U.S. Co-working Industry Report Q3 2025,' CoworkingCafe (Oct. 28, 2025), (accessed January 28, 2026)

280. Yardi Kube, 'Home vs. Office Preference Survey,' Yardi Kube (Oct. 21, 2025), (accessed January 28, 2026)

281. JLL, 'Hybrid is driving the adoption of flex space' (n.d.), (accessed January 28, 2026)

282. CBRE, '2024 Americas Office Occupier Sentiment Survey: Driving Strategic Change' (Aug. 13, 2024), (accessed January 28, 2026)

283. World Economic Forum, 'The Future of Jobs Report 2025', PDF (Jan. 7, 2025), (accessed January 28, 2026)

284. NJBIA, 'Survey: 46% of Remote Workers Would Quit if Told to Work in Office Full Time' (Published Jan. 27, 2025; updated Jan. 28, 2025), (accessed January 28, 2026)

285. Fortune Business Insights, 'Flexible Office Market' (report page), (accessed January 28, 2026)

286. Moody's, 'U.S. commercial real estate vacancies: downtown vs. suburbs' (Data Stories), (accessed January 28, 2026)

287. Bloomberg News, 'Offices will be even more empty in 2026' (June 27, 2024), (accessed January 28, 2026)

288. Erica Xuewei Jiang, Gregor Matvos, Tomasz Piskorski, and Amit Seru, 'Monetary Tightening, Commercial Real Estate Distress, and U.S. Bank Fragility' (NBER Working Paper No. 31970, Dec. 2023; revised Dec. 2024), PDF, National Bureau of Economic Research, (accessed January 28, 2026)

289. NYC 311, 'Find a housing complaint or report building conditions' (Knowledge Article KA-03604), (accessed January 28, 2026)

290. Hannah Ritchie, 'Urbanization' (Our World in Data, 2024), (accessed January 28, 2026)

291. UN DESA, 'Around 2.5 billion more people will be living in cities by 2050, projects new UN report' (May 16, 2018), (accessed January 28, 2026)

292. U.S. Census Bureau, 'ACS-32: Selected Economic Characteristics (2013–2015)', 2015 (American Community Survey report page), (accessed January 28, 2026)

293. Office for National Statistics (UK), 'Trends in self-employment in the UK: 2001 to 2015' (ONS), (accessed January 28, 2026)

294. 'Great Resignation,' https://en.wikipedia.org/wiki/Great_Resignation/ (accessed January 28, 2026)

295. Federal Reserve Bank of Kansas City, 'Is Remote Work Turning the Screw on Labor Market Tightness?' (Rocky Mountain Economist), (accessed January 28, 2026)

296. Boulder Weekly, 'No chasm to cross' (Boulder Weekly archives), (accessed January 28, 2026)

297. Michael B. Kelley, 'Uber's autonomous cars could destroy 10 million jobs and reshape the economy' (Business Insider, Feb. 2015), (accessed January 28, 2026)

298. GeekWire, 'Amazon patent for subterranean delivery network' (GeekWire, 2017), (accessed January 28, 2026)

299. Fox Business, 'Atlanta suburb becomes first to test underground consumer delivery system' (Fox Business), (accessed January 28, 2026)

300. Staten Island Advance (SILive), 'Year-round outdoor dining could return to NYC under proposed plan' (Dec. 2025), (accessed January 28, 2026)

301. 'Game B,' https://www.gameb.wiki/index.php/ (accessed January 28, 2026)

Chapter 25 (Notes 302-321)

302. McKinsey Global Institute, 'Jobs lost, jobs gained: What the future of work will mean for jobs, skills, and wages' (Nov. 2017), (accessed January 28, 2026)

303. Damian Carrington, 'Human race just 0.01% of all life but has destroyed over 80% of wild mammals – study' (The Guardian, May 21, 2018), (accessed January 28, 2026)

304. Live Science, 'Humans are causing species to go extinct 1,000 times faster than natural rate, study suggests' (Live Science), (accessed January 28, 2026)

305. Wikipedia, 'COVID-19 pandemic deaths' (Wikipedia entry), (accessed January 28, 2026)

306. World Health Organization, 'Obesity and overweight' (WHO fact sheet), (accessed January 28, 2026)

307. Kristalina Georgieva, 'AI will transform the global economy. Let's make sure it benefits humanity' (IMF Blog, Jan. 14, 2024), (accessed January 28, 2026)

308. McKinsey Global Institute, 'Retraining and reskilling workers in the age of automation' (McKinsey), (accessed January 28, 2026)

309. McKinsey, 'Five lessons from history on AI, automation, and employment' (McKinsey), (accessed January 28, 2026)

310. IBM, 'The enterprise guide to closing the skills gap' (IBM PDF/doc), (accessed January 28, 2026)

311. Jack Kelly, 'Unbridled adoption of artificial intelligence may result in millions of job losses and require massive retraining for those impacted' (Forbes, Sept. 30, 2019), (accessed January 28, 2026)

312. Neil Savage, 'How AI is improving cancer diagnostics,' Nature 579, S14–S16 (2020), https://doi.org/10.1038/d41586-020-00847-2, (accessed January 28, 2026)

313. CIO, 'Demand for junior developers softens as AI takes over' (Sept. 24, 2025), (accessed January 28, 2026)

314. Wikipedia, 'Universal basic income' (Wikipedia entry), (accessed January 28, 2026)

315. Carrie Arnold, 'Pandemic speeds largest test yet of universal basic income,' Nature 583, 502–503 (2020), https://doi.org/10.1038/d41586-020-01993-3, (accessed January 28, 2026)

316. BBC News, 'Finland basic income trial left people 'happier but jobless'' (Feb. 8, 2019), (accessed January 28, 2026)

317. GSDRC, 'Jobs, unemployment and violence' (Professional Development reading pack), (accessed January 28, 2026)

318. The Atlantic, 'Free Time Doesn't Make People Happier' (Feb. 2019), (accessed January 28, 2026)

319. Business Insider, 'Universal basic income guy standing quantitative easing' (Jan. 2017), (accessed January 28, 2026)

320. U.S. Social Security Administration, 'Cost-of-Living Adjustments (COLA)' (SSA), (accessed January 28, 2026)

321. APFC, 'Fund structure' (APFC (site page)), (accessed January 28, 2026)

322. Oren Lyons, "The Faith Keeper on the Future," in Exiled in the Land of the Free: Democracy, Indian Nations, and the U.S. Constitution, ed. Oren Lyons and John C. Mohawk (Santa Fe, NM: Clear Light Publishers, 1992), 1–12. (accessed February 4, 2026)

ACKNOWLEDGMENTS

This book is the product of many years of reading, listening, questioning, and unlearning. While the arguments and conclusions are my own, they were shaped—often decisively—by thinkers, institutions, and practitioners whose work helped me see more clearly what was broken, why it broke, and what might be possible if we chose to redesign the systems we live inside.

I am particularly indebted to Viktor Frankl, whose insights into meaning, agency, and responsibility I first learned of as a student, and which continue to reaffirm the human capacity to choose differently, even under extreme duress. James P. Carse's articulation of finite and infinite games provided me with a language for understanding much of what drives both human conflict and human connection, and remains a conceptual backbone of this book, and my thinking. Jeff Booth's work on deflation and technological progress helped clarify how deeply misaligned our economic systems have become with physical and technological reality and generosity, and his thinking informs much of this book's economic structure. Hans Rosling's insistence on data, context, and proportion offered a necessary antidote to despair. And the work of systems thinkers in particular—Jonas and Jonathan Salk, and separately, Everett Rogers—provided graphic devices that distill incredible complexity into simple frameworks. The Salks framed our present moment not as an anomaly, but as a predictable inflection point in the longer arc of human development, while Rogers framed all of human innovation in the context of how we relate to one another, new ideas, and time. I return to their thinking regularly.

I am also grateful to the voices—ancient and modern—that remind us that these questions are not new. Marcus Aurelius, writing from the center of power, and Leonard Cohen, writing about the poetry of fractures in the human spirit, each offered words that continue to resonate across time. E. O. Wilson's clear-eyed observation about our Paleolithic emotions, medieval institutions, and godlike technologies remains one of the most succinct diagnoses of our predicament. The work of Gaia Vince sharpened my understanding of climate-driven migration, while Sebastião Salgado's images, reflections, and own pivot toward direct action are not only inspiring, they restored a measure of my faith in the resilience of the natural world, even as they underscored the cost of human excess. Maxwell Maltz's early work on self-image and perception helped illuminate the quiet but powerful ways in which internal narratives shape external outcomes. And Nikola Tesla's life and ideas remain a reminder that technological possibility and human institutions are often misaligned—sometimes tragically so.

Beyond individual thinkers, this book draws heavily on the work of institutions and organizations that have translated ideas into practice, often in defiance of prevailing incentives. In economics, the work emerging from communities engaged with deflationary theory and post-scarcity thinking—particularly those influenced by Jeff Booth's analysis—helped ground abstract arguments in material reality. In addressing homelessness, the evidence-based, housing-first approach advanced by organizations such as Y-Foundation, under the leadership of Juha Kaakinen, provided a clear demonstration that homelessness is not an intractable condition but a solvable multi-system failure. In matters of housing affordability and access, the research, advocacy, and lived analysis by a sizable contingent of community activists, builders, and journalists I reference in this book helped expose the structural roots of exclusion, speculation, and scarcity, while systems innovators like ICONBuild and Broad Sustainable Building have shown that technology can disrupt housing, at scale.

I am similarly indebted to the many practitioners, designers, planners, technologists, and policymakers whose work rarely fits neatly into ideological categories, but who nonetheless continue to experiment with better ways of provisioning shelter, food, energy, education, and care. Their efforts—often incremental, often underfunded—form the practical substrate beneath many of the ideas explored in these pages.

It would be impossible to acknowledge the formation of this book without noting the role of the COVID-19 pandemic. While the human cost of that period—measured in lives lost, livelihoods disrupted, and communities strained—cannot and should not be minimized, the pandemic nonetheless acted as a seismic interruption of the status quo. It exposed, with unusual clarity, which systems were resilient and which were brittle; which forms of work were essential and which were performative; and how quickly norms long treated as immovable could, under pressure, change. For that unmasking—painful though it was—I am grateful, not for the event itself, but for the lessons it forced into view.

Beyond books, data, and institutions, I am grateful to the many collaborators, colleagues, clients, and friends with whom I have worked over the years, often across disciplines and cultures. Designing complex environments is never a solitary act, and whatever clarity I have gained about systems, incentives, and human behavior has been forged in conversation and practice, not in isolation.

I owe Jamie Wheal special thanks for nudging me toward Burning Man, and Tony Greenberg for being my co-pilot on the adventure. It was there that this book was truly born, even if I didn't know it at the time.

Most of all, I am grateful to those who forced me—intentionally or not—to confront my own assumptions, blind spots, and unfinished work. This book exists because certain stories I once told myself no longer held. Any value it has lies in the hope that others may find, within these pages, not answers, but better questions.

About the Author

Anthony Fieldman is an architect and systems designer whose career has focused on large-scale, complex projects that shape how people live, work, learn, and gather. Over several decades of professional practice, he has worked across continents and sectors, partnering with multidisciplinary teams to rethink the built environment as a driver of human behavior, wellbeing, and collective outcomes.

Trained in design and guided by systems thinking, Fieldman approaches global challenges—housing, climate, food, education, work, and economic structure—not as isolated problems, but as interdependent design failures capable of being re-imagined. *Everything Is Broken* reflects his long-standing interest in how incentives, narratives, and institutional frameworks shape human flourishing, and how redesigning those systems can unlock more abundant and humane futures.

Fieldman lives in New York City, at least when he isn't traveling for work, spending time with his daughter and other loved ones, exploring the world with his cameras, or building outlandish things in the Black Rock desert.